Y0-ARP-959

Courtesy of Metropolitan Museum of Art, N. Y.

PORTRAIT OF NERO

Louvre

NERO

THE SINGING EMPEROR OF ROME

BY

ARTHUR WEIGALL

Late Inspector General of Antiquities, Government of Egypt, and Member of the Catalogue Staff of the Cairo Museum; Officer of the Order of Medjidieh

ILLUSTRATED

GARDEN CITY PUBLISHING COMPANY, INC.
GARDEN CITY NEW YORK

NERO

Published, Fall, 1930
First Edition

Made in the United States of America

CONTENTS

CONTENTS

NERO

THE SINGING EMPEROR OF ROME

CHAPTER I

History's Two Contradictory Estimations of Nero's Character—Events before the Birth of Nero—The Early Life of his Mother, Agrippina, under the Emperors Tiberius and Caligula.

In the year A.D. 64 Rome was partly destroyed by fire, and the little sect of the Christians was accused of having deliberately caused the conflagration. A brief but terrible persecution ensued, in which St. Paul is thought to have lost his life; and Nero, Emperor of Rome from A.D. 54 to 68, came to be regarded by the survivors as the first great enemy of the new faith.

In A.D. 68 the Emperor was dethroned and is supposed to have committed suicide in a house in the suburbs of Rome, whither he had fled; but a great many people, passionately loyal to him, believed that he was alive, that his self-inflicted wound had been healed, that he had escaped to the East, and that he would return one day in triumph.

Just at the time when this rumour had gripped the mind of the public, and when the talk of his escape and of his imminent reappearance was in every mouth, that astonishing work *The Apocalypse,* or *Revelation* of St. John, was written; and its author, deeming Nero responsible for the Christian persecution, introduced him into its pages in the guise of the Beast—the Beast which was wounded unto death, but whose deadly wound was healed, [1] "the Beast that was, and is not, and yet is," [2] whose number is 666. [3]

But Nero had not only caused the deaths of the Christian martyrs: he had also been the enemy of the conservative element in the old Roman nobility, whose traditions he had flouted in many ways, particularly by his appearance on the stage as a singer; and since the chief historians of his life belonged to the patrician section of society, an extremely unfavourable view of his character came to be held by later generations of Romans. Thus, when Christianity became the state religion this hostile pagan view was united with that of the Christian Apocalypse; and thenceforth Nero was to all men the Beast, the Antichrist, the hair-raising embodiment of the sins of the world and the flesh.

For this reason, though the cause is usually forgotten, his name now brings before the mind the vision of a monster of iniquity, a fiend incarnate, only human in outward appearance and anything but pleasantly so at that. But the question is whether Nero would be regarded today as such an unspeakably villainous creature if the horror of the early Christians at his violent action against them had not passed into a tradition of detestation. Christian writers throughout the ages have heaped abuse upon him, and historians have blindly followed their lead, hardly knowing that they were prejudiced, and realizing not at all that his villainy, or, at any rate, its degree, was open to question.

These writers, of course, have had the support of the three non-Christian ancient authorities who provide us

[1] References are to notes given at end of volume.

with the bulk of our information about him—Tacitus, Suetonius, and Dion (or Dio) Cassius—for they are unanimous in representing him, if by no means as the Apocalyptic Beast, certainly as a fantastic scoundrel and murderer, a traitor, moreover, to the aristocratic ideal, who imperilled the entire fabric of empire by his wildly unconventional life, and by his insistence upon his right to make public use of his abilities as a singer and musician. Pliny the Elder, too, calls him the enemy of the human race; and Marcus Aurelius speaks of him as an inhuman monster. [4]

After his death it was undoubtedly the opinion amongst patrician Romans, though not amongst the people, that he had callously and unnecessarily murdered his foster-brother Britannicus, his mother Agrippina, his first wife Octavia, his aunt Domitia, his cousins Sulla, Rubellius Plautus, and the Silani, his tutors Seneca and Burrhus, and scores of others; that he had kicked to death his second wife Poppæa; that he had himself set fire to Rome; and that he had intended to slaughter the entire Senate, burn Rome again, let the wild beasts loose on the people, and so forth. He was accused of all kinds of horrible immoralities; his character was described as cruel, bestial, vicious, vain, cowardly, and utterly irresponsible; and he was thought to have degraded the dignity and status of Emperor, as has been said, by singing in public theatres. His soiling of the imperial purple by appearing on the stage, and the murder of his mother, were his two outstanding crimes; and he was alternately howled at as "the Matricide" and "the Musician."

Thus, quite apart from the Christian legend, there was enough to damn him in the general talk about him in upper class Roman society which at length took definite shape in the histories of Tacitus and others and the biography of Suetonius. But these writers made far more terrible accusations against other Emperors—Caligula, for instance; and it can hardly be supposed that Nero would have come down to us at the present day as the most monstrous character in Roman history if early Christianity had not identified him with Antichrist. It is more likely that he would have been regarded simply as *one* of the bad or criminally foolish emperors.

In the following pages, however, I want to show that there is another side of the picture altogether, a side which can now only be rendered apparent by recognizing the cause of the prejudice against him, by piecing together the many admissions of his merits grudgingly made by various ancient writers, and by interpreting Nero's character and the motives of his actions in the light shed both by these, and by the undoubted fact that he was beloved by the bulk of his people.

It is not that, in this age of whitewash, a merely fashionable attempt is here to be made to show him in the best light. The fact is that the unbiassed historian is confronted with incontrovertible proofs of Nero's wide popularity; and the problem has to be faced as to why a man who is regarded by historians as a monster should have been so much beloved. It is unquestionable that in the opinion of many people who lived during the first centuries after his death, Nero was almost a celestial figure, a friend of the poor, an enemy of the stiff-necked rich, an Emperor who had also been a great artist, and who had travelled through his dominions singing to his people with a voice the like of which would never be heard again.

In order to explain this dual and contradictory estimate of the Emperor's character one is obliged in fairness to look for the good in him as well as the bad; and if, as a result of this search, the unspeakable Nero is found to be a fantastic but understandable, and in some ways sympathetic, character, not often, though a little more frequently than most of us, suited to the part of the Beast, the fact must not be imputed to any preconceived desire to allow him the Devil's prerogative of being not so black as he is painted.

. . . .

Nero was born in A.D. 37, a few months after the death of the Emperor Tiberius, the successor of the great Augustus; but to comprehend the intricacies of his position, and to view his behaviour—as I think it should be viewed—in the light of the struggle he was making against that noble yet narrow-minded Roman Traditionalism which he could not in the least understand, we must, at the outset, hark back to the dictatorship of the picturesquely shameless Julius Cæsar, and particularly to the year 47 B.C., when, having gone to Egypt to regulate its chaotic court affairs, the Dictator interested himself in Queen Cleopatra's troubles to such purpose that she presented him with a little son, Cæsarion.

Cæsar, who cared neither for God nor man, has been called "the inevitable co-respondent in every society divorce"[5]; but so great was the glamour of his brilliant personality that, in spite of his championship of un-Roman customs, and his love of the unconventional life which in all ages leads the man of artistic temperament into mischief, his power, even in conservative Rome, was absolute. He daringly conceived the idea of abolishing the Roman Republic, and establishing a monarchy instead, on the Egyptian model; and it was his intention to force the people to recognize the dazzling Cleopatra as his legal wife.[6]

Although Egypt was her kingdom, Cleopatra was not an Egyptian; she was a pure Greek, descended from a long line of Greek kings, or Pharaohs, of Egypt, whose capital, Alexandria, was the Paris of the ancient world, the main seat of that gaiety, culture, and social elegance, which made Rome's ideal of respectable austerity seem so provincial to Cæsar, and which, still keeping ahead of the times, impressed itself in like manner on Nero's mind.

Cleopatra with her baby followed her lover to Rome, and it was mainly because he intended to create a Roman throne for himself and her, and to introduce a spice of Greek brilliance and light-heartedness into the drab and tasteless mediocrity of the capital's best society, that he was murdered in 44 B.C. by Brutus and his friends, the Egyptian Queen being obliged to make a bolt for it back to Alexandria, with the curses of men like Cicero falling about her ears. Cæsar, it must be explained, had been given the military title of *Imperator,* or Commander-in-Chief; but the word had not yet assumed the meaning which our rendering of it, *Emperor,* implies, and, when he died, he had in no sense established by law a ruling dynasty.

His legal heir was Octavianus, afterwards known as Augustus, the son of the daughter of his sister Julia; but his old friend Marcus Antonius (Antony, as we now call him) disputed the high powers conferred by the Senate on this young man, and finally it was agreed that Augustus should govern Rome and the hidebound West and Antony the easy-going and artistic East, where the civilization was Greek and not Roman in character.

To cement this superficially friendly arrangement between these twin lords of the earth, Antony married Octavia, the sister of Augustus; and the two daughters of this union, both named Antonia, became respectively Nero's grandmother on his father's side and great-grandmother on his mother's.

Antony then espoused the cause of the little Cæsarion, married Cleopatra, and declared war on Augustus, his avowed object being to make himself monarch of Rome, with the Egyptian Queen as his consort and his stepson, Cæsar's child, as heir to the throne, [7] the boy being the Dictator's only acknowledged son. Augustus, on the other hand, believed himself to be defending the Republic and its stern and uncompromising traditions against the luxury and emasculating Hellenism of this new autocracy of the East. It was a fight on behalf of that familiar social phenomenon which we term Respectability, and in the time of Nero the battle, though no longer in armed array, was still in progress.

In 31 B.C. Augustus was victorious, Antony and Cleopatra committed suicide, Cæsarion was murdered by the victor's orders, and the Republic was saved. But, actually, Augustus now became the autocratic ruler of the whole West and East, including Egypt with its gay Greek capital, Alexandria; and the Egyptians, refusing to admit that they had been conquered, told themselves that Julius Cæsar had really been married to Cleopatra, that he had consequently been their rightful king or Pharaoh, and that Augustus, being his heir, was likewise their Pharaoh.

Thus Augustus, while being only a sort of President of the Republic at home, was an actual monarch in the most up-to-date part of his Greek dominions; and gradually the hereditary idea, with perhaps a tendency towards the Egyptian matriarchal system of inheritance through the female line, began to influence his status in Rome itself. Though republican forms were maintained, his title *Imperator* assumed the significance which *Emperor* now has for us; and there was little doubt that the supreme power would remain in his family after his death.

As the direct result of Rome's connection with the Greek and Oriental world, a new elegance, both mental and material, a new recognition of the artistic professions, and a new indifference to sex-morality, swept over Italy, at which old-fashioned people very naturally held up their hands in dismay; and Augustus was kept busy in his later years trying to purify Rome of this contamination, closing certain establishments of the kind now known as night-clubs, limiting the sale of intoxicating drink, and punishing people involved in society scandals, even his own free-thinking daughter, Julia (Nero's great-grandmother), the leader of the smart and fashionable life, being banished under his stern laws against that immorality which is always the curse of emancipation.

He issued a decree forbidding young people to go to evening performances at the theatres except when accompanied by elderly chaperones, and he showed his contempt for the dramatic art by snubbing actors, banishing one, in fact, for having had the effrontery to point his finger at a noisy member of the audience, and flogging another for going about with a girl who was so indecent as to dress almost like a boy. He could not abide the irregular habits of the artist; he exiled Ovid for being improper; he set up a censorship of morals, obliging people to answer a *questionnaire* regarding their private lives; he passed a number of anti-luxury laws; and so forth

He fought hard for the old austerity and simplicity which fostered moral uprightness and duty to the state even at the expense of self-expression and consequent progress in art and culture; but the fight was in vain: and, though he went down to posterity as a national hero, a celestial figure standing like a rock at the foundations of the family pedigree, he could not prevent the general trend of Rome's fashionable society in the direction of the loose, elegant, and artistic life of the

Greek world, of which Antony and Cleopatra had been the bright particular stars.

When he died in A.D. 14 he was succeeded, for want of an heir, by his stepson, Tiberius Claudius Nero, the son of his wife Livia, now always spoken of as the Emperor Tiberius, whose tenure of the imperial office made it still more of an autocracy. The throne, be it understood, was even then not hereditary: Rome was still a Republic in name; but in actuality the Emperor was an absolute monarch, and could at least propose his own heir to the Senate. Tiberius did not belong by blood to the family of Julius Cæsar and Augustus—the Julian House as it is called: his family is known as the Claudian House, and this distinction must be kept in mind.

The character of Tiberius was horrible in the extreme, and the number of people murdered or executed by him was enormous, while the tortures inflicted by his orders and often carried out in his presence, indicate that he was a sadistic maniac. The Romans nicknamed him "Mud-and-Blood," [8] and they also called him "The Goat" [9] on account of his sexual excesses and perversions. His palace at Capri was full of obscene paintings and statues, and orgies were conducted there which are quite unfit to be recorded, and, indeed, are only mentioned here for the purpose of establishing the background for the study of Nero, in which connection it is interesting to notice, too, that the relationship of Tiberius to his mother, Livia, was one of cruel hatred and oppression which fell short of actual murder only by the chance that she died a natural death.

He had a brother Drusus, who had married Antonia, one of the two daughters of Antony and Octavia; and this exalted couple had a son, Germanicus, who was the most popular Roman who ever lived. He had married Agrippina (the Elder), granddaughter of the revered Augustus; and the children of this union were very much in the public eye, partly because their father was a national hero, and partly because through the maternal line they were representatives of the glorious Julian House. There were three surviving sons, Nero, Drusus, and Caius or Caligula, and three daughters, Agrippina, Drusilla, and Julia Livilla.

This Agrippina (the Younger) was born on November 6th, A.D. 15, and was three years the junior of Caligula, who had been born in A.D. 12. In A.D. 19 their father Germanicus died of poison, and Agrippina (the Elder), his widow, was convinced that the infamous Tiberius had ordered his death, being afraid of his tremendous popularity with the army.

Tiberius had a son, also called Drusus, who had married his cousin Livia, sister of Germanicus; but he was murdered in A.D. 23 with the connivance of his wife, who committed suicide when her guilt became known, and Gemellus, the son of this unhappy pair, Tiberius's only grandson, shared with the three sons of Germanicus the chance of being chosen by Tiberius as his successor.

In the year A.D. 28 much scandal was caused by the behaviour of the young Agrippina, who was then no more than twelve years of age but, with that precocity not infrequently found in southern races, was already sufficiently developed to want to encourage the attentions of the other sex. Her brother, Caligula, then fifteen years of age, took advantage of this tendency in her, and, being a youth devoid of any sexual restraint whatsoever, seduced her. Shortly afterwards, she turned her eyes upon Æmilius Lepidus, her cousin, the son of her mother's sister, Julia, and permitted him the same intimacies which she had allowed in Caligula.[10] Tiberius, therefore, hastily married her off to another cousin of hers, Cnæus Domitius Ahenobarbus, a red-haired[11] young man, who, from being a youth of simple and noble nature,[12] soon developed into a hard-drinking, evil-living scapegrace, typical of the Ahenobarbi, the Bronze-Beards, of whom the orator Crassus once said that no wonder their beards were of bronze, since their faces were of iron and their hearts of lead.

The family was old and illustrious, tracing its descent back to 500 B.C., but its men had the reputation of being reckless and unreliable, the grandfather of this Cnæus, for instance, having gone from one side to the other in the civil war which followed Cæsar's death, and having finally deserted Antony and Cleopatra just before the battle of Actium. Lucius, the father of Cnæus, married Antonia, daughter of Antony and Octavia, the sister of the Emperor Augustus; and this union may well have introduced something of the wildness of Antony into its progeny.

Lucius had been a devotee of the stage, and a great lover of horses and chariot-racing; and his son Cnæus was also a racing man, but came into ill repute owing to certain financial transactions in connection with racing matters, and also on account of his having failed to pay his debts to money-lenders. He was a man of violent temper: he knocked a gentleman's eye out once in the Forum, murdered one of his servants for refusing to drink as much as he had drunkenly ordered him to do, and deliberately—so it was said—ran over and killed a boy who had annoyed him by getting in the way of his chariot.

The little Agrippina, in spite of her moral behaviour in the case of Caligula and Lepidus, must nevertheless be pitied on account of the unhappy life she led with him; but her domestic troubles may well have seemed insignificant as compared with those of her family. Her mother, the elder Agrippina, had fiercely hated the terrible Tiberius ever since she had begun to suspect him of having poisoned her husband, and at length, in A.D. 29, after nearly ten years of widowhood, her unquenchable thirst for revenge led her to involve herself in a conspiracy against him, the object of which was to bring his reign to a close and to elevate her son, Nero, to the imperial dignity without waiting upon tardy nature to effect the change in due course. The young Nero was an unpleasant and dissolute fellow, and nobody was particularly sorry when, having been clapped into prison on the island of Pontia, he starved himself to death so as to cheat his gaoler of the pleasure of killing him.

Nor was there much regret when the second brother, Drusus, who had been imprisoned in Rome, in the dungeons of the palace, was done to death in A.D. 33 under revolting circumstances; yet when the Emperor told his friends how the young man, emaciated by torture and finally deprived of food, had tried to prolong his miserable life by eating the stuffing of his mattress, not a few persons were shocked. The general opinion was that Drusus was mad, and that his insanity ought to have been respected.

Agrippina, the mother of these boys, was kept in exile until both were dead; and having had one of her eyes knocked out by the Emperor, so it is said, [13] in a hand to hand fight with him when he was visiting her, she suddenly began a hunger-strike, daily struggling against forcible feeding until her heart failed, and she died.

Thus, the third brother, Caligula, was alone left as the alternative to Gemellus in the succession; but, owing to the fact that he had a thoroughly perverse nature, and was, moreover, subject to fits, Tiberius could never bring himself definitely to announce that he had chosen him irrevocably as heir, though he let it be understood that he intended to do so.

The aged Emperor was always looking askance at the young man; and one day when he observed the malicious glance he gave his cousin and rival Gemellus, he exclaimed, "You'll kill him one day!—and then somebody will kill *you*." There were tears in his eyes as he spoke; for he was sick of the quarrels and intrigues which had brought death to so many of his relations and friends, and he earnestly desired to leave Rome a heritage of peace, now that old age was dulling his enjoyment of the pain of others.

Early in the year A.D. 37 there were more troubles in the family. Agrippina (the Younger) had had to put up with the many infidelities of her husband, Cnæus, but now she discovered that he and his red-haired sister, Domitia Lepida, had been guilty of an incestuous relationship, and, probably at Agrippina's instigation, he was publicly accused both of this and of adultery in general, to which was added a charge of treason against the old Emperor Tiberius. Everybody knew, however, that Agrippina herself had, in bygone years, been guilty of a like relationship with her perverted and odious brother Caligula; and perhaps on this account the charge against Cnæus was not pressed.

To the end of his days Tiberius could not make up his mind about the succession. He was puzzled by the contradictions in Caligula's character. At times the young man appeared to be modest and dutiful, and even weighed down by his responsibilities; but at other times he was brutish and savage, and alternated a boisterous licentiousness with a scowling gloom. He was quite good-looking, being tall and slender; but his hair was too thin on his head and too abundant all over his body, and his complexion was sallow. The expression of his face was sinister, and there was often a look of madness about his heavy brows and wide-open, unblinking eyes; while his cruel little mouth had a way of opening at one corner in a most unpleasant snarl. Yet in the rare moments when he was in repose he was undoubtedly handsome.

He had at this time a great friend, Herod Agrippa, nephew of that Herod to whom our Lord was sent for trial; he was some twenty years older than Caligula, and he appears to have taught the young man not only the vices of the East but also the Oriental view of kingship—a teaching which bore fruit in later years in Caligula's insane enjoyment of despotic power. Herod used to make him talk of what he would do when he came to the throne; but they knew the danger of such conversation—for the terrible Tiberius would not be likely to show mercy on anybody who wished his death—and they spoke of these matters only in whispers.

Once when the two friends were out driving, Herod whispered to Caligula that he hoped it would not now be long before the old fellow died, and he added that Gemellus could easily be got rid of. The driver happened to overhear this remark, and informed the Emperor, who promptly put Herod in prison.

Then, in the spring of A.D. 37, came the day when Tiberius was thought to be dying, for he was nearly eighty years of age and was constantly suffering from attacks of extreme weakness and illness, while, as he himself said, he was weary of life, and was weighed down by the memory of his sins and cruelties. The rumour spread, presently, that he had expired, and at once one of Herod's friends hastened to the prison, and whispered in his ear in the Hebrew tongue: "The old lion is dead."

The centurion on guard asked the Jewish prince what had been said to him that was evidently causing him such unbounded joy; and thereat Herod revealed the secret, and ordered a fine supper to be spread, to which he invited all the officers in the place. But in the midst of the feast, news was brought that the story was untrue; and instantly his guests, almost scared out of their wits, swept away the plates and dishes and loaded their bewildered host with chains.

As a matter of fact, Tiberius, though not dead, was really dying; and as he lay upon his bed that night he gave orders that both Gemellus and Caligula should be brought to him early in the morning, saying to those around him that he had prayed heaven for a sign as to which of the two he should finally choose as his successor. He said that he had asked the gods to signify their choice by causing the youth they had selected to enter the room first; and he revealed the trend of his thoughts by sending a message to the tutor of Gemellus, telling him to bring his pupil as early as possible.

But, next day, Gemellus overslept himself, and Caligula entered the dying man's room before him, at which Tiberius sighed, and, accepting the decree of destiny, commended the Roman Empire into the morose young man's hands. When Gemellus came in, the Emperor implored Caligula to love him and to look after him; but he must have known in his heart that the boy had not a chance.

When the young men had left the room, Tiberius lapsed into unconsciousness, and those around his bedside, thinking that he was dead, went helter-skelter down the passage to congratulate Caligula, who, on hearing the news for which he had been so anxiously waiting, hastened back to the bedroom, his sullen face for once wreathed in smiles as he acknowledged the salutations of the company. Everybody was fawning upon him and saying how glad they were to have such a fine young man as Emperor, when suddenly the supposed corpse sat up in bed, and asked for something to eat.

For a moment Caligula stood speechless with angry disappointment and also with fear lest Tiberius should have observed his manifest delight, and should still have strength to disinherit him. The courtiers, too, were embarrassed and frightened; and, edging away from the young man, they slipped one by one out of the room.

Caligula, nervous and impatient, thought that the best way to settle matters would be to get possession of the dying Emperor's signet ring to show that the sovereignty had now changed hands whether the aged man were alive or dead. He therefore approached the bed, and attempted to pull the ring from the gnarled old finger; but Tiberius grimly clenched his fist, and glared at him with hate in his fading eyes.

A tense struggle ensued, but the accounts of what then happened vary. Seneca, reported by Suetonius, [14] says that the Emperor shouted for his attendants, and, as a result of the effort, fell lifeless over the side of the bed; Tacitus and Dio state [15] that Caligula caused the bedclothes to be thrown over the old man's head, and left him to smother; and Suetonius records the belief that Caligula held a pillow over his face until he was suffocated.

There was a horrified servant in the room at the time, and the new Emperor's first command was characteristic: he gave orders that the man should instantly be taken away and executed.

Tiberius had come to be feared and hated by his subjects during the last years of his life; and when Caligula, who was now five-and-twenty, appeared as the chief mourner at the funeral, the crowds gave him an ovation, calling him by all kinds of pet names. He then went at once to the mausoleum wherein the ashes of his mother and his brother Nero rested; and, while tactfully showing every respect to Tiberius who had caused their deaths, paid equal honour to these two unfortunates whose attempts to murder the old man had miscarried. It was rather an awkward situation, and he handled it with skill.

In fact, during the first seven months of his reign, his conduct was for the most part exemplary. He dramatically burnt the records of the trial of his mother and brothers, saying that he had not read the names of those who had laid information against them (which was untrue, for he afterwards had them all put to death). He made polite speeches to the Senate, telling them that he was under their guidance. He gave magnificent entertainments for the public in the arena, and made himself very popular with the senators and high officials by permitting them, for the first time, to sit upon cushions at these shows.

But in the late autumn he had a dangerous illness of a mysterious kind, and when he recovered he threw off all pretence of being benevolent or conscientious. The kindest thing to say is that from this time onwards he was mad; and yet he was not really insane, and, indeed, the fact that he used to say himself that there was something wrong with his head shows that he was sane enough, at any rate, to have some fears about his sanity.

At the best of times, nevertheless, he was a nervous wreck, unable to sleep at nights, and the victim of terrible nightmares when he did.

The first indication of his eccentricity was his falling passionately in love with his sister, Drusilla, a girl of twenty, who was married to a certain Cassius Longinus. He obliged her to leave this personage, and then announced that he was going to marry her himself, pointing out that the Pharaohs of Egypt used to marry their sisters, and that, since Egypt was now an imperial possession, he was in fact a Pharaoh, and indeed had already been crowned as such by proxy at Alexandria, as had Augustus and Tiberius before him.

Roman society, although used to every kind of abnormality, criminal or otherwise, was decidedly shocked; and the young Emperor's grandmother, Antonia, widow of Drusus, who was still living and was a lady of great influence, so warmly protested to him about the matter that he angrily told her to go and poison herself, which she did, and Caligula had her cremated in front of his dining-room window, but showed no interest in the proceeding.

Meanwhile, Agrippina had been reconciled to her husband at about the time when the charges against him had been dropped, and as a result of their renewed conjugal life she found that she was going to become a mother. She therefore left Rome and went to reside at their country house near the little seaport town of Antium, the modern Anzio, 35 miles south of the capital; and there, in the middle of December, A.D. 37, her confinement took place.

As her hour approached it may well be imagined that she asked herself what kind of a child she was likely to bring into the world. She knew already that her brother, Caligula, was more or less insane, and was at that time living openly with their sister, Drusilla, calling her his wife. She knew that her brother Drusus had been practically insane, and that her other brother, Nero, had been licentious to the degree of eccentricity. Her mother, Agrippina (the Elder), she recalled as a ferocious woman, burning with unbalanced hatred of the Emperor Tiberius; her uncle Agrippa, Agrippina's brother, was little short of a half-wit; and her mother's mother, Julia, the daughter of Augustus, had been one of the most immoral women of her time, and had been banished from Rome as an unlimited adulteress. Her aunt Julia, the daughter of this other Julia, had been exiled for the same reason, one of her lovers being the poet Ovid; and her cousin, Lepidus, that Julia's son, had shared with her brother in the corruption of her morals.

Her father, Germanicus, it is true, had been a gallant and charming personage, but his surviving brother, her uncle Claudius, was so stupid as to be almost imbecile, and at the same time was notorious for his immoralities; while his sister, her aunt Livia, had allowed her adulteries to make of her a murderess in the end.

So much for *her* side of her unborn baby's parentage; and what that was better was there to be said of its father? Cnæus was an Ahenobarbus, a family notorious for instability, treachery and licentiousness. He had never pretended to be faithful to her, and his guilty relationship with his sister, Domitia Lepida, could hardly be excused, as her own with Caligula could be, on the grounds of youth and inexperience.

What chance, then, was there that this coming child of hers would grow up to be a decent member of society? There was only this slender hope, that he would take after her father Germanicus. "It is generally agreed," says Suetonius,[16] "that Germanicus possessed all the noblest endowments of body and mind in a higher degree than had ever before fallen to the lot of any man." He was frank, affable, and modest; extraordinarily kind-hearted and humane, yet very brave in battle; dramatic and inspired, romantic and idealistic; a poet who wrote his verses equally well in Latin or Greek; a keen scholar; an eloquent speaker; and a passionate defender of the poor and the oppressed.

In spite of the otherwise shocking record of the family, there was, therefore, just this one hope for the newcomer; and in the following pages it will be seen that the hope was not entirely vain.

CHAPTER II

Nero's Birth, December, A.D. 37—His Infancy under the Emperor Caligula—The Exile of Agrippina, A.D. 39—The Death of Caligula, January, A.D. 41—The Accession of Claudius, and the Recall of Agrippina.

THE child, a boy, was born as the sun rose on December 15th, A.D. 37. He came into the world feet first, which was considered a very bad omen[1]; but the rising sun happened to strike upon him at the moment of his birth, and this was regarded as a favourable portent. But when the household went to congratulate the father, telling him what a fine baby was his, he only laughed, and remarked that nothing that was not detestable and a public menace could possibly be born of two such people as Agrippina and himself. He was a simple, unabashed, downright man, perfectly aware of his sins, and quite frankly untroubled by them.

Nine days later, in the presence of the Emperor Caligula, the boy was formally given the name Lucius Domitius Ahenobarbus, all his paternal ancestors having been called either Lucius Domitius or Cnæus Domitius; but later on he came to be known as Nero, and by this name, in anticipation, it will be more convenient to speak of him in these pages.

Caligula, as has been said, was at this time living openly with his sister Drusilla, with whom he was passionately in love; but as he had "lived in habitual incest with all his sisters,"[2] it may be that he was not unprepared to regard himself as the father of the child. If this be so, however, his interest in the infant no doubt declined when he observed that the downy hair on the baby's head was bright red, like that of all the Ahenobarbi. The little Nero was an Ahenobarbus surely enough, and the fact was somewhat disconcerting to Caligula, who had yet no child, and who therefore saw in this baby an elder cousin and rival of any future son of his own. A feeling of resentment against Agrippina and Cnæus, and this baby of theirs, began to grow in his dark and suspicious mind; and soon there was undisguised hostility between them.

A few months later Drusilla suddenly fell ill and died. Caligula was wild with grief. For weeks he refused to shave or have his hair cut, and he wandered from city to city, morose and savage, violently abusing and sometimes condemning to death those who did not seem to share his sorrow with sufficient demonstration. A certain senator, probably wishing to curry favour, declared that he had had a vision in which he saw Drusilla ascending to heaven in the company of the whole pantheon; and thereupon Caligula decreed that she should henceforth be worshipped as a goddess, and a golden statue of her was set up in the Forum.

It was shortly after this that his cousin, the eighteen-year-old Gemellus, met his end. The boy was suffering from a persistent cough, and one day he came into dinner smelling strongly of cough-mixture. Caligula accused him of having taken the medicine not to relieve his chest, but to protect himself against poison, it being quite a common practice in Rome at that time for one who was about to dine with an enemy to swallow an antidote before the meal.

Gemellus protested against the accusation, and a quarrel ensued, as a result of which Caligula sent a message to him after dinner, telling him to kill himself. The messenger handed the boy a sword, but Gemellus, weeping and coughing, said that he had never seen anybody commit suicide, and tremblingly asked what was the best way to do it. The messenger, it seems, explained that the point of the weapon should be held to the heart, beneath the ribs, and that one should then fall forward upon it; and thereupon the unfortunate youth did as he was bid, and expired in a pool of blood.

Finding his orders so instantly obeyed, Caligula now amused himself by telling all manner of people to commit suicide, and he was highly diverted when one by one they killed themselves. It made him feel entirely god-like thus to dispense life and death, and soon he began to declare that he himself was a god. He said he was in constant communication with Jupiter, and sometimes he could be seen with his hand to his ear and his brows knit, pretending to listen to some divine remark, after which he would nod gravely and whisper a reply. When the moon was in the sky he would call her his beloved, and would loudly demand that she should come to his bed.

He caused statues of himself to be placed in the temples, to be worshipped, ordering that only the best birds—peacocks, flamingos, pheasants, and so forth—should be sacrificed to him; and the next step, of course, was to constitute himself high-priest of himself, a seeming paradox which on closer investigation is seen to be logical, and was a theological commonplace in the ancient East—the earthly incarnation of a divine entity doing homage to that entity itself. But sometimes Caligula was puzzled to know whether to dress up as a high-priest and say prayers to himself and the other gods, or to put on a false beard like Jupiter's, and climb up onto a pedestal to receive as a god the adoration of the assembled mortals. He had a thunder-machine installed which, by the turning of a handle, could be made to rumble and roar as he stood glaring down on the congregation, and sometimes he used to challenge Jupiter to a friendly contest; but when there was a real thunderstorm, he was generally so scared that he used to crawl under the bed.

Once when he was posing as a god in the temple, and was wearing his false beard, an old working man burst out laughing. Caligula sent for him, and shouted at him: "Do you know who I am?" "Yes, I do," the man replied, still chuckling. "You're a priceless fool!" The Emperor, thoroughly staggered, turned in dismay to those around him. "Who is this man?" he gasped. Somebody explained that he was only one of those ignorant Celtic fellows from northern Gaul or Britain or somewhere; and, to everybody's surprise, Caligula waved him away unpunished.

He was passionately fond of the theatre, especially enjoying the music and dancing; and it is said that he could not keep from joining in the singing or imitating the gestures of the performers. He liked to take part in private theatricals, particularly if his rôle gave him the opportunity to dress up, preferably in women's clothes; and in everyday life his garments were often startling in their jewelled splendour.

It seems that he had a sense of humour of sorts. Once when a certain gentleman had made an unnecessary bustle in taking his seat at the theatre during a performance, Caligula sent for him and ordered him to proceed at once to North Africa, carrying a letter to the King of Mauritania. The letter, scribbled on the spot, contained only these words: "Do neither good nor harm to the bearer." At his parties he used to be inspired sometimes by the music to mimic the professional dancers, and he would make everybody laugh by his absurd contortions. Or he would dress up as Venus or one of the other goddesses, and stare with his curious snake-like and unblinking eyes at his friends, who never knew whether he were in fun or in earnest. Or, again, he would make terribly ferocious faces at those around him, as though he were about to have them all murdered; but it soon began to be known that he rehearsed these grimaces before a mirror in his room.

On one occasion he burst out laughing at dinner, and on being asked by his unctuous friends what it was that had tickled him, shocked them by replying that it was so ludicrous to think how, at a single nod from him, they might all have their throats cut. He had a favourite horse, named Incitatus, to which he assigned a beautifully furnished house and a retinue of servants; and supper-parties were given whereat it was supposed to be host. To crown the joke he made this horse a priest in his own temple, and he even suggested that he should make it a consul.

His immoralities were far worse than those of his predecessor, Tiberius, and he indulged in all sorts of vices. He assumed that others were as vicious as himself, and the presence of decent men or women imposed no restraints upon his words or actions. He used to declare with amusement that his mother was the daughter of an incestuous relation between Augustus and his daughter, Julia; nor did he deny his own acts of incest. He was completely shameless in this respect, and the stories told of him are unfit to be repeated.

His cruelty was his outstanding characteristic, and he prided himself on his pitilessness. "There is nothing in myself I find so admirable," he said to the Senate, "as my inflexible rigour." Bored with telling people to commit suicide, he had men and women of all ranks tortured and put to death before his eyes with every kind of indignity and cruelty; and he often caused people to be burnt alive in the amphitheatre. Slow deaths were most to his liking, and he would often declare that he wished his victims to feel themselves die.

The effect of his conduct upon his sister Agrippina was remarkable: she became extremely and exaggeratedly respectable. She objected not only to her brother's moral life, but also to his whole conception of his office. Caligula based his idea of sovereignty on that of the Greek Pharaohs of Egypt, he himself as Emperor being a hereditary Pharaoh; and he introduced into the court an Oriental atmosphere of splendour and licentiousness, and a crazy personal despotism, which made the Republic look like the ghost of a half-forgotten dream.

All the servants at the palace were Egyptians, and Helicon, his favourite freedman,[3] was a native of Alexandria. He prohibited the annual celebration of the victory of Actium, the battle at which Augustus defeated Antony and Cleopatra. He recognized the worship of the Egyptian goddess Isis as one of the official cults in Rome, and decreed an annual festival in her honour,[4] this being in direct contrast to the attitude of Tiberius, who had caused the Roman temples of Isis to be destroyed.[5] His relationship with Drusilla was justified by him on the grounds that the Pharaohs of Egypt married their sisters; and before her death, he declared her heiress of the empire, since, under the Egyptian matriarchal system, the descent of the crown and of all property passed through the female line. The great stress laid by him on his godhead was due to Egyptian influence, the Pharaohs being regarded as actual gods on earth; and it may be that the false beard he wore when dressed as a deity was the sacred plaited beard which the Egyptian Pharaohs and gods wore strapped on to their chins.

The introduction of these foreign ideas was deeply offensive to the old-fashioned patricians of Rome, and Agrippina and her husband now came out on the side of traditionalism. But in so doing they were obliged to declare for domestic morality also, since the old Roman virtues were inseparable from conservative society's conception of citizenship and patriotism.

Caligula, on the other hand, had, to some extent, the support of the younger and more fashionable set in Roman society; for, however tyrannical he might be, however mad and perverted, at least it was to be said of him that he encouraged the gaieties, the frivolities, and the luxuries which Augustus had endeavoured to suppress. He wanted to make an Alexandria of Rome, a bright city of hectic days and prodigal nights; and the "smart set" was with him heart and hand in this respect. Tiberius, with all his despotism, had been a Roman through and through, just as Augustus had been before him, and had even refused to use a Greek or other foreign word in conversation when a Latin one would serve; but now the conservative leaders of society, the traditionists, were in eclipse. The younger set had the bit between its teeth, and was going the pace, led by this young Emperor whose murderous excesses it was prepared to overlook provided that he conformed to the extravagant spirit of the times, gave Rome an air of Greek smartness and gaiety, and fostered in particular that night-life which Augustus had checked.

Thus, by a curious turn of fortune, the immoral Agrippina and her lawless husband—but especially Agrippina—came to be the main support of the old school, upholding the austerity, the purity, and the narrow conservatism of traditional Rome. Perhaps the new experience of motherhood had something to do with her outward reformation; or perhaps that boundless ambition which Tacitus believed to be the mainspring of all her actions had caused her to throw in her lot with the decent, if narrow-minded, element of society, in the belief that a wave of popular enthusiasm for reform might carry her and her husband to the imperial throne itself. Cnæus, after all, was the grandson of Octavia, the sister of Augustus: the Julian blood was in his veins, and the aristocratic party might see in him a possible Emperor.

Caligula, at any rate, recognized in their new posture a definite menace to his position; and suddenly, in the autumn of A.D. 39, like a threatened snake, he struck at them. Cnæus he flung into prison on a charge of treason, and Agrippina he consigned to exile upon the island of Pontia, 50 miles off the Campanian coast, while his other sister, Julia Livilla, who appeared to him to be involved in this plot against him, was also banished.

Both the sisters were accused also of improper relations with a handsome Sicilian horse-breeder, named Sofonius Tigellinus; and this man, of whom we shall hear again, was banished. He then put to death his cousin, Æmilius Lepidus, who had apparently still played the part of an occasional lover to Agrippina up to the time of her outward reformation.

The infant Nero, not yet two years old, was torn from his mother's arms, and was sent to the house of his father's sister, Domitia Lepida, a red-haired, fat, and unpleasant woman, accused by rumour of the most appalling immoralities. On December 11th, A.D. 40, Cnæus, the child's father, died of dropsy, and another typical member of the Bronze-Beard family at once stole the boy's inheritance—a pretty big fortune. Meanwhile, Agrippina ate her heart out in exile, deprived of the luxuries of life, and separated from the only human being she cared for—her red-haired little son, not even knowing how he was being treated by her disreputable sister-in-law.

Thereafter, Caligula continued his insane career. Such remaining popularity as he enjoyed was due to the magnificent entertainments he provided for the public, and to the dazzling splendour of his court. His extravagances in this respect are exemplified by the famous bridge of boats which he built across the Baian Gulf, from Bauli to Puteoli, a distance of some two miles. For this purpose he commandeered the boats from the harbours all round the coast, and in so doing partially paralysed sea-going traffic and nearly caused a famine in Italy.

The vessels were fastened together in a double line, and across them the road was laid, consisting of a wooden structure paved with stones and earth, there being "stations" at short intervals, supplied with drinking water by an aqueduct, and the entire length being illuminated at night by torches.

At the opening of this bridge—which was only intended to be a temporary structure—the Emperor rode on horseback from one end to the other at the head of his troops; and in the evening he gave a great public banquet, at which most of the guests were grouped in small boats beside the bridge. Somebody, however, started a panic, and a great many people were pushed off the bridge into the water, while several boats were upset. Caligula was drunk at the time, and it is said that he was riotously amused at the accident, and watched the victims drown with the greatest excitement, pushing them back into the water as fast as they scrambled out.

Having executed, murdered, or tortured to death most of his relations and friends, he entertained the frightened remainder to wildly extravagant feasts, at which the honour of no woman-guest, and the life of no man, was safe from him. He was endlessly building wonderful palaces; and his pleasure-galleys or barges, studded with precious stones, carrying sails of many colours, and containing baths of warm, scented water, became legendary. The hulls of two such barges, one certainly, and the other probably, built by his orders, have recently been reclaimed from the bottom of Lake Nemi, near Rome.

Philo, the Jewish philosopher of Alexandria, has left us a vivid description of the Emperor busy supervising the rebuilding and decoration of his villas and palaces. There had been trouble in Alexandria owing to the fact that while the Egyptians had readily accepted the idea of the divinity of Caligula, since their ancient Pharaohs had always been regarded as gods, the Jews of that city refused to worship any but Jehovah, and for that reason had been much persecuted. Philo, therefore, headed a deputation to Rome to explain to the Emperor in person that while they would always pray *for* him they could not possibly pray *to* him; and, with perhaps pardonable narrowness of religious understanding, he thought that Caligula would of course see his point at once.

When the deputation arrived in Rome, an audience was obtained in the palace gardens; but the Emperor, who was doing a little landscape gardening that day, merely waved his hand to them, and told them that he would hear what they had to say some other time. He then went off on a long tour of his villas and pavilions in the Bay of Naples, and these anxious Jews were obliged to follow him from place to place, hoping for the promised interview. At length they came trailing after him back to Rome, and, having endured many further disappointments, they were brought into his presence in the grounds of the palace on the Esquiline, where he was giving directions to the architects, artists, builders, and decorators engaged upon its renovation.

Philo and his friends at once prostrated themselves on the pathway; but Caligula made a terrible face at them, and demanded at once to know whether it were really true that they refused to acknowledge his godhead, adding such a string of blasphemous oaths that the Jewish chronicler says he could not possibly set them down in writing.

The Emperor then turned his back on them, and hurried away to examine the newly decorated rooms, while the deputation followed at a respectful distance. Suddenly he became aware of their presence once more, and, pointing his finger at Philo, snapped out: "Why don't you eat pork?"

This led to so much laughter on the part of the courtiers, who were always endeavouring to outdo one another in their appreciation of their master's jokes, that the officers of the guard ran about pushing and cuffing everybody, and telling them to behave themselves; and by the time that quiet was restored the Emperor was moving on into the next room.

After an hour or so the deputation, now frightened and weary, again passed under his notice, and he flung a question at them about their political organisation; but before they could answer, his attention was distracted once more, and many minutes elapsed before, suddenly, he turned to them again. "What were you saying?" he asked, as though the interruption had been momentary.

Philo began to explain at some length the Jewish constitution; but the Emperor, after staring at him blankly for some moments, wandered away. It was just like a farce at a theatre, says the chronicler. Caligula's friendship for Herod Agrippa, however, had given him a feeling of some tolerance towards Jews; and presently he remarked that Philo and his friends were more to be pitied than blamed for being so foolish as to deny his divinity, and with that he dismissed them. He could not resist teasing them, nevertheless, by giving orders that his statue was to be placed in the Holy of Holies in the temple of Jerusalem, upon hearing which Philo says that he and his friends were stupified with horror, and stood for some moments rooted to the spot.

One can hardly paint Caligula's character too

darkly, and it is not necessary to repeat the many stories of his cruelties and vices to support the opinion of Suetonius that he was "a monster rather than a man."[6] One more tale will suffice. The Emperor took it into his head to enter the arena at the public games, and to fight with a professional gladiator, who had been told to handle his imperial antagonist with the utmost care. The man parried all Caligula's blows, but refrained from striking back; and at the end of the fight he knelt down to ask his sovereign's pardon for opposing him at all, whereat the beastly young man ran him through with his sword, and, leaping up, shouted out that he was the victor, and strutted off, waving the palm-branch of victory above his head.

Curiously enough there was one person who loved him, namely a woman called Cæsonia, who was neither particularly young nor beautiful, and who was already the mother of three children by somebody else. He had had three or four wives, but now he married this woman on finding that she was going to have a child by him; and she managed to retain his affections for the remainder of his life. He used to mutter that he was quite astonished at his feelings for her; and though he would take her sometimes by the throat and remind her that one day he would cut it from ear to ear, she only smiled, and he never hurt a hair of her head.

For a while longer, Caligula pursued his horrible career of cruelty and oppression, but at last, at the beginning of A.D. 41, he made the mistake of insulting beyond endurance an officer of his bodyguard, a certain Cassius Chærea; and when, at the close of a performance in the amphitheatre on the evening of January 24th, the Emperor once too often held this old soldier up to ridicule, and mimicked his rather shrill voice, Chærea suddenly drew his sword and struck a blow at him which cleft deep into his shoulder.

Caligula was too dumbfounded even to cry out, and Chærea too horrified at what he had done to repeat the blow. The next moment, however, the Emperor was running for his life; but, as though a spell had been broken, other officials now drew their swords and struck at him, for the proposal to assassinate him had long been discussed, though nobody until now had dared to put it into execution.

Caligula fell to the ground, streaming with blood. "I am alive! I am alive!" he shrieked, but whether to ask to be saved or to be put out of his agony, cannot now be decided. At any rate, everybody hacked and thrust at him, and when his lifeless body was dragged away there were more than thirty gaping wounds in it. His wife, Cæsonia, flung herself upon his corpse, and her baby rolled from her arms into the pool of blood. The wretched woman was left there for some time in semi-darkness, moaning and wailing; but at length a soldier came to her and told her to prepare to die, too. She at once, almost gladly, bared her neck to him, and when he had despatched her, he took the baby by the heels and dashed its brains out against the wall.

Meanwhile, in the back premises of the house of Domitia Lepida, the infant Nero was being brought up in the care of a dancing-master and a hairdresser; and so little consideration was given him that Suetonius describes his condition as being almost that of a pauper. He was a trifle over three years of age at the time of the murder of Caligula, and had then been in his aunt's house some fifteen or sixteen months.[7]

Domitia Lepida had a pretty daughter, a well-developed, precociously erotic, weak-faced girl, named Valeria Messalina, who was some thirteen years older than her infant cousin Nero, and who, at just about the time of Nero's birth, had been married off to Claudius,[8] the brother of the late Germanicus, and nephew of the Emperor Tiberius, that is to say the little Nero's great-uncle, who, at Caligula's death, was fifty years of age.

This Claudius was generally regarded as an incorrigible fool. As a child he had been so sickly and so backward in his mental growth that his widowed mother, Antonia (daughter of Antony), spoke of him as "an abortion of a creature, only begun, but never finished by nature," and she gave him as a tutor a former mule-keeper, accustomed to deal with refractory mules, who thrashed him at the least provocation.

His mother married him at an early age to Æmilia Lepida, the great-granddaughter of Augustus, but she was snatched away again, before the marriage was consummated, owing to that Emperor's sudden disapproval of the young woman. Much bewildered, he was then betrothed to Livia Medullina, who, however, fell sick and died on the actual day fixed for the marriage. Next, he married Plautia Urgulanilla, and had two children by her, a boy, Drusus (who died in infancy, choked by a pear he was eating), and a girl, Claudia; but some months after the latter's birth he found that his wife was unfaithful to him, and, suspecting that he might not be the father of Claudia, he divorced her and left the baby, naked, on her doorstep. He then took to wife Ælia Pætina, but after she had born him a daughter, Antonia, divorced her on the grounds that she was a lewd woman, his actual reason being, however, that Domitia Lepida had offered him her pretty daughter, Messalina.

In spite of the slow development of his intelligence he had now become a fairly reasonable being, and lived a mild and quiet life, doing a little literary work now and then, and indulging a turn for historical research by preparing a history of Etruria and other antiquarian studies, all of which are lost. He was very susceptible, however, to the charms of women; and his excesses in the bedroom were only equalled by his intemperance in the dining hall. Daily he used to drink and eat until he fell asleep and snored, whereupon the guests would pelt him with olive-stones or pellets of bread, or would play some joke upon him such as putting slippers upon his hands so that, upon awaking, he might rub his eyes with them. The lack of respect with which he was treated is vividly revealed by the statement of Suetonius that "if at any time he chanced to be late for dinner, he was obliged to walk round the room some time before he could find a place at table."[9]

Messalina had presented him with a daughter, Octavia, in A.D. 39, when she was fifteen years of age; and now at the age of seventeen she was about to have her second child when the death of Caligula suddenly and quite unexpectedly brought the foolish Claudius into prominence. He happened to be at the palace at the time of the assassination, and, being terrified lest he, too, should be murdered, he hid himself behind a curtain; but a passing soldier saw his feet protruding from beneath its trembling folds, and, pouncing upon him, dragged him forth. Claudius was panic-stricken, thinking his last hour was come, and his teeth chattered in his head; but the soldier was still more frightened on recognizing him, and, in his excitement, threw himself at his feet, hailing him as Emperor. Claudius, however, was more popular with the troops than he knew, for he was the only surviving brother of their hero, Germanicus, and they liked him, moreover, as an easy-going, good-living, bawdy fellow, about whom they could make their improper jokes, just as their fathers had joked about Julius Cæsar whom they used affectionately to call their bald-headed old adulterer.[10] The consequence, therefore, was that Claudius was induced to face the other soldiers of the guard who were angrily roaming about the palace trying to prevent the servants from running away; and these men, half in jest, also hailed him as Emperor.

The Senate, as a matter of fact, was at a loss to find an Emperor, and next day there was much talk of abolishing the imperial office and restoring the Republic to a full use of the functions which, since the time of Augustus, had been merely nominal; but at last it was decided that the troops should have their way, and the honour was offered to the agitated Claudius, who had spent a night of mental agony locked up in the barracks.

For the first month of his reign he remained hidden in the palace, his knees knocking together in the fear that some other claimant to the throne would rise up and slay him; and it was during this period—on February 12th, to be exact,[11]—that Messalina's second baby was born. The child was a boy, who was named Tiberius Claudius, but came to be known afterwards as Britannicus in celebration of the conquest of Britain which took place in A.D. 43; and when at last Claudius found the courage to appear in public, he carried the baby in his arms so as to appeal to the sentiment of the people. They would hardly kill him, he thought, while he was nursing a baby; but, actually, nobody wanted to hurt him. Caligula had been such a disgrace to the Julian line that they were willing enough to revert to a Claudian, the nephew of the late Emperor Tiberius, fool though he was.

One of the first acts of Claudius was to recall from exile his nieces Agrippina and her sister Julia Livilla, as well as the horse-breeder, Sofonius Tigellinus, who had been accused of being their lover.

CHAPTER III

Nero's Boyhood from A.D. 41 to 48—The Struggle between his Mother Agrippina and the Empress Messalina—The Character of the Reigning Emperor Claudius.

For a year and a half Agrippina had been an agonized exile, daily expecting to receive the dread order from her brother to commit suicide. Daily she had no more than the hope of surviving until the morrow; for at any time somebody might lay information, false or true, against her, declaring that she had been in communication with one of the many people who were suspected of plotting the overthrow of the Emperor, or that she had cursed him or wished him dead. A single story of this kind about her, told, for instance, by a disgruntled servant, would have been sufficient to terminate her life; one little word uttered in anger, and reported by a slave or a soldier desirous of a reward, might have led to the arrival on her lonely island of an officer bearing the Emperor's orders to her to open the veins of her wrists and bleed to death in the customary manner. Scores of people had received such orders from Caligula, or from Tiberius before him; and she could not expect to escape.

When, therefore, the news of her brother's murder,

of the accession of her easy-going uncle Claudius, and of her recall to Rome, was brought to her by one of those messengers whose arrival on the island was the cause of recurrent terror to her, it must have seemed that the heavens had suddenly and blindingly opened and that the appalling cloud of impending doom had been miraculously dispersed. She was twenty-five years of age at the time, and was a woman of considerable beauty, the squareness of her jaw and the firmness of her mouth being tempered by her wide-set eyes and the softness of her hair which grew low upon her forehead, and was parted in the middle, waved down over her ears, and fastened at the nape of her neck. In her joy and relief she must have appeared radiant indeed as she was brought into the presence of Claudius at the palace; and the welcome he gave her was, doubtless, extremely affectionate. He had always been fond of this niece of his; and, in fact, when he was staying with her at Antium just after the birth of her boy, Nero, there had been a proposal that the child should be given his name, Claudius—a suggestion which she had scorned at the time, her uncle being regarded then as a nonentity, and no one having dreamed that he would one day be Emperor.

Agrippina's meeting with the new Empress, Messalina, however, can scarcely have been cordial, even when the eternal fraudulence of one woman's salutation to another is taken into account. The beautiful Messalina, as has already been said, was then seventeen years of age, and had just become the mother of a boy, the ill-fated Britannicus. She could hardly yet have been able to credit her good fortune in finding herself mistress of the Roman Empire; and, feeling still that her position had the insecurity, the unsubstantiality, of a wonderful dream, she may well have seen in the arrival of Agrippina the intrusion of a hard and disconcerting fact into her fantastical felicity.

This exile returned from the grave—who, curiously enough, was at once her aunt and her niece [1]—was the daughter of Rome's most idolised hero, the late Germanicus, and was, moreover, the descendant of the great Augustus, and hence a representative both of the Julian and the Claudian House; whereas neither Messalina nor Claudius could claim such illustrious lineage. Agrippina was still young and beautiful, and, being a widow, would soon find herself another husband, who, by virtue of his wife, might become a rival to Claudius, a man so weak-minded that he could hardly be expected to hold the imperial office for long. And then, again, Agrippina's son, the little Nero, would grow up to be the inevitable rival of Messalina's boy, Britannicus.

The enquiry as to the welfare of this Nero must have been Agrippina's first question; and though Claudius and Messalina were able to reply that he was safe in the care of the latter's mother, Domitia Lepida, the young Empress must have known that Agrippina would soon find out that he had been grossly neglected. There were thus present the possible causes of serious enmity between the two women; and in the following pages we shall see the development of these hostilities.

From the palace Agrippina went to the house of

her sister-in-law, Domitia Lepida, and was shocked to find the three-year-old Nero in the neglectful charge of the above-mentioned barber and dancer—a sad little red-haired child, underfed, unloved, and treated with all the poverty of benevolence so often extended to a poor relation. The grandson of Germanicus, the direct descendant of the divine Augustus, treated as a pauper! Agrippina's heart flamed with unaccustomed fires; and from that moment, so it seems to me, her self-control, her dignity, her show of morality which her repugnance to Caligula's way of life had forced upon her, were but the disguises of a ruthlessness, cruel and calculating, which had no plea to offer except the example of the female animal defending its young.

She wanted money with which to rehabilitate the boy and herself: at all costs she must have money, cart-loads of it, mountains of it. When Caligula had banished her, he had sold all her belongings by auction, and had quickly squandered the proceeds: her house, her furniture, her jewelry, her slaves, her horses—all had been sold; and now she found that her husband's lands had been seized by his surviving brother, and that her boy's heritage had been taken from him.

She appealed, of course, to her uncle Claudius to recover the lost inheritance; and he was able to give her back some of the Ahenobarbi lands. But that was not enough: she wanted to be second in wealth only to the Emperor—not altogether for herself, but for the sake of her boy, and for the honour of the Julian House. The love of money was a family trait. Her brother, the late Caligula, had rolled about upon the great heaps of gold pieces in his treasury, in order to feel the coins pressed against his body; he had taken off his shoes so as to experience the sensation of wading in gold; and the subconscious impulse behind these antics had been the sheer delight in the possession of wealth. But whereas he had enjoyed the prodigal spending of it, the wasting of it, the tossing it into the air for his slaves to catch, the flinging it to the crowds in dazzling showers, Agrippina had the instincts of the business woman. She was never generous, never prodigal; she was mercenary, thrifty, and parsimonious; she knew what it was to be in want; she knew the power of money, and she needed it desperately just now for the purposes of her ambition.

She had in her veins, it must also be remembered, the blood which in the case of her brother had led to every sort of crime; and though her horror at his conduct had made of her a very pillar of that old school of simplicity and respectability of which her great-grandfather, Augustus, had been the corner-stone, she was prepared to go to any lengths to gain her object. A cynical remark of Tacitus in regard to her,[2] that she would suffer no departure from her chastity unless it were likely to further her power, explains her conduct.

There was a man called Passienus Crispus, who was married to another sister-in-law of hers, Domitia (sister of the above-mentioned Domitia Lepida), and who was one of the most wealthy men in Rome. If she could only win his love she would not only obtain the money she required, but she would revenge herself upon her sister-in-law whom she happened heartily to dislike. She therefore set herself to gain the affections of this desirable Crispus; and, in accomplishing his seduction, the fire of ambition which illuminated the frozen caverns of her heart may well have been mistaken by him for passion, and may have inspired a reciprocal passion in his own heart. It was no little thing to be loved by a Julian princess.

He divorced the infuriated Domitia at Agrippina's command, and married his seducer; but not long afterwards, as soon, in fact, as he had made a will leaving her his vast fortune to add to the salvaged Ahenobarbi inheritance, he died mysteriously, and Agrippina, bland and unembarrassed, was enabled to reappear in Roman society as quite the most important, and probably the wealthiest, lady in the land, with the exception of her niece, the Empress Messalina, and the ex-Empress Lollia Paulina, divorced wife of the late Emperor Caligula, who was notoriously the richest woman in the world. Everybody said, of course, that Agrippina had poisoned Crispus to make way for some still more desirable husband; but she had now resumed her armour of frigid and haughty propriety, and the arrows of scandal could not harm her.

Before the year 41 was out Messalina had struck the first blow in her war with Agrippina. Fearing, as has been said, that the latter's son might one day put forward a claim to the throne at the expense of her own son—the imperial office being in no legal sense hereditary—she took steps to have the child murdered; for though she was still in her 'teens, and had been Empress but a few months, she was already familiar with the habits and usages of the imperial family, and was aware that private murder was always resorted to when the personage to be removed did not lend himself to formal execution or to enforced suicide.

One day when Nero was asleep in his cot, an attempt to strangle him was made by some men, apparently in the pay of the Empress, who had concealed themselves near by; but the approach of his mother frightened them, and they decamped. It was then discovered that an old snake-skin [3] had been placed under the boy's pillow, probably by his nurse, as a magical protection against harm; and Agrippina was superstitious enough to attribute his escape to the power of this charm.

But a snake-skin had also another occult quality, according to the folk-lore of the time, namely that of bestowing upon its possessor great honour through the medium of an elderly man, this fancy having its origin in the belief that an old snake renewed its strength and youth by shedding its skin.

Agrippina therefore took comfort in the thought that her boy was evidently going to be honoured in the future by the already middle-aged Claudius; and she caused the snake-skin to be made into a bracelet which she obliged Nero always to wear. Nevertheless, she was fearful for her little son's safety, and for her own; and the terrible danger in which they stood was again revealed to her by Messalina's next move.

As has been said, Agrippina's younger sister, Julia Livilla, had also been recalled from banishment by Claudius; but this young woman, being of the brood of

Caligula, led astray by him in her early youth, encouraged by him in her subsequent love-affairs,[4] and now, after months of enforced continence in exile, given the freedom of the palace once more, was soon involved in amorous intrigues, in which respect she vied with the young Empress herself, who had quickly reverted from the emotions of recent motherhood to those to which motherhood is the not uncommon sequel.

Now, Agrippina was much attached to the philosopher Seneca, and both she and Julia, it would seem, had been seen a good deal in his company; for he was a courtly man, much in evidence in society. Suddenly Messalina, as though in warning to Agrippina, caused Julia to be accused of improper relations with Seneca; and the bewildered Emperor, who was entirely under his wife's thumb, reluctantly gave the order for Julia to be banished once more, and for Seneca to be sent into exile on the wild island of Corsica. A few weeks later the unfortunate girl was done to death.

To Agrippina the blow must have been staggering. It would be her turn next, she felt, for she and her son were now the last of the main Julian line, and Messalina's dread of rivalry was far more active than was the family affection of Claudius, and her will far stronger than his. Obviously the only course for Agrippina to take was that of leading as quiet and inoffensive a life as possible, remaining unmarried, and limiting the number of her friends; and thus, during the next few years, history has nothing to record about her. Aware of her deadly peril, she seems to have gone into retirement, devoting herself to the upbringing of her son, and yet not daring even to do this with any conspicuousness.

She was a woman of no great intelligence, but she kept herself closely in touch with current opinion. She knew that the public was sick of the licentiousness of high society, and was veering back to the old morality. She saw clearly that the people were in no mood to stand any further behaviour in their princes such as that of Caligula; and she realized that Messalina's action against Julia Livilla had been a cynical attempt to demonstrate the moral reformation of the court at the same time that it was a blow struck in private hostility. Messalina, however, was now gathering a crop of scandals around her own name; and as the years went by the outrageous situations in which she was discovered multiplied. Already the number of men whom she had seduced from the path of virtue, under the nose of her weak and doting husband, had become a matter of general talk; and Agrippina, quietly watching the movement of events, could see that the Emperor was liable to lose what popularity he had by his blindness to the excesses of this silly and headstrong wife of his.

She therefore determined to bring up her son Nero in the straight and narrow way, educating him to be a second Augustus, an ultimate leader of a moral reformation, which, in the seemingly inevitable debacle to come, would bring him triumphantly to the throne. No less than this was her ambition for her son: he should be the next Emperor, if only Claudius should live long enough to see him grown to manhood. Diligently and even harshly she trained the boy to be the future reformer; and so severe was she with him, and yet so completely the fount of his existence, that she inspired an awe in him which he never overcame.

Controlling the tendencies of her nature—a nature at once mentally heartless and physically sensual—she presented a cold and virtuous face to those around her, a hard, unimpassioned, thin-lipped face. Inwardly she might burn with the fires of unindulged passion, of thwarted ambition, of half-concealed devotion to her little son, of impotent hatred towards those who menaced him; but outwardly she was a calm and chaste young widow, leading a life which the tongues of scandal could not reproach.

So, at least, I read her character in an effort to reconcile her position as a pillar of propriety with her shocking moral record. Clearly she was outwardly pious and chaste. Tacitus says that her manner was grave, frigid and ostensibly virtuous, and, in a public speech, she was described as of unblemished purity and of strict moral behaviour,[5] while, as we shall presently see, she introduced the severest simplicity into the imperial household, and prosecuted people on the charge of immorality. Yet, at the same time, we have to think of her as a member of an infamous family, the partner of a perverted brother's and a cousin's lust, the seducer and perhaps the murderess of Crispus, the mistress of at least two other men,[6] and the ultimate villainess of the piece. Passionate, hot-tempered, and high-handed she must have been, and yet at the same time austere, hard, and exaggeratedly respectable; but the contradiction will perhaps be understandable when we remember that a member of a naturally dissolute family who has an unindulged tendency towards immorality and viciousness often becomes the most intolerant opponent of those tendencies when expressed in others. There is no woman so frigidly puritanical as the thwarted sinner.

In A.D. 47, however, when Nero was nearly ten years of age, an incident occurred which was at once a joy and a terror to his mother. In honour of the eighth centenary of the foundation of Rome, the traditional "Game of Troy" was enacted, in which two troops of cavalry, consisting of boys of the noblest birth, fought a mimic battle. It was a dangerous game which so often caused serious accidents to the boys that Augustus had been obliged to put an end to it, after one of the lads had been lamed for life[7]; but it was afterwards revived. In this particular case, one troop, of course, had to be led by the Emperor's little son, Britannicus, then aged six; but to Agrippina's great alarm, the organizers of the fête chose Nero to lead the other troop.

Now Nero had often been told by his mother how his legendary ancestor Julius-Ascanius, the founder of the Julian House, the son of Æneas, had fought upon the plains of Troy; and in this mimic battle, the small, red-headed boy, vain of his ancestry, and encouraged by the approving shouts of the vast concourse of people, conducted himself with great spirit and dash, galloping about the ground, waving his toy sword, and nearly smothering Britannicus with his dust. At the end of the fight he received a tremendous ovation, but his cousin was hardly noticed.

Claudius was too easy-going, or too indifferent, to bear much resentment for the slight to his son; but his wife, Messalina, must have been enraged by it, and, with her ever increasing recklessness which now led her almost as frequently into casual murder as into haphazard adultery, would probably have made a second attempt upon Nero's life had not sudden disaster befallen herself, as will be related in the next chapter.

The Emperor Claudius, born in B.C. 10, was now a man of fifty-seven years of age, and was old for his years at that, being in a diseased condition which was gradually paralysing him; whereas Messalina was twenty-three, healthy, passionate, and romantic—if there can be any romance maintained in multiple infidelity. Her love affairs were now so notorious that even her infamous mother, Domitia Lepida, would not speak to her; but her husband either did not know about them or else was too sick, or perhaps too deeply hurt, to make any protest. So tattered was her reputation that libidinous gossip credited her with frequenting the crowded houses of ill-fame whenever there was a shortage of lovers at the palace; but since this is the stock story told of the famous loose women of antiquity, we may regard it less as a fact than as an indication that the public's imaginary conception of nymphomania was evoked by her behaviour.

The Emperor, who was still very much in love with her, was a ludicrous yet pathetic figure. He was a tall, heavily-built, grey-haired, clean-shaven man, who, "whether standing or sitting, but especially when he lay asleep, had a majestic and graceful appearance, though his knees were feeble and failed him in walking,"[8] so that his feet dragged and his shoes shuffled. The expression of his face was one of puzzled bewilderment; his forehead was wrinkled, his blue and bleary eyes curiously sorrowful, his mouth tremulous, and his chin small and weak. A nervous affliction caused his head to shake perceptibly; and he was always starting at the slightest unusual sound, or staring about him uncomprehendingly as though something were worrying him. His stammering speech, too, was very indistinct, and he often failed to make himself understood.

Usually he was good-tempered and well-meaning, and he was famous for his frequent fits of loud and rather idiotic laughter. Once, for example, when he was reading one of his own historical essays to a solemn assembly, the weight of a certain fat man caused the bench on which he was seated to collapse, and the Emperor burst thereat into paroxysms of mirth which were renewed again and again whenever he thought of it. Sometimes, however, he lost his temper, and in his wrath his appearance was very disgusting, for he foamed at the mouth, his eyes rolled, and his head twitched.

The most unpleasant feature of his character was a half-witted, but probably not sadistic, enjoyment of the infliction of pain, by reason of which he was often seen shuffling off to the prison so as to be present at the torture or execution of criminals; and in the arena he seldom permitted a defeated gladiator to escape butchery. He took great pleasure in watching people given to the wild beasts, and when the men employed about the amphitheatre were careless in their work he would suddenly order a stage-carpenter, a scene-shifter, or, maybe, a call-boy, to be thrown to the lions. He was ruthless, too, in his judicial condemnations to death, and no less than thirty-five senators and three hundred Roman gentlemen [9] were executed by his orders—these orders being given so recklessly that he had afterwards no memory of many of them, and used to send for men whom he had thus murdered, quite forgetting that they were no longer alive to answer his summons.

In other respects, however, he was kindly, considerate, and laughably human. Once, when one of his guests at a big dinner-party had stolen the golden cup from which he had been drinking, Claudius punished him merely by inviting him a second time and placing only earthenware before him. Upon another occasion a guest was taken seriously ill as a consequence of a good-mannered attempt to suppress his eructations, whereupon the Emperor immediately wrote an edict to the people of Rome—which, however, was never issued—granting them permission "to give vent at table to any distension occasioned by flatulence." [10] He was an inveterate gambler, and was endlessly shaking the dice-box; and, in fact, he had a gaming-board fixed in his chariot, so that he could throw the dice with a friend even while taking the air or making a journey.

He was extremely greedy at meals, and the smell of cooking always set him sniffing excitedly. Once, when he was judging a case in court, the pleasant savour of the priests' dinner in the temple across the way drifted to his nostrils; and, to the dismay of the litigants, he rose in a sort of rapture from the magistrate's seat and hurried over to ask a share of the meal. He was tipsy every evening, and often fell asleep on his dining-couch with his mouth open, whereupon his physicians would take the opportunity to tickle his throat with a feather so that his over-loaded stomach might painlessly relieve itself as he lay dreaming. Sometimes he would fall asleep while transacting business, and his ministers were obliged then to speak loudly or bump the furniture about in order to wake him.

His increasing years and his infirmity did not correct his improper interest in the other sex, and the best that can be said of him in this regard is that he showed no inclination towards the perverted vices of the time, and that the homosexual tendencies of Julius Caesar, Tiberius and Caligula were completely absent in him. He was, in fact, the typical roué, tipsily ogling every pretty woman he saw, yet maudlin in his affection for Messalina and greatly elated when she condescended to take any notice of him. He was devoted to their two children, Octavia and Britannicus, and to his daughter by an earlier marriage, Antonia, all three being with him at the palace and usually having their meals with him. He was fond of animals, too, and a white poodle, who never knew that he was an Emperor, remained his friend until the end from motives of pure affection.

The lack of respect in which he was held led to two

or three attempts at rebellion; and he was always so afraid of assassination that he caused everybody to be searched for concealed weapons before coming into his presence. Roman society in general, however, tolerated him as a well-meaning, vulgar, simple-minded man, though the fact that he so often said the wrong thing or forgot to conduct himself with proper dignity caused the old-fashioned nobility to shake their heads over him. He was too fond of Greek culture and the Greek language, moreover, to please the narrow-minded patriots, in whose opinion nothing that was not Roman was worthy of admiration; and the great respect he showed for the memory of his grandfather, Antony, was regarded as something of a slight upon that of Augustus.

Apart from being at the beck and call of Messalina, he was entirely in the hands of three aged freedmen—ex-slaves who had been manumitted and raised to high office: Narcissus, Pallas, and Polybius, the first-named being, one might say, the actual ruler of the Roman Empire. Narcissus had the merit of being fond of his master; but the other two seem to have bullied and pestered the weak-minded Emperor with their demands, and made fun of him behind his back—in which they were not alone, for Claudius was the butt of a thousand jokes, and, indeed, was often treated with contempt in public. On one occasion, for instance, when he was judging a case in court, an angry litigant called him "an old fool," to his face; and on another occasion an exasperated petitioner threw his writing materials at his head.

Agrippina watched the trend of events with intense and impotent anxiety. If Claudius were soon to die or to be dethroned the chances of her son Nero becoming Emperor would be exceedingly slender. Neither he nor Britannicus were old enough to be given the throne, and quite possibly the imperial office would be abolished, and the Republic restored to its lost authority. Her only hope was that her uncle would live until Nero had attained his manhood or something like it, and that he would not too dismally fail to maintain the prestige of his office.

His health was becoming more and more precarious, but with care and attention surely his physical collapse, if not his mental, could be staved off for a few more years; but who was there at court to nurse him? Not Messalina: she could not stand the sight of him. Not those three freedmen who were always at his elbow: they had all made their fortunes, and were ready to retire.

If only she could take up her residence at the palace herself, take charge of him, look after his health, and keep him from making a fool of himself, all might be well. After all, he was her uncle; and what could be more proper than that a man should be looked after by his niece? First, however, she would have to get rid of her enemy, Messalina: there was no room for both of them, and she knew quite well that any interference on her part in the affairs of the palace would mean that Messalina would employ all her power in effecting the intruder's destruction.

CHAPTER IV

The Plot Against the Empress Messalina—Her Marriage to Silius—Her Death, A.D. 48—The Coming of Nero and his Mother to the Palace.

In A.D. 48 Messalina was in her twenty-fourth year, and a bust of her,[1] sculptured at about this time, shows her as a comfortable, voluptuous, pleasant faced but somewhat brainless-looking woman, with a low forehead, heavy brows, large, bovine eyes, and soft, curly hair parted in the middle and drawn loosely over her ears. Her hair was of the red-gold colour,[2] typical of her mother's family, and, indeed, she was in other respects also an Ahenobarbus, having the full-blooded, corporeal appearance noticeable in Domitia Lepida and Nero, but lacking both the brightness of expression which animates the faces of these two, and also their hint of good breeding. She gives the impression of being a healthy, lazily lustful, self-indulgent, careless soul, intended by nature—as are the majority of immoral women—for prolific motherhood. One might say, perhaps, that she was rather a fool.

Her position as Empress, and wife of an Emperor in his too early dotage, had engendered in her mind an unbounded belief in her licence to amuse herself to her heart's content without consideration of the consequences, and she now thought nothing of sending discarded lovers and other troublesome persons to their deaths by the simple expedient of having them accused of treason, the fear of assassination being her husband's darkest dread. She felt that she could do as she pleased with Claudius, and, indeed, she must have known by constantly recurring experience that she had but to show a voluptuous interest in him when they were alone together to win from him whatever she desired to obtain.

She was wildly extravagant, and spent money like water, much to the distress of Pallas, the keeper of the Emperor's private purse, who, nevertheless, was obliged to humour her, though daily he became more ready to procure her downfall if ever the chance to do so with impunity should come his way. Narcissus, too, was sorely tried, and was on the verge of an open rupture with her, for, as has been said, he was a man who seems to have had the interests of Claudius sincerely at heart.

But it was Polybius who precipitated matters by actually quarrelling with the wayward Empress. He was a man of learning, who had translated Homer into Latin and Virgil into Greek, and whose chief business it was to help the Emperor in his historical and antiquarian studies. He had been a great friend of the exiled Seneca, and therefore was by no means well-disposed towards Messalina, who had caused the philosopher's banishment; and lately he had been indiscreet enough to show a growing friendship for Agrippina and her son, Nero.

On this account the Empress had regarded him for some time with suspicion, and now she suddenly bestirred herself to accuse him of treason, whereat the Emperor, shocked, bewildered, and flung into a panic at the thought of an assassin at his very elbow, ordered him instantly to be put to death.

His place at court was filled by another freedman, Callistus, a jovial old soul who, if he could not discuss historical problems with his imperial master, at least could make him laugh; but upon Narcissus and Pallas the effect of the fate of their colleague was more than Messalina had bargained for. They were thoroughly scared, and, knowing that their turn might come next, they began to give secret and nervous consideration to the matter of ridding themselves of this menace to their lives. Agrippina, on her part, must also have been thrown into a state of intense anxiety by the death of Polybius; and, realizing that he had forfeited his life by showing friendship towards herself, she determined to be revenged upon Messalina and to put a final stop to her protracted hostility. If only Claudius could be induced to divorce her; if only his eyes could be opened to her infidelity! But who would dare to tell him, and risk Messalina's wrath and the terrible consequences of her probable ability to hoodwink her husband once more?

The Empress's latest lover at this time was a certain Caius Silius, a handsome and extremely attractive young man of aristocratic family, who was shortly to be raised to consular rank; and though the Emperor, in his blindness, did not permit himself to think that there was at present anything but the merest friendship between his wife and this personage, he was undoubtedly jealous of him and wished him no good. Nor was jealousy the only feeling aroused: he always experienced a sense of uneasiness, too, in regard to Messalina's men friends, for, as has been said, the dread of assassination was ever with him, and who more likely to wish him dead than a man attracted to his wife?

One day it came to the knowledge of Agrippina [3] or the conspiring freedmen that there was a prophecy being whispered around the city, which predicted that "the husband of Messalina" would die within the year. By some means or other this omen was brought to the Emperor's attention, and his fears were worked upon with such cunning that he was almost scared out of his wits. Narcissus then boldly carried out the plan agreed upon between himself and his friends: he whispered to the frightened Emperor that his only hope of escape lay in his ceasing, only temporarily of course, to be Messalina's husband; and to the query as to what "husband," then, the curse would fall upon, he replied that Messalina could be married off to somebody else—Caius Silius, for example—who would thus be the fated victim.

Claudius no doubt protested that he would not dream of hurting Messalina's feelings by discharging her in this manner, and, anyhow, he did not want to lose her. He had been, and perhaps still was, very much in love with her, and, after all, she was the mother of his two children. But Narcissus, it seems, blandly pointed out that she need never know anything about it. The Emperor would merely have to put his seal to a document marrying her to another man, after which life at the palace would proceed as before; and when the fatal year was over, and this other man presumably dead, he could sign another document remarrying her. Not a word need be said to her about it from beginning to end.

Claudius was greatly intrigued. He was tickled to think that the predicted blow could be so easily deflected from his own head to that of one of his wife's admirers: it was the kind of quibble which pleased him, one of his idiosyncrasies being his love of precisionisms and petty technicalities, and his enjoyment of scoring off his friends or foes by sophistry and hair-splitting. Like so many persons of restricted mental range he had what is called a legal mind; and the extension of this propensity into the realm of necromancy was quite natural to him.

A point which, I think, has been overlooked by historians is that in ancient Roman law a husband was entitled to give his wife in matrimony to another man, furnishing the dowry which the transaction legally required: Augustus, in fact, had received his wife, Livia, in this manner from her former husband, and other cases are also on record. Claudius, therefore, at once and with childish glee signed the necessary papers, mischievously choosing Caius Silius as the "husband of Messalina" who should be the victim of the prophecy. He had no idea that this young man was his wife's actual lover: he imagined him to be just a foolish and tiresome admirer of hers who had merited his fate by being a little too free and easy with the Empress. The joke would be that neither Messalina nor this shadow-husband of hers would ever know that he, Claudius, had made them temporary man and wife; and in the ensuing months Messalina would have no idea that in sharing as usual the Emperor's bed she would be, for the time being, an adulteress.

"What is beyond all belief," writes Suetonius,[4] "is the fact that Claudius himself should have actually signed the documents relative to Messalina's dowry for her marriage with her adulterous lover, Silius, induced, as it is supposed, by a scheme for diverting from himself and transferring to another the danger which the omens seemed to threaten." But Suetonius did not realize that Messalina and Silius themselves were not in the secret; yet to me it seems that this ignorance on their part is the only available key to the riddle presented by the events about to be recorded. I have no authority for the assertion that Claudius intended to keep them ignorant of the fact that they had been technically united; but, as will presently become apparent, no other solution of the problem meets the difficulty.

Having signed the document, and being temporarily a bachelor, Claudius went away for a few days' visit to Ostia, sixteen miles from Rome. The month was October, and the annual festival of the Vintage which coincided with the full moon was to be celebrated on the morrow; and the Emperor had arranged, this year, to be present at Ostia to conduct there the religious service which began the day. He was going to enjoy himself, and he took with him two ladies of easy virtue, by name Calpurnia and Cleopatra, to make merry with him in the absence of Messalina, who remained in Rome. But no sooner was he gone than the conspirators carried the plot to its diabolical conclusion by telling Messalina that very thing which was to be kept from her knowledge, namely that the Emperor had made the necessary arrangements for her transfer to a younger and more capable husband—to wit, Caius Silius.

It was a move of surprising boldness, and its chances of success lay in Messalina's indignation against Claudius and her acceptance of Silius in matrimony. The freedmen must have known that, this time, she was violently in love, and desired more than a passing affair with the man of her choice; but it may well have seemed to them that, even so, she would attempt to revenge herself upon Claudius for the affront to her dignity. They had surrounded her with *agents provocateurs* who were ready to charge her with conspiracy against the Emperor should she show the least sign of active resentment; and they hoped that she and Silius would do something spectacular to cover her shame. With luck, Messalina might even try to raise a rebellion, for the purpose of dethroning Claudius and acclaiming the infant Britannicus as Emperor-elect, with herself and Silius as regents, just as Queen Cleopatra and Antony had once aimed at seizing the sovereignty of Rome so as to hand it over to Cæsarion, Cleopatra's son by Julius Cæsar, when he should come of age.[5]

As was expected, Messalina was indignant at the

news that she had been given to Silius, but at the same time her passion for the young man induced her to make no protest. Very well, then, she seems to have said: she would call all Rome to her wedding, and would let it be understood that the transfer of her affections from a half-witted Emperor to a virile and fascinating young man was her own doing.

Agrippina and the freedmen with bated breath must have watched her walk into the trap. Claudius in my opinion, as I have already said, did not know that Messalina had been told of his action in technically handing her over to Silius; and when the report of her public wedding should reach his ears the conspirators knew that he would think she had married the young man in full consciousness that she was committing bigamy, deliberately offering the Emperor this crowning slight. Surely, they said to themselves, he would never forgive her.

The wedding took place within a few hours, and was celebrated in public. "I am aware that it will appear incredible," says Tacitus,[6] "that any human beings should have exhibited such recklessness of consequences, and that, in a city where everything was known and talked of, any man, much more a consul elect, as was Silius, should have met the Emperor's wife, as for the purpose of procreation, on a stated day and in the presence of persons called in to witness and seal the deeds, and that she should have heard the words of the augurs, as at a wedding, entered the house of the husband, sacrificed to the gods, sat down with the guests at the wedding-breakfast, exchanged kisses and embraces, and, in fine, passed the night in unrestrained bridal intercourse."

Tacitus evidently was unaware of the fact which Suetonius records, namely that Claudius himself had signed the marriage-deed; and he was thus justified in regarding the wedding as one of almost incredible audacity. On the other hand, our authorities make it certain that Claudius was dumbfounded when the news of the marriage was brought to him; and this discrepancy, in my opinion, can only be explained in the way I have suggested above, namely that Messalina had been told of the Emperor's transfer of her to Silius, but that Claudius did not know that she had been told, and thought she had acted in scandalous disregard of her marriage vows to himself.

Tacitus thinks that Silius was as much to blame as Messalina in hurrying on the wedding and making it as public as possible. He felt, says this historian, that Claudius in any case would presently turn upon him; and he thought that it would be wiser to act with daring and even make a bid for the throne, or, rather, the regency, forcing Claudius to abdicate, and adopting Britannicus as his own son, proclaiming him Emperor-to-be. At any rate, it is agreed that Claudius, when he was told of the wedding, was quite certain that Silius aspired to nothing less than the throne.

The news was broken to him in the following manner. On the morning after the wedding the three freedmen, Narcissus, Pallas, and Callistus, had discussed the situation; and while Pallas and Callistus, fearing Messalina, were for allowing the Emperor to find out for himself what had taken place, Narcissus had thought that it would be best to go to Ostia at once and tell him. The latter course was adopted, but on arriving at Ostia Narcissus' heart had failed him, and, having told the news to the two courtesans, Calpurnia and Cleopatra, he had persuaded them to go in first to the Emperor.

Claudius, in a frenzy, ordered Narcissus to come to him, and the freedman at once begged the Emperor's forgiveness for having concealed from him Messalina's many infidelities, adding that, so as to spare him pain, he would have attempted to conceal even this affair, had not the matter been so serious. "Messalina has married Silius," he groaned, "in the presence of senators, military officers, and citizens; and unless you act with speed, her husband will be master of Rome." [7] At this, Claudius "was so dumbfounded and panic-struck that he asked over and over again whether he were still Emperor."

That was his first bewildered thought, and he instantly gave his agitated attention to the overthrow of this unexpected rival. His feelings in regard to Messalina were not so definite: he saw that she was perhaps to be excused for marrying the man, for he must have guessed that somebody had told her that he, Claudius, had intended her to do so when he drew up that secret document which he now so heartily wished he had never been induced to sign. Narcissus, of course, assured him that she did not know of this document, and that she had acted in total disregard of her marriage vows; but Claudius could not be brought to believe entirely in her guilt, and thus the plot against her looked for a while as though it were going to miscarry. At one moment the Emperor was swearing that he would have no mercy upon her; at the next he was tearfully recalling the happiness of their married life, and bemoaning the fate of his two children, who would be left motherless if he were to take drastic steps against her.

One thing he realized, that he would have to go at once to Rome to assert himself and nip this potential conspiracy in the bud. Silius would have to be arrested: that was certain. But who could be trusted to seize him? The Emperor felt himself to be surrounded by secret enemies: even Lucius Geta, the commander of the Prætorian Guard, was not to be trusted. No one was to be trusted, in fact, except his faithful Narcissus, upon whose shoulder he could not restrain himself from sobbing out his grief and his anxiety.

Narcissus then suggested that for one day Geta should be suspended, and that he, Narcissus, should be given the command, and with it the responsibility of rounding up the supposed culprits. To this Claudius, in his perplexity, agreed; and thereupon Narcissus at once sent officers galloping off to Rome with orders to surround the house of Silius and to arrest everybody within it. Shortly afterwards—presumably in the afternoon of the day following the wedding—he and the Emperor set out for Rome, Narcissus riding with his distracted master in the imperial chariot.

Meanwhile, in the city, the golden haired Messalina, flushed and excited by the events of the previous day, and thrilled by the authorized and even ceremoniously conducted lechery of her bridal night with Silius, had been unwilling to call a halt to the headlong progress of this frenzied debauch. As has been said, this was the day of the annual festival of the vintage, when all Italy lawfully misbehaved itself in a tipsy and lascivious carousal in honour of the gods of the vine. Few people were sober on that day, but Messalina was drunk with more than wine: she was feverishly in love, and since she was a woman accustomed to express every sort and degree of amorous emotion in immediate adultery, it may be understood that this exceptionally violent attack of her chronic malady of physical desire was only to be appeased in an unprecedented orgy of erotic excitement. "Never," says Tacitus, "had she wallowed in such voluptuousness."

In the name of the vintage-gods, who were patrons, too, of sexual licence and fertility, she summoned her friends to the palace, where she and Silius announced that they would continue the wedding-revels of the day before in the appropriate guise of a Bacchic festival. The anxious business of arousing the people to dethrone the foolish Claudius would have to wait until the morrow: today the whole country was given up to merry-making, and here at the palace the Dionysian madness in all its habitual obscenity should be unchecked by thought of the political convulsion so near at hand. The dangers and the hoped for triumphs to come should be but their aphrodisiac, and defiance of their crazily unbalanced fate should be their incentive to unheard of excesses of salacity.

Tacitus [8] describes the ensuing scene. In the gardens of the Palatine the wine-presses were set up, the troughs being heaped high with grapes upon which almost nude slaves, chosen, as was the custom, from the most handsome of the palace-youths, leapt and capered, pressing the squelching grapes with their feet until the juice ran out into the vats. Around them danced intoxicated women, scantily begirt with skins in the manner of Bacchanalians, and maddened to sexual frenzy by the worked-up excitement which was regarded as the inspiration of the unseen yet present god of the festival. Leading the wild and wanton dance "Messalina herself, with her hair loose and flying about, waved the thyrsus—the wreathed staff of Bacchus; while at her side Silius, crowned with ivy and wearing buskins, tossed his head to and fro." The beating of tambourines and the rhythmic clapping of hands made noisy accompaniment to the Bacchanalian songs sung by the onlookers, who thronged about the dancers, collectively inciting the crowd to the individual depravities in which the festival should culminate.

At the height of the orgy a certain doctor, named Vectius Valens, who, like many other men present, had a particular interest in the proceedings by reason of the fact that Messalina had from time to time taken him to her bed, climbed to the top of a high tree in the garden to exhibit his agility and nerve. Somebody called up to him, asking him what he could see from his lofty perch; and in reply he laughed, "A hurricane from the direction of Ostia"—ominous words which had hardly been spoken when messengers came panting into the garden, crying out that the Emperor was returning to Rome, bent on immediate vengeance.

In an instant all was confusion. The dancers dispersed; the intoxicated guests staggered off this way and that; Silius hastened to the Forum, hoping to establish an alibi; and Messalina, whom one is compelled to picture as rather drunk, betook herself to her villa in the Horti Luculliani, the Gardens of Lucullus,[9] on the Pincian Hill, north of the city—an estate which had become her private property on the death of its owner, Valerius Asiaticus, whom she had caused to be executed on a charge of treason, in order, so people suspected,[10] that she might obtain possession of this most beautiful suburban retreat. It seems that her mother, Domitia Lepida, and her two children, Octavia and Britannicus, were staying there at the time, and that the elderly Vibidia, the "mother-superior" of the Vestal Virgins (the famous nuns of Rome), was a guest at the villa, probably so that she might avoid the noises and disturbances of this bibulous holiday.

Domitia Lepida received her flushed and befuddled daughter with stern reproval, and told her that the best thing she could do would be to take the two children with her and go to meet the Emperor as he approached along the Via Ostiensis, the highway which ran beside the left bank of the Tiber, connecting Rome with Ostia. Messalina had been on rather bad terms with her mother for some time, but at this crisis she was willing enough to do what the elder woman told her; and she persuaded the good Vibidia to accompany her so as to intercede for her in the event of her being unable to appeal successfully to the Emperor's affection. It was not her marriage to Silius which was on her conscience: *that* could surely be justified, since Claudius had himself handed her over to the young man, and, so she supposed, had expected her to celebrate the wedding at once, if not quite so publicly or so riotously. What troubled her was that the Emperor had apparently been told of her previous infidelities, and was furious with her both on this account and also because her rudimentary plans for dethroning him had been reported to him. Heaven knows what she had said to her friends in this regard under the combined influence of love, indignation, and drink!

But now, as she was about to set out, the terrible predicament in which she stood became clear to her rapidly sobering brain: nobody answered her call for her litter. The household slaves had nearly all fled, and those who remained told her, in abject terror, that the soldiers sent ahead by Narcissus had seized the house of Silius, and were arresting her late guests wherever they came upon them.

There was nothing to be done but to traverse the city on foot, and make her way as best she could to the Ostia road. Fortunately, the streets had suddenly become almost deserted; for the arrival of the soldiers had substantiated the wild rumours which were flying about, and there had been a general rush for cover: home was the safest place for every man. By lucky chance she and Vibidia, holding the frightened little Octavia and Britannicus by the hand, were not accosted as they hurried along, though many must have recognized them with astonishment and fear; but as they approached the gate in the city walls the danger of arrest or detention became imminent.

Here, however, they came up with a gardener's cart, loaded with refuse which was being taken out of the city from one of the public gardens; and, Vibidia—so I suppose—having revealed her identity, the driver allowed them to scramble in, thinking that the kindly Vestal was conveying some nervous woman and her two children out of danger's way. The guard at the gate, paying like respect to the venerable nun, allowed the cart to pass; but they had not gone far along the Ostia highway when, in the distance, they saw the Emperor's cavalcade approaching, whereupon they alighted, and while Vibidia and the two children remained at the side of the road, Messalina boldly went forward to meet him.

An outrider recognized her, and galloped back to the main party with the news that the solitary woman standing in the roadway was Messalina herself; and at this Narcissus, who, as has been said, was riding in the Emperor's chariot, must have felt, with beating heart, that the crisis of the whole affair had arrived. If her pathetic distress were to arouse the Emperor's pity, all would be lost: she would be forgiven, and his own life would not be worth a day's purchase. Hastily he took from the folds of his gown a writing-tablet upon which he had scribbled the names of some of the Empress's lovers, and began feverishly to recite the list in his master's ear. He was thus engaged when Messalina ran towards the chariot, holding forth her hands in supplication, and crying out that Claudius would surely listen to the mother of Octavia and Britannicus.

But Narcissus whispered to him, telling him not to look at her, and the Emperor, unable in any crisis to act on his own initiative, obediently stared straight in front of him, his mouth fallen open and his head twitching; and presently the cavalcade had passed, leaving the fallen Empress obscured in its dust.

A few minutes later Vibidia and the children stepped out into the roadway, but at once Narcissus ordered an officer to take the boy and girl and their mother back to the Pincian villa, while in response to Vibidia's entreaties he gave the promise that the Emperor would grant Messalina an opportunity of clearing herself on the morrow. Claudius himself spoke not a word, and, as Tacitus tells us,[11] "his silence while all this was going on was matter of astonishment"; but it is possible, of course, that he was drunk.

Narcissus then caused him to be driven to the house of Silius, and in it the Emperor was shown various objects belonging to himself, and many of his family heirlooms, which Messalina had taken from the palace and had given to her lover. This at last aroused him from his lethargy, and, uttering a string of oaths, he went back to his chariot and was driven to the barracks of the Prætorian Guard; yet, all the way there, he kept nervously asking those around him whether the throne were still his, and whether there was any danger to be feared from these troops.[12]

The soldiers, of course, were flattered that he had come to them for protection, and when he had made a brief and halting speech to them, they all shouted out that Silius and his friends, who had been arrested and were now in the guardroom, should be immediately tried and punished. Thereupon, Claudius shuffled up the steps to the tribunal-bench, and, as soon as he was seated, the wretched Silius was dragged before him.

The young man made no defence and asked no mercy; he only begged to be put out of his misery quickly; and a few moments later he was dead, the prophecy that "Messalina's husband" should soon die being thus fulfilled. Then, one by one, those of the guests at the recent wedding, and at the orgy which had followed it, who had not made good their escape, were brought in and executed in the Emperor's presence, only his fears for his own safety marring the excited interest he always displayed in the infliction of capital punishment.[13] Senators, high officials, and military officers were butchered in turn, many of them on the grounds that they had at one time or another shared Messalina's bed, amongst these being the doctor, Vectius Valens, who, from the tree-top a few hours previously, had so ominously reported the coming of the storm from Ostia.

One shy and good-looking youth, named Traulus Montanus, declared "that he had been summoned by Messalina to her embraces without any solicitation whatsoever on his part, and after one night had been cast off, such was the wantonness with which her passions were inflamed and surfeited"; but this defence did not save him. An extremely effeminate young man, however, named Suilius Cæsoninus, was spared amidst loud guffaws, for the reason that none of the company could credit him with behaviour other than that of a woman.

The case of Mnester, a celebrated actor, is less obvious. He had been one of the favourites of the Emperor Caligula, and it seems [14] that he was always more attracted by persons of his own sex than by women. Nevertheless, there was a great deal of talk about his intimacy with Messalina, and he appears to have had the freedom of her bedroom,[15] though whether as a lover or as a friend of nondescript sex is not clear. At any rate, when he was brought before Claudius he said that the Emperor himself had ordered him to do the Empress's bidding in all things, and that he had merely obeyed instructions too literally, yet, even so, under compulsion. He then tore off his clothes, and revealed his body marked by the red welts of a recent lashing; and he declared that the iniquities into which others had been tempted by presents or by hopes of gain, he had been forced to commit by thrashings such as this.

It was evidently not clear to Tacitus [16] whether the iniquities referred to were those of aiding the Empress in her plans for raising Silius to imperial status, or those of helping her to pass the time in her habitual manner while Silius was unavoidably absent from her. Be this as it may, however, Claudius would have pardoned him, had not those present pointed out that after so many gentlemen had been put to death it would be extremely bad form to spare a mere actor.

When the slaughter was stayed for lack of further victims, Claudius returned to the palace, where he ate a particularly sumptuous dinner, and drank himself into a state of benevolence towards all men. In this condition he enquired what had become of Messalina, and was told that she had been conducted back to the villa in the Gardens of Lucullus, where she was being tended in her distress by her mother. At this the tipsy Emperor ordered somebody to go and tell "the poor creature" to come to him next morning and plead her cause.

That message was never delivered. Narcissus, frightened by this change of attitude, and deeming it better to act on his own responsibility, immediately hurried out of the room, and told a military officer that the Emperor commanded him to go at once with his men to the villa, and to put Messalina to death; and at the same time he dispatched a freedman, named Euodus, to see that the deed was duly accomplished. Euodus arrived first at the house, and found Messalina lying on the floor, weeping, while her mother was seated beside her, trying with maternal solicitude to persuade her to kill herself, saying that the course of her life was evidently run, and that her only object now should be to die like a lady rather than to wait for the expected executioner.

Euodus at once began vulgarly to abuse and upbraid her; but suddenly the door was flung open, and the military officer, followed by his soldiers, burst into the room. Only then did the miserable Messalina realize that there was no escape; and, grasping the dagger which her mother was holding out to her, she made a trembling and feeble prod at her throat and then at her breast. The blood spurted from the wounds, but they were not deep enough to kill her; and the officer, shocked by her screams, hurried forward, took hold of her, and drove his sword through her body.

Claudius had not yet finished his dinner when Narcissus came in to him, and whispered, "Messalina is no more." The Emperor stared at him, with his mouth open, but made no reply, nor asked whether or not she died by her own hand. He merely called for another cup of wine, and went on eating and drinking, until, according to his usual habit, he fell asleep where he was, and lay snoring upon his back.

The news was at once conveyed to Agrippina, who, concealing her unbounded satisfaction, came next day to the palace with the ostensible purpose of consoling her bewildered uncle. At first, upon awaking, he could not be brought to believe that Messalina was dead, and later, when he realized it, he took refuge in complete silence in regard to the whole affair, giving never a sign either of sorrow or of any other emotion. When his two motherless children were brought in to him he kissed them without any unusual display of feeling; and in Agrippina and her boy Nero, who accompanied her, he showed no unwonted interest.

The Senate, which had been deeply shocked by Messalina's wild behaviour, was greatly relieved at her death, and at once decreed that her name should be erased from all inscriptions, and her statues removed. High honours were paid to Narcissus for the courageous manner in which he had brought the Empress to book, risking his own life to serve his master and the State;

and on all sides the utmost satisfaction was expressed at the outcome of the whole terrible business.

Meanwhile, at the palace, Agrippina eagerly discussed the situation with Narcissus, and his two colleagues, Pallas and Callistus. The danger was that the scandal of Messalina would lead to a new revulsion of feeling in favour of a Republic without an Emperor, unless the court could quickly reform itself; and these three men realized that Agrippina, whatever might be her private life, stood for the old austerity of the days of Augustus, and that was just what the people wanted. She was outwardly so chaste, so pious, such a model of propriety: she would exert an influence upon the palace which might save it from disaster.

They asked her, therefore, to remain: and she, the frigid, hard-faced woman, who by intrigue and perhaps by murder had raised herself to this commanding position, graciously consented to do so. Her only thoughts were for the advancement of her son, whose growth she watched with the one tender impulse of her icy heart, and for the increase of her own power through him. Surely it would not now be difficult so to force him upon the Emperor's attention that at length his ultimate accession to the throne would be secured. Only the unhealthy Britannicus stood in the way; but he, as the faithless Messalina's son, could be continuously disparaged, and, if necessary, removed altogether.

Upon two things all her schemes depended. Firstly, Claudius would have to be kept alive until Nero was old enough to be accepted as Emperor by the Senate and the people; and, secondly, Nero himself would have to be forced by the sternest of upbringings into the semblance of a second Augustus, a model young man, an upholder of the ancient traditions of Rome. Only in this guise would he be acceptable to the nation, tired as it was of scandals.

History does not tell us definitely that she at once took up her residence at the palace, but this is to be inferred from the statement of Tacitus that she was now constantly in and out of her uncle's apartments, and quickly began to exercise over him the influence practically of a wife.[17] Her one great enemy was dead, her triumph was at hand: for the first time in years she could breathe freely. It is not to be supposed, thus, that she would content herself with less than actual residence under one roof with her uncle, whom she was now determined to bend to her imperious will.

CHAPTER V

The Marriage of Nero's Mother to the Emperor Claudius, A.D. 49—The Betrothal of Nero to Octavia, Daughter of Claudius—The Adoption of Nero by Claudius, A.D. 50.

It is impossible to decide whether the display of frigid morality, and the puritanical attitude of propriety, which, in a dissolute age, so clearly marked Agrippina's outward behaviour as that of a lady of the stern old Roman school, were now entirely a political pose or in part an inclination of her cold and overbearing mind, triumphant over her sensuous nature. Certainly she knew the importance of moral decency at this juncture; yet an outward show of this kind of thing, and even something deeper than that, had probably been forced upon her, as has been said, by her disgust at the appalling vices of her brother, Caligula, and later by the abominations of court society in general, particularly those in which Messalina, her hated enemy, had been involved. She had been frozen by horror, and later by personal hostility, into an appearance of the most rigid virtuousness, intended to contrast with the licentiousness of her foes; but, as in the case of a snow-covered volcano, there were fierce fires hidden below the surface which ultimately burst out, and one cannot say whether their concealment at this period of her triumph were due to an actual dislike of, and revulsion from, the loose manners of the "fast" set, or to mere political cunning.

Those, indeed, who believed later that her chastity was fraudulent, declared that, soon after her arrival at the palace, she had begun to carry on a secret love-intrigue with Pallas, the most engaging of the three freedmen who ruled the Empire in the name of Claudius; but this story may well have had its origin in a misinterpretation of her diplomatic cordiality to this enormously wealthy and powerful minister, who was in charge of the Emperor's private treasury. Pallas, it may be mentioned, was the brother of Felix, the Governor of Judæa, before whom St. Paul was once brought as a prisoner[1]; and the high regard in which such freedmen were held may be judged from the fact that this Felix married in turn three royal ladies: Drusilla, the granddaughter of Antony and Cleopatra, and hence the cousin of the Emperor himself, who was the grandson of Antony and Octavia; another Drusilla, sister of King Herod Agrippa, and widow of the king of Emesa; and a third princess whose identity is unknown.[2] In view of these family connections, and having regard to the fact that Pallas was now declaring himself the descendant of the kings of Arcadia, it is not outside the bounds of probability that Agrippina had deemed him a fitting object of her seductive overtures, whether or not these overtures were intended to lead to their natural consequences.

Suetonius tells us that Agrippina did not hesitate also to make improper advances to Claudius himself, "taking advantage of the kisses and endearments, which their near relationship permitted, to inflame his passions,"[3] and Tacitus says much the same[4]; but to credit such statements is to place a merely alternative construction upon an affectionate attitude which may well have been due to Agrippina's unbounded elation at finding herself at last installed as a kind of combined nurse, housekeeper, and companion of the unfortunate Emperor.

But whatever view be taken of her actual behaviour, it is clear that her apparent and outward respectability was her strength. It was because she came into the imperial palace in the guise, or disguise, of a disciplinarian, a God-fearing, sober-minded young matron and widow, that the three tacticians behind the throne—Narcissus, Pallas, and Callistus—were unanimous in welcoming her and her son Nero. They saw that the late Emperor Caligula and the foolish Messalina had, between them, caused the palace to appear to the public as an aggrandised bawdy-house, and that their master, the Emperor Claudius, who was little more than a figure of fun, could of himself do nothing to set matters to rights. It seemed to them that the only hope for the imperial prestige lay in the court's ability to make a show of reformation and of a return to the morality of the days of Augustus; and here was the notoriously virtuous Agrippina, a great-granddaughter of Augustus, ready to devote herself to the task of setting her uncle's house in order. And if this stiffly pious lady showed an inclination to unbend to Claudius or to Pallas, what did it matter so long as she did so in strict privacy?

True, her girlhood's relationship with her brother, Caligula, and her cousin, Lepidus, had not been wholly forgotten, and many people believed her to be the seducer and murderess of her husband Crispus, but her years of secluded widowhood had caused these unfortunate incidents to be relegated to an obscure background. True, too, she had shown a dangerous cunning in her attack on Messalina; but perhaps she was justified. Moreover, it was obvious that she would use her position to further the interests of her boy, Nero; but he was not a bad young fellow, and, as grandson of the never-to-be-forgotten Germanicus,[5] he would probably make a more popular Emperor, when the time came, than anybody else, particularly in view of the fact that he was being so strictly brought up.

At length it came to be agreed amongst these three that a new wife must be found for Claudius, for it was felt that a kindly companion would help to prolong his life, and consequently to prolong their tenure of office, in the preservation of which they now felt a renewed interest since the death of Messalina. Narcissus suggested that the Emperor should re-marry Ælia Pætina, the lady who was the mother of his daughter Antonia, but whom he had divorced several years ago at the request of Domitia Lepida, so that he might marry the latter's daughter, Messalina. Callistus, however, opposed the project on the grounds that a woman who had been divorced and then taken back would tend to become quite insufferably vain; and he made the alternative suggestion that the Emperor should marry Lollia Paulina, Caligula's ex-wife, whose wealth, as has been said, was so enormous.

But Pallas, the remaining member of the trinity, had his own axe to grind. Agrippina had made a particular friend of him, if no more; and he felt that this intimate relationship between them could hardly be better turned to account than by the elevation of his new ally herself to the position of Empress. She was the direct descendant of Augustus, and such a marriage would unite the Julian and Claudian lines. She was no more than thirty-three years of age at this time, and if she did not marry Claudius she would certainly marry somebody else, who, through this exalted union, might aspire to the throne and thereby cause trouble.

It seems to me that the idea was novel to Agrippina, for she may well have supposed that her marriage to her father's brother would be vetoed by public opinion. But now that the suggestion had been made by Pallas, and had finally obtained the support of his two colleagues, she immediately gave her undivided attention to the business of seducing Claudius as she had seduced Crispus. The task was made somewhat difficult owing to the Emperor's attitude towards her which, according to Suetonius, was one of ostensibly paternal affection, in spite of the fact that he was beginning to find her unexpectedly attractive as a woman.[6] He kept on calling her his "daughter," his "baby," whom he had "nursed upon his knee"; and it must have been some time before it dawned upon his slow mind that the caresses they now so often exchanged were leading towards a closer relationship—a relationship all the more enticing[7] to him because it was forbidden as between a niece and her uncle. But when at last some particular occasion of privileged fondling caused him to realize the potentialities of the situation, and led to the discovery that Agrippina was more than ready to help him to misbehave himself, he ceased to play the part of a fatherly uncle to her, and became her ardent, if not very sprightly, lover.[8]

Inwardly triumphant, but outwardly resigned, she then told the three freedmen that she would accept the duty imposed upon her by destiny; and she gave them her permission to propose the marriage to Claudius. But the Emperor was not at first enraptured by the idea: it had interested him and had flattered his vanity to beat down, as he supposed, the defences of his niece's notorious chastity; but to make her his wife in defiance of the law in regard to incest was quite another matter.

In certain respects the proposal appealed to him. He was no longer capable, sick man that he was, of indulging what had once been the ruling passion of his life—the pursuit of woman, and he felt that an understanding and not too exacting wife would fulfil a long-felt want in his life. She evidently found him irresistible, he told himself; and yet she was not too temperamental: she was quiet, tactful, and considerate. She would not jeer at his infirmity as Messalina had done, nor hurt him by conducting love-affairs with other and more able men under his very nose. She would loyally defend his honour, and protect him from the slights which he now so often received.

On the other hand she was undoubtedly a woman with a will of her own; and he heartily disliked the thought of being disciplined by a strong-minded wife. He prided himself that he had succeeded in overcoming her puritanical scruples, but he was conscious that her outward air of ostentatious virtue, which he could not abide, had been unaffected by her private submissions to his lust. He had no taste for the austerities of the traditional Roman life: he liked, within proper bounds, the easy-going ways of the Greeks, which Caligula had introduced. He liked rich food, and he was afraid that Agrippina was the type of woman who would prefer plain cooking; he liked to get drunk, but Agrippina was almost invariably sober. He liked to have pretty women around him, and jovial men, and it did him good to laugh at the improper jokes and antics of low comedians from the theatre; but Agrippina would object to all that sort of thing.

And then there was her boy, the red-headed young Nero, whom he would be expected to father, to the detriment of the interests of his own son, Britannicus. Still, whether he married her or no, she would undoubtedly oblige him in the end to consider Nero as a potential heir to the throne; and, after all, he might do worse, Britannicus being certainly extremely delicate.

Unable to make up his mind, he said at last that he would abide by the wishes of the Senate; and at this Agrippina sought the good offices of a certain Vitellius,[9] who was a senator, had been consul, and was now Censor of Rome—an unctuous man who had shown himself very willing to do anything to ingratiate himself with the new mistress of the palace. He had once been Governor of Syria, and it is interesting to recall that it fell to his lot to remove the unpopular Pontius Pilate from the office he was holding when Jesus Christ was tried and crucified.

Vitellius went to the Emperor, and asked him whether he would really submit to the authority of the people and the Senate in this matter, to which Claudius replied in the affirmative, remarking that he was himself but one of the people—for he was always very precise about legal definitions, and the imperial office was technically a position open to any citizen who might be so acclaimed. Having received this answer, Vitellius told him to remain in the palace while he put the matter before the Senate; and therewith he hurried off to that assembly which was then in session, and interrupted their deliberations by asking permission to address them immediately on a subject of the highest importance.

He began his speech by saying that the overpowering work of governing the earth would be much lightened for the Emperor if he were to marry again, but that the choice of a wife was a difficult matter, since a lady had to be found who combined the qualities of noble birth and perfect chastity with some definite proof that she was not barren. What high-born lady could they think of, he asked, who could give them evidence that she was not sterile without compromising her position as a single woman of strict moral virtue? He then called the attention of the Senators to the widowed Agrippina whose virtuousness was well-known, whose splendour of lineage was unparalleled, and who had proved that she was fertile by bringing a son into the world. Of course, he added, it was a novelty in Rome for an uncle to marry his niece, but the practice was common in other countries, and was not specifically forbidden by any written law. After all, the marriage of cousins had once been illegal, but now was fully accepted; and the union of uncles and nieces would, if now legalized, soon be a commonplace.

Vitellius then pointed out, to the astonishment of his hearers, that, unlike other Cæsars, Claudius had never been known to steal a wife from her husband, and therefore could not now adopt that means of obtaining a consort of proven chastity and fertility. But the high-born Agrippina, as by a special dispensation of Providence, was a pious widow who had borne a son; and in taking her to wife the Emperor would establish a precedent of cautious conduct and careful selection in the choosing of a bride.

This remarkable speech had an immediate effect. A number of Senators, eager for a moral reform after the excesses of Messalina, followed by a like-minded crowd of townspeople, hastened to the palace, where Claudius uncomfortably awaited the outcome of the matter, and shouted, outside its windows, that they wanted Agrippina as their Empress, by which they meant to say that they would tolerate no more scandals in the imperial household, and urgently demanded its purification.

The betrothal was announced forthwith, and Rome was agog with this new wonder—an incestuous marriage between an Emperor and his brother's daughter; but a law was quickly passed which made such a union legal, and soon, indeed, it was realized that in future all things would be conducted with a show of the strictest legality and decorum at the palace. The engagement, in fact, seemed to sound the death-knell of the power of the frivolous and lawless section of society; and old-fashioned people, speedily recovering from the shock of this extension of the marital licence, were delighted to think that the court was going to become a pattern to the nation. Very conveniently they forgot Agrippina's former relationship to her bestial brother, and her behaviour to her late husband, Crispus; nor did they listen to the gossip which said that already she had prostituted herself to the Emperor, if not also to Pallas. They chose to see her only in her outward aspect as a cold and moral widow, the descendant of the austere Augustus, and the daughter of the beloved Germanicus; and as such they hailed her gladly in their revulsion from the licentiousness which had so nearly brought about the collapse of the imperial throne.

Agrippina was elated by her good fortune so long postponed, and if she felt any disgust at her new relationship to the drunken and prematurely senile Emperor, she may well have consoled herself with the thought that that relationship need not be much prolonged beyond the day of her marriage. As soon as she was Empress she would be able to take a grip of her afflicted and weak-minded husband which would shake out of him all desire to play the lover.

Only one matter remained to be settled. The little

Octavia, the daughter of Claudius and Messalina, was nearing her tenth birthday, and Agrippina felt that the girl ought most certainly to be betrothed to her boy Nero, who was now eleven years of age, so that there might be yet one more reason why he should in due course become Emperor, there being a strong feeling that a sovereign's daughter was his heiress in the sense that she would convey to her husband a sort of right to the throne. Claudius, however, had promised Octavia to Lucius Silanus, a brilliant young man of twenty-four, already conspicuous in public life, and related to the imperial family, his mother being Æmilia Lepida, daughter of that Julia who was the granddaughter of Augustus, and sister of Agrippina's mother. This Æmilia having died, her husband, Junius Silanus, had married the widowed Domitia Lepida, mother of Messalina, and thus Lucius Silanus and Messalina were step-brother and sister. It may be mentioned in passing that Messalina had taken a fancy to Junius Silanus, her step-father, and had invited him to join the ever-increasing number of her temporary lovers; but, being her mother's husband, he had been unable to oblige her, whereupon she had caused him to be put to death. In spite of this contretemps, the Empress and her husband, in choosing Lucius Silanus as their future son-in-law, had thought of him as the possible successor to the throne, should Claudius himself die before Britannicus or Nero were old enough to be acclaimed; but Messalina's death put an end to these plans. Agrippina could brook no rivals to her son, and she applied her mind at once to the task not only of cancelling the engagement of Lucius Silanus to Octavia, but also of removing him altogether from the pathway of her ambition.

Once more she sought the aid of Vitellius, who had a particular interest in the case because his son had married Junia Calvina, the sister of Lucius, but had divorced her for some now forgotten reason. Vitellius, therefore, having employed detectives to smell out the sins of this young man whom Agrippina wished to destroy, learnt that he was on particularly affectionate terms with this sister of his, Junia Calvina; and he at once brought the fact to the attention of the future Empress whose reputation for stern morality was now turned to good account. In great indignation Agrippina broke the news to Claudius that this man to whom he had affianced the poor little Octavia was morally unfit to be the girl's husband, for he had committed incest with his sister; and Claudius, entitled to be shocked now that his own incestuous relationship to his niece had been declared legal, at once ordered Lucius Silanus to be deprived of his public offices, this command being carried out, at the end of December, A.D. 48, by Vitellius himself in his capacity as Censor of Rome.

The charge seems to have been quite unfounded, for not only does Tacitus repudiate it,[10] but Seneca speaks of Junia Calvina affectionately as "most beautiful and most playful of all girls."[11] Love affairs between brothers and sisters, however, were then very fashionable in Rome, having been made popular by Caligula, who, regarding himself as the hereditary Pharaoh of Egypt, had invoked the traditional Egyptian custom of brother-and-sister marriage to justify his abnormal love for his sister Drusilla. Queen Cleopatra, wife of Claudius's grandfather, Antony, for example had been married to her brother. Agrippina herself as a girl had borne this relationship to her brother, though, no doubt, she was saying at this time that it had not been her fault; her first husband, Cnæus Ahenobarbus, had been accused of a similar impropriety with his sister, Domitia Lepida; and her second husband, Passienus Crispus, had been believed, by Caligula at any rate, to be addicted to this practice. On all sides it was rife, and Agrippina appeared to be striking a blow for purity when she thus caused Lucius Silanus to be disgraced.

The unfortunate young man could not at first believe that his degradation was final, but at length he realized that his offence was his being descended from Augustus and hence his being a possible claimant to the throne; and seeing that he could expect no mercy from Agrippina if she were to become Empress, he made up his mind to kill himself on the day on which her marriage to Claudius was celebrated. Junia Calvina, meanwhile, was banished from Rome, and, in anticipation, it may be mentioned that she remained in exile for ten years, being at last recalled by Nero upon the death of Agrippina.

Agrippina's marriage to Claudius took place at the beginning of the year A.D. 49; and on her wedding day Lucius Silanus cut his throat. In the following October Nero's betrothal to the little Octavia was announced, and was popularly acclaimed.

There was now no further doubt that, should Claudius live long enough, Nero would be the next Emperor, and not the unhealthy Britannicus. It is true that Lucius Silanus had been survived by two brothers, who, as descendants of Augustus, might ultimately cause trouble; but they were marked men, and Agrippina seems to have regarded their brother's fate as sufficient warning to them for the present.[12] Nero's elevation to the position of prospective heir was assisted, of course, by Pallas, Narcissus, and Callistus, the three great powers at court; for these men had all helped in the overthrow of Messalina and hence could expect no mercy from her son Britannicus were he ever to become Emperor. Thus it was essential to them that not he but Nero should succeed; and this necessity, involving, as it did, their very lives, obliged them to champion the cause of the Emperor's new stepson at all costs.

A few months later, on February 25th, A.D. 50, the certainty of the boy's ultimate accession was made more certain by the Emperor's formal adoption of him as his son. Until then, as has been said, his name had been Lucius Domitius Ahenobarbus; but at his adoption he was renamed Nero Claudius Cæsar Drusus Germanicus. He was now beginning his thirteenth year, and he was still too young for Claudius, even if he were so inclined, to announce him to the public as his chosen heir to the throne; for the imperial office was regarded as a leadership of the nation, a grown man's job, not by law hereditary. But in the family circle the matter was a foregone conclusion.

Meanwhile, however, Agrippina had to rid herself

of any danger to her own position due to the unexpected circumstance that Claudius, now that they had been married a year, was showing increasing restlessness under the new régime. In spite of the fact that he had conferred upon her the title of Augusta, never before given to an Empress during her husband's lifetime, and had, in other ways, demonstrated the high regard he felt for her, there could be no doubt that he found her interference in domestic and state affairs a little trying.

He did not like the curtailment of his amusements; and, reform or no reform, he did not see any reason why the palace should be deprived of all its gaiety. Agrippina, working hand and glove with Pallas, the custodian of his private fortune, had established a régime of strict economy: she examined the household accounts, kept herself informed of all that went on in the kitchens, and cut down the Emperor's entertainments to a minimum. Moreover, she was no longer his "baby" and his "darling" who permitted herself to be petted and fondled by him as once she had done: she had become his implacable keeper, cold and unloving, and it was clear that she was never going to allow herself to have a child by him, even if he were still capable of becoming a father. Yet she would not permit him any dalliance with other women. There was, for example, a beautiful woman named Calpurnia upon whom the Emperor, in this mood of rebellion, cast his roving eye; but Agrippina promptly caused the unfortunate lady to be banished from Rome as an undesirable character.

The activities of the wealthy Lollia Paulina, however, gave her more serious reason for anxiety: she was the lady, it will be remembered, whom Callistus had at first favoured as a wife for Claudius; but being disappointed in her hope of becoming Empress she had consulted some Chaldæan fortune-tellers in her desire to find out whether the Emperor's married life with her rival was likely to last long. The fact was reported to Agrippina who, implacable in her hate of a woman-rival,[13] at once caused her to be accused of an attempt to employ magic to upset the existing union; and Claudius, who, through Callistus, may well have given the unfortunate woman a hint of encouragement, was now forced to banish her from Rome, confiscating the bulk of her vast fortune.

This, however, did not satisfy Agrippina, who sent her own officers post haste after the miserable exile, with orders to put her to death; nor would she rest until she had actually seen her rival's severed head. When it was brought to her she could not at first recognize it; but she knew that Lollia Paulina's teeth had certain peculiarities, and she thereupon prised open the mouth with her fingers and thus satisfied herself.[14] Callistus, the former supporter of the dead woman, died at about this time; and though it is said that his end was due to natural causes, the suggestion that it was connected with the affair of Lollia Paulina is not without some probability.

Utterly heartless in all but her love for her son, Agrippina stuck at nothing to secure her position so that she might be free to revive the good name of the imperial house, to advise and direct her foolish husband, and to keep the breath in his decrepit body until her beloved Nero, trained to be the perfect puritan, should be ready to present himself to the people as a worthy successor of Augustus, with herself as the all-powerful Empress-mother.

Nero was now twelve years of age. He was a rather fat little boy, with a freckled face, short-sighted, blue eyes, and hair which may be described as of a reddish-bronze colour. Already he was showing signs of a taste for the arts, for he loved to draw and paint, or make figures in clay; and he was beginning to try to write verses which he would sing to himself as he twanged the strings of a small harp. All that sort of thing would have to be knocked out of him.

He wanted to read books on philosophy and art, but his mother would not let him. Sternly she trained him to become a gentleman of the old school, that is to say one who, like Augustus, should turn his back on the adventures of the brain and the talents, and should devote himself to the simple tradition of good citizenship; one should ever keep his wayward proclivities or his little sins secret and show an expressionless and puritanical face to the world.

For the sake of Rome, for the glory of the imperial house, she desired, yet did not know that she desired, to make of him a conventional hypocrite; but that was the one thing she could not do. Nero remained all his life an honest man, sincere in his virtues, and barefaced in his vices; and upon the solid substance of this peculiarity his and his mother's lives were shipwrecked.

CHAPTER VI

The Appointment of Seneca and Burrhus as Nero's Tutors—The Marriage of Nero and Octavia, A.D. 53—Nero's Apprenticeship—The Struggle between Agrippina and Narcissus—The Death of Claudius and Accession of Nero, A.D. 54.

One of the first steps taken by Agrippina after her marriage to Claudius was the recall of her old friend, the philosopher, Lucius Annæus Seneca, then some fifty years of age, [1] who had been banished to Corsica eight years previously at the instigation of Messalina, having been accused of adultery with Julia Livilla, Agrippina's sister, a charge of which he neither affirmed nor denied the truth.

He was a short, stout man of Spanish origin, who looked very much like a modern Jewish financier, with his dark, thoughtful eyes, his bald head, his fleshy cheeks and neck, and his slight, pointed beard. His father had been an advocate of the old Roman school, who disliked all things foreign, and detested Greek philosophy and the Greek language; and his mother was a typical Roman matron who was wrapped up in her children and was deeply loved by them in return. Seneca, however, had been very delicate in his youth, and there was one period at which he was only prevented from committing suicide by the thought of the distress he would cause his parents by so doing. All his life he suffered from weak lungs and asthma, but his habitual abstemiousness prolonged his years, and he was able to accomplish a great deal of literary and other work.

It may be mentioned in passing that his elder brother, who had been adopted into the Gallio family, and was made Governor of Achæa in A.D. 52, was that same Gallio who "cared for none of these things,"[2] before whom St. Paul was once accused of heresy by the Jews.

Seneca came to Rome when he was a boy, and studied the philosophy of Pythagoras under Sotion of Alexandria, as a result of which he believed for some time that the human soul transmigrated into the bodies of animals, for which reason he became a vegetarian, his teacher saying that even if the doctrine were extravagant the diet was cheap. Later he studied the philosophy of the Stoics under Attalus, and for the rest of his life slept on a hard mattress, abstained from too many hot baths, used no perfumes, drank no wine, and, in accordance with the peculiar dietetic principles of his instructor, cut out oysters and mushrooms from his otherwise generous menu.

He was by no means an ascetic, and enjoyed the good things of this life as much as any man, though he was moderate in this enjoyment. He was comfortably married to a lady named Pompeia Paulina, by whom he had two sons, both of whom, however, died young. Nor was he above amassing a very large personal fortune, a fact which led many people to regard him as a philosophical humbug,[3] though he defended himself by saying that great possessions were a matter of indifference to him, and that if chance brought them his way it would not be in keeping with the Stoic faith for him to attribute to them the importance implied in renouncing them. Nevertheless, the fact that he lent out money at interest can hardly be justified on philosophic grounds, [4] and there can be no doubt that in later life he was an enthusiastic exponent of Stoicism rather than a strict adherent to its doctrine. His voluminous writings are full of quiet, rambling, idealistic thought, and chapter after chapter might well have been written by some kindly bishop of today.

His manners were polished and charming, his conversation eloquent and thoughtful, and at the time when Agrippina recalled him from exile his hard and lonely life on the then barbarous island of Corsica had made him very appreciative of kindness and very ready to flatter his benefactress. Indeed, during his banishment he had composed a very grovelling document for Messalina's reading, full of gross flattery of which he must afterwards have been mightily ashamed, and which leaves upon the mind the impression that he was by no means a Stoic hero. [5]

Agrippina, however, decided that he would be just the right man to act as tutor to Nero, for he would naturally be devoted to her interests and would have a strong antipathy to Britannicus, the son of his enemy, Messalina. His devotion to the memory of his mother would predispose him to the teaching of filial affection to his pupil; and though she determined never to allow him to instruct Nero in philosophy—a subject foreign to the Roman mind, and held in contempt by patricians of the old school—she was willing enough to let the boy benefit by Seneca's example of sobriety, simplicity, and hard work. He was a good Roman, too, and, like his father, had little taste for the elegance and luxury of the Greeks against which Agrippina had set her face.

Having established him at the palace, as tutor to her boy, she selected as his colleague in the work a fine old soldier, Afranius Burrhus, whom, shortly afterwards, she persuaded the Emperor to appoint as commander of the Prætorian Guard, a force of some twenty thousand picked troops stationed in Rome, every man of which was, by this clever move, made the devoted protector of their leader's pupil.

Thus her son, bursting with high spirits, now found himself in the hands of these two masters, one of them a wordy, if somewhat insincere, professor of that ideal of simple and austere Roman life towards which the boy had no natural bent; and the other a bluff and laconic martinet, with a hand maimed in the wars, whose military outlook was opposed to everything the artistic and rather feminine-minded young Nero most enjoyed. And behind these two men stood the awe-inspiring figure of his mother, hard and unyielding, and yet his all-in-all. He loved her deeply; but already his childish mind was aware that there was some frightening difference between their two natures. She did not understand him; she was driving him towards a place whither he had no wish to go; and yet in his youthful eyes she could do no wrong. "Her despotism," as Tacitus says, "was as strict as though it were that of a man"[6]; and to this sensitive and repressed boy she must have seemed indeed to be overpowering in her demands upon his obedience, and yet herself only obedient to the strange and terrible ogre, Duty, which had them all in thrall.

On December 15th, A.D. 50, Nero's thirteenth birthday was celebrated; and less than three months later, on March 4th, A.D. 51, he was allowed to assume the *toga virilis,* the dress of a grown man, although this change of costume, which was equivalent to a coming-of-age, was not customary until a boy's fourteenth year was ended. Agrippina, in fact, was hastening him feverishly towards manhood because of her fear that Claudius might die.

The Emperor himself presented the boy to the Senate, and conferred on him the title of *Princeps Juventutis,* other honours also being bestowed upon him, after which he was exhibited to the public marching at the head of the Prætorian Guard, and, later in the day, he attended a tournament at the Circus, dressed in imperial robes, while his cousin and now foster-brother, Britannicus, who at this time was in his eleventh year, sat beside him still wearing the dress of a child.

Nero, in fact, now held the centre of the stage; and the senile, bleary-eyed Claudius, with his shambling gait and his foolish smile, was merely tolerated as one keeping the throne warm for this bright and eager boy whose lineage was so much more splendid than his own. And while the sickly Britannicus was at a disadvantage owing to the foul reputation of his late mother, Nero, on the contrary, had the powerful support of *his* mother, who was ever at his side, resplendent in cloth of gold and blazing with jewels, presenting him to the people as, in so many religions, the mother-goddess presents her son, the eternal hope of the world.

In her capacity as mother of the future Emperor she was now assuming more and more power, and demanding ever greater honours. She was even permitted to enter the precincts of the Capitol riding in her golden carriage, a privilege never yet allowed to any but the priesthood; and she was enthroned beside her husband at functions over which no woman had ever before presided. "In her public conduct she was grave and rigid, frequently haughty and overbearing," says Tacitus.[7] "She had control of everything," he tells us; and it is clear that this was not so much because she was the wife of the reigning Emperor, the despised Claudius, as because she was the mother of the future Emperor, the brilliant Nero, in whom was centred the nation's hope.

In A.D. 53 Agrippina decided that her son, who would be sixteen towards the end of that year, and Octavia, who was approaching her fourteenth birthday, were old enough to be married; and their wedding was therefore celebrated with great pomp. Nothing is known of Octavia's appearance, but her subsequent actions indicate that she was a girl of passionate disposition, sullen, reckless, and perhaps a little queer in her head, having regard to the facts that her mother, Messalina, was a nymphomaniac, her father, Claudius, in some respects a half-wit, and her brother, Britannicus, an epileptic. She was devoted to this brother, and one gathers that she was always smouldering over the slights which were so constantly offered him. She does not seem to have liked Nero; and he, on his part, was not in the least fond of her. They had been betrothed, however, for four years, and they accepted the marriage as part of the inexorable fate which had them in its grip. Nero was to be Emperor—there was now no reasonable doubt about that; and this immature, loveless, and embarrassing union was one of the penalties of the position which had to be faced.

At about this time Nero began to find an unexpected friend in his aunt Domitia Lepida, his father's sister, who was doing her best just now to engage his youthful affections, petting him and giving him little presents. She was an evil woman, but he was too young to realise that her behaviour was prompted not so much by her interest in him, as by her desire to be revenged upon her sister-in-law, who had been instrumental in bringing about the death of her daughter, Messalina, and the shelving of Messalina's son, her grandson, Britannicus.

"Violent was the fight between Domitia Lepida and Agrippina," says Tacitus,[8] as to whether aunt or mother should obtain predominance over Nero"; and for the first time in his life the boy now heard his mother's character disparaged. Domitia Lepida seems to have warned him that Agrippina was actuated only by her own desire for power; and she represented his irksome form of education to him not as a necessary training for the duties of his high office, but as a cruel method of suppressing him and breaking his will.

At the same time this embittered lady renewed her friendship with Narcissus, to whom, naturally enough, she had shown considerable enmity ever since he had ranged himself against her daughter, Messalina; and in this coming together of these two old enemies I think we may find the explanation of the events which immediately followed. Narcissus, in fact, seized the opportunity to turn to his own advantage the interest shown in Nero by his aunt. The position of Narcissus had been increasingly uncomfortable ever since Agrippina's marriage to the Emperor—a marriage which he himself, it will be remembered, had at first opposed; for he was genuinely fond of his master and resented the harshness of Agrippina's behaviour to the unfortunate man, and, at the same time, he felt that his influence with the Emperor was being undermined by the new Empress.

Narcissus, in fact, was out of sympathy with Agrippina except in regard to the selection of her son as the future Emperor, a matter upon which he ardently agreed with her, for if Britannicus were to succeed, Narcissus would probably be condemned at once as the man responsible for the death of Messalina. On the other hand, the accession of Nero while still under the tutelage of his mother, would with equal likelihood bring about his downfall, since his loyalty to Claudius, and the love of the power he derived from him, were inevitably converting Agrippina into an enemy.

In this dilemma he appears to have realized that the ultimate accession of Nero *without* Agrippina was the only solution of his difficulty; and hence he conceived the idea of getting rid of the troublesome Empress by estranging her both from her husband and her son, making use of Domitia Lepida for the latter purpose. Domitia Lepida, as has been said, seems to have had no object more far-reaching than that of hurting Agrippina by opening Nero's eyes to his mother's crimes; but Narcissus was securing his own future welfare and perhaps his very life, and his plans were directed at nothing less than the complete overthrow of Agrippina.

The tension steadily grew. Agrippina, with all her show of outward chastity, with all her cold and calculating heartlessness, was a woman who took pleasure in privately using her sexual charms to excite the amorous passions of the men of whom she wished to make use. By this means she had deliberately won her two husbands Crispus and Claudius; and now she seems to have converted her dalliance with the powerful Pallas into an actual illicit relationship with him, for Tacitus says that he was "notoriously her lover." [9] She had formed a coterie consisting of Pallas, Seneca, and Burrhus; and, Callistus being dead, Narcissus found himself alone, excluded from this group because of his loyal devotion to Claudius, of whom he was the only friend left in the palace, everybody else being under Agrippina's thumb.

The Emperor at this time was a pathetic figure. His strong-willed wife would never let him out of her sight, because, so she said, he was always making a fool of himself. When guests were being entertained she insisted upon sitting beside him and telling him what to do; and she was incessantly pushing herself forward at his expense, treating him either as an invalid or as an idiot. He had nobody to confide in except Narcissus, and even he was now maintaining his position with obvious difficulty.

Agrippina was frightened by the intrusion of Domitia Lepida into these affairs, and when it dawned upon her that the object of Narcissus was to bring about her banishment from the palace, so that Nero might ultimately succeed to the throne without her controlling hand upon him, she was thrown into a frenzy of alarm. Nero detached from her!—she had never thought of that.

To save herself, she acted with typical daring and ruthlessness. She suddenly caused a charge of treason to be brought against Domitia Lepida on the grounds that her comment on the marriage of Agrippina and Claudius had been a string of oaths, damning it and them to eternal perdition—which was probably quite true; and that she was attempting to disturb the peace of the empire. Agrippina then explained to her bewildered son that his aunt had tried to win his love solely to be revenged on her, and that the wicked woman had actually intended to murder her; and so deeply did she work on his feelings that Nero, much shocked and disillusioned, impulsively gave evidence against his aunt, admitting that she certainly had said things calculated to alienate him from his mother.

Domitia Lepida was sentenced to death, and was duly executed. Agrippina then turned her attention to Narcissus, whose death-sentence she endeavoured to obtain from Claudius. But the Emperor, sick though he was, and cowed by his wife, was not yet bereft of all power to fight for his friend; and he valiantly refused to allow any accusation to be made against the man. Narcissus, however, knew that his life was no longer safe at the palace; and, pretending to be ill, he asked permission to leave Rome and retire to Sinuessa, on the coast of Campania, on the road to Naples, to take the waters for which this popular resort was famous. [10] This was granted, and thus Claudius, having lost the support of his one remaining friend, passed entirely under the control of Agrippina, whom he now detested.

Meanwhile the training of Nero proceeded. He was a brilliant youth: already like his grandfather Germanicus, he could speak Greek as fluently as his native Latin, and the poetry which he wrote by the yard seems to have been not without merit, though it was faulty in scansion and rather grandiloquent. He was beginning to paint, too, and he showed some talent as a sculptor; but interest in these arts was vigorously discouraged by his mother and his tutors. It was useless for him to tell Agrippina that these had been the interests of his popular grandfather: she was blind to the fact that his nature was exactly like that of Germanicus. She was bent upon him being an Augustus.

The practice of public speaking, however, was regarded as useful, and whenever the boy displayed particular interest in any subject the open discussion of which would be proper, Seneca used to help him to prepare a speech, and Nero would then deliver it before the Emperor and his council, while Agrippina listened with pride and approval behind the curtains. Nero had a very good memory, being easily able to make himself word-perfect in these carefully prepared orations, and since he was also a born actor, he generally surprised his hearers by his apparent eloquence, earnestness, and wisdom.

At this time, he was unquestionably a good-hearted, generous-minded youth, who responded with particular warmth—again like Germanicus—to any subject which involved the righting of a wrong; and Seneca's teaching in regard to philanthropic and humane ideals always found in him a ready listener. Thus, when he was told that the city of Apamea in Phrygia had been damaged by an earthquake, he prepared and delivered a glowing speech in which he successfully pleaded for five years' remission of taxes for its citizens. On another occasion he pleaded in Greek for the immunity of Ilium (Troy) from taxation; and at another time he asked for and obtained a grant of money for the city of Bononia which had been partially destroyed by fire.

His greatest forensic success at this time, however, was a public speech made by him on behalf of the Greek city of Rhodes which had lost its municipal independence. Nero successfully pleaded for the restoration of its freedom; and the members of the deputation of Rhodians then present were so enraptured by the eloquence and the dramatic fevour of this red-headed youth that they hailed him as their own particular sun-god come to earth, and went away deliriously singing his praises, while Nero, tremendously thrilled, decided in his own heart that these cultured and artistic Greeks were evidently closer to him in their mentality than his own people.

Thus he advanced by leaps and bounds in public favour, until everybody was hailing him as a prodigy—

everybody, that is to say, except Agrippina, who did not allow her love of him, and her pride in him, to interfere with her cold and disciplinary attitude towards him. She saw, all too clearly, that he was temperamentally an artist—as we should now describe it; but she wanted him, and old-fashioned Rome wanted him, to grow up into a stern, unemotional, and modest gentleman of the old school, and she was afraid of all this adulation.

Britannicus, meanwhile, was relegated to complete obscurity. The public hardly knew that he existed at all: many actually did not know, and those who did were inclined to believe that he was not right in his head, for it was common knowledge that he suffered from epileptic fits. Some time ago Agrippina had had his tutor, Sosibius, put to death on the grounds that the man was encouraging the boy to dislike his cousin Nero; and one by one she had removed by execution or dismissal every member of his staff, putting in their place her own creatures who would report his every action to her. Moreover she was doing her best to prevent Claudius from seeing more of his son than was unavoidable.

One day there was a sharp quarrel between the two boys, and Britannicus was rash enough to call Nero by his real name, Ahenobarbus, the implication being that he was not, on his father's side, a member of the imperial family; and Nero shouted back that Britannicus was a bastard, the son of one of Messalina's lovers, not of Claudius. Both youths took their troubles to the Emperor and Empress, the result being an increased estrangement between the two parents. Britannicus, of course, could see that Agrippina disliked him, and in future when she attempted, for appearances' sake, to kiss him or put her arms about him, he revealed the bitterness of his young heart by turning his back on her.

Matters came to a head in the autumn of A.D. 54, when Nero was getting on for seventeen, and Britannicus was about thirteen and a half—a tall, lanky, pale-faced boy. At this time Claudius, who was sixty-three years of age, was in a condition of impotent revolt against Agrippina, into whose dark heart he thought that he now saw clearly. He felt that her piety, her respectability, even her chastity, were fraudulent—a pose intended for the public eye, a means of obtaining the support of the old-fashioned nobility who were at present in the ascendant.

All his pleasures had been taken from him by this flint-hearted wife of his; the palace, it seemed to him, was a stifling hot-house, a forcing-house, of smug propriety, completely governed by the intolerant Agrippina, aided and abetted by that glib humbug, Seneca, by Pallas who had become her very slave for his bread-and-butter's sake, and by Burrhus, a man without a thought beyond those of his strict military training. Everlastingly he, the Emperor, was being corrected because of his so-called breaches of conventional etiquette, his vulgar manners, and his lack of dignity. Dignity be damned!—what he wanted was good food, good wine, and good company. He was a simple soul, bereft of his health but not of his interest in life; and his rebellion is entirely understandable.

I think there is reason to suppose that he was in

touch with Narcissus at this time, and that some scheme for freeing him from his difficulties was afoot which put new heart into him. One day at dinner, at any rate, when he had been drinking somewhat heavily, he had the courage to remark in Agrippina's hearing that he had got rid of one wife, and was quite prepared to get rid of another. On another occasion, meeting Britannicus in one of the corridors of the palace, he clasped the boy in his trembling old arms, and cried out passionately: "O, grow up quickly, my son, so that you can right these wrongs!"[11]

During the first days of October, A.D. 54, he announced that he was going to allow the boy to assume the *toga virilis* and come of age at once; and when Agrippina coldly asked him why he wished to do this, he retorted: "So that the Roman people may at last have a real Cæsar," meaning by this that in his opinion Britannicus was likely to grow into a man of the world after his own heart, whereas Nero was soft, and a willing pupil of this unbearable puritanism. He did not see that Nero was almost as ready for revolt as himself.

Agrippina was terrified, and when, shortly afterwards, the Senate issued a new coin with the head of Britannicus upon it, her anxiety knew no bounds. She had forgotten that Claudius was still able to assert himself; and suddenly she saw the possibility that he would ask the people to accept Britannicus as his heir at his coming-of-age, in spite of the fact that a child-Emperor would be a complete novelty. In her agitation the thought of murder entered her heart. She had caused many a man and woman to be put to death; and why now should she hesitate to clear this menace to Nero and to herself from her path?

The burning question in her mind, however, was whether Nero himself was yet old enough to ascend the throne; and, unable to answer this question with certainty, she fell back on the argument that at any rate he was older and more acceptable at the moment than Britannicus, but that this factor in his favour would be considerably lessened as soon as Britannicus had been given the *toga virilis*. . . .

On the night of October 12th there was to be a supper at the palace, [12] on the occasion of one of the annual religious festivals in memory of the revered Augustus. To Agrippina this fact was almost like a sign from heaven: if Claudius were to die on that night, her boy, Nero, whom she had trained to be a second Augustus, would ascend the throne as it were under the auspices of his mighty ancestor. What could be more fitting? It seemed to her that she was the instrument of fate, the instrument of the deified Augustus, chosen by him to strike this blow for the glory of the Julian house, for the good of Rome; and, with cool and deliberate purpose, she made her plans.

When the time arrived and the supper was in progress a dish of mushrooms was placed in front of the Emperor, who was already somewhat tipsy. He loved good food, and mushrooms were a delicacy he could never resist. He ate them now with his usual greed; but presently he complained of indisposition, and, leaving the room, was overcome with nausea. This was not unusual, for his digestion was bad; but as he was now obliged to take to his bed, where he continued to vomit, the party soon broke up.

Agrippina then sent for the court physician, Stertinius Xenophon of Cos, who had served on the staff of Claudius in the army, and had been decorated for his services. This doctor remained with the Emperor for the rest of the night; but in the early morning, finding that his patient was still in great pain, he made him open his mouth, and tickled his throat with a feather so as to cause him to vomit once more. A moment later, Claudius fell back on his pillows, dead.

Nobody can say with certainty that Agrippina had poisoned him. The motive for such an action is clear enough; and Tacitus gives a circumstantial story of how she obtained the poison from an old woman named Locusta, how it was administered by the eunuch Halotus, and how the feather used by the doctor had been dipped in another and more deadly poison. But it is possible that Agrippina's murderous intentions were forestalled by accident, and that Claudius, having eaten a poisonous variety of mushroom, died of heart-failure caused by the strain of the vomiting.

Be this as it may, when the sun rose on the morning of October 13th, he was lying dead upon his bed; but only Agrippina and her immediate circle knew that life was extinct. The gates of the palace were barred, and Burrhus stationed his guards at every door to prevent anybody entering or leaving. It was said that the Emperor was critically ill, and a note was despatched to the Senate, as soon as it assembled in the early morning, bidding the consuls and priests to offer up prayers for his recovery.

To keep up this pretence, while the plans for the proclamation of Nero as Emperor were being perfected, the dead man was propped up on his pillows, and his favourite comedians and dancers were told to go into the room to amuse him. This they did, cracking their jokes and cutting their capers in front of the body, whose eyes stared at them glassily; while, in the corner of the room, the court orchestra made their music and banged their drums. Every now and then Agrippina or one of her friends would go smiling to the bedside and ask the corpse whether the entertainment were amusing him. From time to time, too, hot poultices were applied to the dead man's stomach; and bulletins were issued saying that he was reacting well to the treatment.

This grim farce was enacted not only so that secret preparations for the acclamation of Nero might be made both in the Senate and amongst the troops, but also because the official soothsayers in the palace had declared that the day was wholly ill-omened except for the hour of noon; and that hour, therefore, had been selected for the announcement of the death of the old Emperor, and the proclamation of the new.

During the morning it was necessary to keep Britannicus out of sight, for he had been somewhat troublesome since his father had talked to him about the possibility of his being Emperor one day, and there was now danger that he might break away and raise a rebellion, perhaps with the aid of Narcissus who may have made a bargain with him, and may have been planning some such coup. Agrippina therefore kept Britannicus and his sister Octavia, Nero's wife, close to her; and from time to time she would put her arms around the boy and tearfully declare that he was the image of his dear father, and her chief comfort in her sorrow. But Britannicus instinctively mistrusted her, and did his best to escape her caresses.

In the meantime Nero was pacing about his room, excitedly rehearsing the speeches he and Seneca had composed; and, as the fatal hour approached, he sent for his servants to dress him and to arrange his thick crop of red hair to the best advantage, brushing forward a low-growing curl against his cheek in front of each ear so as to form a smart and grown-up little pair of whiskers. He was a heavily-built young man of average height, a little inclined to be fat; but his flushed and freckled face was full of animation, and his blue eyes, which usually had a dreamy look due in part to short sight, were now bright with excitement.

Exactly at the hour of noon the main gates of the palace were thrown open, and Nero appeared with Burrhus at his side. The guard, already primed by their officers, at once hailed him as Emperor with a great shout; and thereat the doors were shut and barred behind him, leaving Britannicus locked within. Nero was carried in a litter to the Prætorian barracks, where he delivered an excellent speech, promising every soldier a handsome present of money.

He was then conducted in triumph to the Senate, the members of which also hailed him; and there he remained until sunset, returning in the dusk to the palace, where Agrippina awaited him with beating heart.

As soon as she had received from him the assurance that all was well, and that he had been accepted by Rome as Emperor, the cold and revengeful cruelty of her heart impelled her, it seems, to dispatch a messenger to her defeated enemy Narcissus, telling him that his old master and friend was dead, and that Nero had ascended the throne with herself as Regent. Narcissus knew the meaning of the tidings, and prepared himself for any eventuality, setting his affairs in order, and burning all his private papers.

That same evening the officer of the Guard came to Nero to receive from him the watchword. "The watchword this night," said the new Emperor, turning to Agrippina who was at his side, "is 'The Best of Mothers.' "

CHAPTER VII

The Beginning of Nero's Reign, October to December, A.D. 54—The Death of Narcissus—The First Quarrels between Nero and his Mother—Nero's Entrance into Society—His and Seneca's Ridicule of Claudius.

EVENTS had moved with bewildering rapidity, and after an interval had been provided by a night of such sleep as overwrought nerves would permit, one may imagine that the actors in this historic drama resumed their rôles next morning hardly knowing what was expected of them, and being impelled only by their individual desires and needs.

Agrippina, now a woman of nearly forty, must have sighed with deep satisfaction at the thought that for at least two or three years she would in all probability be the absolute ruler of the Roman world, and that even after her son had grown to full manhood she might still be the power behind the throne. She had trained him to love her and to be obedient to her, and she was determined to hold him in unconscious subjection to her so long as it was possible to do so. Seneca and Burrhus, his two tutors, were to be trusted, she supposed, to stand by her, for they were both under deep obligations to her; and Pallas, now the most influential, and perhaps the wealthiest, individual in Rome, was bound to her service by that powerful tie—an ambitious man's pride in the exalted rank of the lady in the habit of spending the night with him. Narcissus, against whom she intended to act immediately, was already as good as dead. Thus, she had but to keep a motherly hand on her dear son's shoulder, never allowing him to forget that he owed everything to her, and her wildest dreams of wealth and dominion would come true. The actions of Claudius had recently disturbed the progress of her ambitions, and she was profoundly relieved at his exit, believing that she would be more powerful as regent-mother of an Emperor not old enough to govern than as the wife of an Emperor not sufficiently imbecile to be prevented from interfering.

Britannicus, four months short of his fourteenth birthday, could hardly have been prostrated by grief at the loss of a father he had never known at all intimately, and he was still too young fully to understand the tragedy of his position; but though he must have been disappointed at the collapse of the exciting hopes held out to him of his being the next Emperor, he looked forward, no doubt, to a reasonably happy life as the new ruler's brother-in-law. He and Nero, in spite of occasional quarrels, did not get along so badly together; and his devoted sister Octavia, as Empress, would assuredly look after his interests. It was only Agrippina whom he feared and mistrusted; but she would probably be kinder to him now that her beloved Nero was safely on the throne.

Octavia, at this time fifteen years of age, must have been frankly pleased to have attained so early that privileged degree of licence and criminal sanction accorded by recent usage to an Empress, for, as the daughter of Messalina, she may well have begun already to flirt with the young men at court, thereby consoling herself for her youthful husband's gauche and awkward indifference to her. One imagines that she felt herself to be far more a grown woman than he was a grown man. The red-haired, freckled Nero was too simple, too shy, too boyish, to fit in with her precocious ideas of romance; but so long as she kept the friendship of Agrippina by showing respect to her and by not interfering in state affairs, she was sure that she would without difficulty amuse herself. She felt indignant, no doubt, at the treatment of her ailing brother Britannicus; but she may well have realized that had he succeeded to their father's throne, she herself would now neither be enjoying the grandeur nor anticipating the latitude of being the first lady in the land.

Nero, on his part, must have been dazed by the sudden cessation of his apprenticeship and by his realization that today, for the first time, it was his to command rather than to obey. He could hardly believe it. His education had been so irksome: there were so many things he had wanted to do which had been forbidden, but to which, with a little courage, he could now demand the right to give his attention. He wanted to study music, to write poetry, to paint, to sculpture. [1] Of course, he said to himself, he would be a wonderful Emperor: he would pass a lot of laws relieving people of oppression; he would see that there was no more tyranny, no more squandering of human lives, no more unnecessary taxation and poverty; he would carry out the humane reforms which Seneca had so often told him were desirable. He would make himself immensely popular—and he loved the thought of popularity; but so that he should not be overburdened with the labours of governing the civilized world, he would assign greater powers to the Senate, and would make Seneca and Burrhus do all the spade-work for him.

They were a fine combination, these two: the suave Seneca, with his diplomatic skill in handling people, his philosophic, thoughtful consideration for all men's rights, and his not too strict adherence to his Stoic principles; and the honest Burrhus, with his blunt loyalty, his military discipline, and his ability to command the devotion of the army. They would be shocked, perhaps, when he told them he was going to devote himself to the arts; but they would enjoy the great powers he was going to place in their hands. Pallas, he did not like: the man was too wealthy, too arrogant, [2] too fond of intrigue, and very much too familiar with his mother. [3]

His mother! There lay the difficulty. He knew well enough that he owed his position to her: it was she who had defended him against the murderous designs of Messalina; it was she who had obliged Claudius to adopt him and make him his heir; it was she who had turned upon this same Claudius at the first indication that he was inclining towards Britannicus, and perhaps had poisoned him. True, she denied emphatically that she had done so, protesting that a dish of noxious mushrooms had accomplished by accident that which she would have shrunk from achieving by design; but Nero did not know what to think.

He loved his mother, and felt great respect for her forceful will, yet he was painfully uneasy about her. She had caused so many people to be put to death; and though she always said she had done so for his sake, there was, on this account, an element of horror in the awe she inspired in him, for with all his heart he hated bloodshed.[4] And his late aunt, Domitia Lepida, had told him some terrible stories about her—how she had prostituted herself first to Crispus and then to Claudius to gain her ends; and he could see for himself that her relations with Pallas were not all that they should be.

In spite of the fact that he was now Emperor, and that the whole Roman world was at his beck and call, he feared that he was not truly a free agent; for his mother would still continue to stand over him like a tribal deity, and he shunned the thought of hurting her feelings. She had established such a position of dominance in his emotional life, she had used so incessantly every manœuvre of motherhood—excepting neither stern and matriarchal correction nor tender and even sensuous caresses—to create an unbreakable bond between them, that it seemed to him almost impious to drag his fettered individuality from her insufferably loving grip. Yet what he wanted to be, and what she desired him to be, were two utterly different things.

In these first hours of his sovereignty, when his brain was reeling with the possibilities of his unimaginable power, when the amazing fact was dawning upon him that every wish expressed by him would be fulfilled if man could fulfil it, when the dazzling thought was ascending into his consciousness that at last he might dare to be himself, he was aware of that opposing maternal force, dreaded yet loved, beating down his aspiring spirit, suffocating the artist's enthusiasm within him, so that from the wreck of his individualistic freedom there might arise a parody of himself, a crowned hypocrite, capable of any secret crime necessary to imperial ambition, but outwardly upholding with expressionless face the dead weight of the Roman tradition of lordship.

In the immediate needs of the moment, however, the conflicting interests of mother and son were served by a single line of action. It was necessary for Nero to create a favourable impression of filial piety by officiating at the funeral of his step-father, and giving the ceremony an air of solemn pomp and magnificence; and this he willingly did, himself delivering the customary panegyric on the dead man's character. He was proud of his literary and oratorical talents, and he had spent many hours in the preparation of this effusion, which, with youthful vanity, he doubtless deemed to be a most creditable piece of work. Tacitus, indeed, thinks that the composition was Seneca's rather than Nero's, for he points out that the young Emperor was from his early childhood more inclined "to turn his vivid intellect to other pursuits, such as sculpture, painting, singing, and horsemanship," though he admits that his composition of poems showed that he had the gift of words.[5]

The speech has not been preserved, but Tacitus says that "so long as he was recording the antiquity of the late Emperor's lineage, and the consulships and triumphs enjoyed by his ancestors, he spoke with fervour, and the whole assembly listened with deep emotion; while the mention also of the dead man's liberal accomplishments, and the observation that during his reign no calamity from foreign enemies had befallen the state, met with a ready response in the minds of his hearers. But when once Nero turned to a commemoration of the wisdom and foresight of Claudius, not a soul could refrain from laughter, though the speech showed every indication of good taste."

Thus far Agrippina and her son were at one; but now their interests diverged. When the funeral was over, Nero went to the Senate where he delivered a second speech, which aroused the utmost enthusiasm. "He set forth," says Tacitus, "the principles and models by following which he hoped to administer the affairs of the empire in the best manner. His youth, he declared, had not been mixed up with civil dissensions or domestic quarrels, and, therefore, he brought with him no animosities, no sense of injuries received, and no desire of revenge. He then laid down his future plan of government, pointedly repudiating those evil practices the odium of which was still fresh and strong in the minds of his hearers. In his house, he said, there should be no bribery nor corruption, nor anything open to the wiles of ambition, and his family concerns should be kept distinct from affairs of state. The Senate, he added, should be restored to its ancient authority."

In the preparation of this address he may well have been helped by Seneca, but it seems to have reflected, nevertheless, his own enthusiastic ideas, for, in the coming years, he fulfilled all that he had promised. [6] The applause was vociferous; and the Senators, in their unbounded delight, ordered the speech to be engraved upon a pillar of solid silver, and to be read publicly once a year. [7] Agrippina, however, who had not been consulted in regard to it, was vexed and troubled, [8] for she regarded the reference to abuses in the palace as a reflection upon her joint rule with Claudius, and, in any event, she did not approve of giving the Senate back its republican powers.

Nor did she think it seemly that Nero should have said so pointedly that he brought no animosities into his new office, considering that she was already taking steps to have Narcissus arrested. It looked as though the boy were attempting to embarrass her in her punitive designs against this dangerous freedman; and she determined to assert her authority at once. Within an hour or two of the reporting of this speech to her, she sent orders for Narcissus to be thrown into prison, on the pretext that he was conspiring against the new Emperor; but Nero, on hearing what she had done, though he had no liking for the fallen freedman, indignantly protested, [9] and it would seem that the matter produced the first definite clash between himself and his mother. One can imagine that she ridiculed his desire to treat his former friend with kindness, and that she defended her action by telling him he was not old enough to realize the dangers which beset him. Narcissus, she said, really meant mischief, and Nero must permit her to do what she, in her wisdom, thought best.

Narcissus, however, was unaware that he had an advocate in the young Emperor; and, finding himself a prisoner apparently without hope of escape from death, he anticipated the executioner by immediately committing suicide, apparently not more than a day or two after the funeral.[10] It is interesting to notice, as we take leave of him, that his name has come down to us as a patron, or at least a tolerator, of that little sect of Christians which was just beginning to find its feet in Rome; for in the Epistle to the Romans,[11] St. Paul sends his greetings to "them that be of the household of Narcissus, which are in the Lord."

It will be recalled that when Agrippina decided to betroth Octavia to Nero, she had been obliged to rid herself of the girl's fiancé, Lucius Silanus, whom she therefore caused to be disgraced on a charge of incest. This Lucius had a surviving brother, Marcus Junius Silanus, who, at the time of Nero's accession, was Proconsul of Asia Minor—a kindly, easy-going man, whom Caligula used to call "the golden sheep." Agrippina had some reason to fear him, for, as Tacitus says, "whereas Nero had hardly arrived yet at manhood, this Silanus was of prudent and mature age, of unblemished character, of illustrious descent, and of the lineage of the Cæsars, being the great-grandson of the revered Augustus."

There is nothing to show that he had aspired to the imperial dignity, but it is not at all unlikely that Narcissus had been in correspondence with him in regard to that possibility; for the fallen freedman, knowing that Agrippina was an implacable enemy, may well have supposed that the only hope for himself, unless he could strike a bargain with Britannicus, lay in bringing about the transfer of the throne to this distant branch of the family. Be this as it may, Agrippina seems to have thought to herself that her best justification for her action against Narcissus—a justification which would put her right with Nero in this startling breach between them—would be provided by her proceeding now against Silanus also. She knew, however, that her son, in this unexpected attitude of his, of conscientious objection to her violent and ruthless policy, would refuse to agree to the arrest of the supposed traitor; and therefore she decided to act without telling Nero what she intended to do. [12]

Secretly she sent two of her officers to Asia Minor with orders to kill this dangerous relation of hers; and these men, without any attempt at concealment, brutally poisoned him at the first meal to which he had unsuspectingly invited them.

The unnecessary crime, which must have become known in Rome some time in November, sent a thrill of horror through the city, and on all sides people asked what sort of a woman, then, Agrippina could be, who had appeared to be a paragon of virtue, but now was guilty of a murder so cold-blooded that her connection also with the death of Claudius could hardly be in doubt.

Agrippina, in truth, had begun to abandon—in the domestic circle, at any rate—the ostentatious practice of the exemplary life now that Nero was safely seated upon the throne. So long as her son's ultimate accession had been in doubt she had taken pains to appear always as a respectable and upright matron of the old school, scrupulously careful of the imperial dignity, because this rôle was likely to enhance her son's chances, Rome being sick of the lawless element in its aristocracy, as has been said, and being desirous of a social reform. But now, having attained the object which this superficial but not altogether insincere punctiliousness of hers had been calculated to secure, she began to allow her real nature to direct her actions. Gradually she ceased to be a self-disciplined follower of the austere Augustus: she showed herself as a true sister of Caligula, outspoken and incautious before her son, and an unashamed perpetrator of any crime which might serve to consolidate the power she had won. She continued, it is true, to present a dour face of disapproval to the broad-minded and frivolous elements in society, but that had become habitual to her, and was a kind of Julian snobbery more than anything else.

She was, in certain respects, dense, obtuse and unable readily to understand the point of view of others; and now she did not trouble to reckon with the peculiar temperament of Nero. She knew that throughout his childhood she had been his goddess who could do no wrong, and she supposed that, in his developing manhood, he would realize the political necessity of the acts of violence she had committed, and would see with gratitude that all had been done for his sake. She had pictured him growing up to be her loving accomplice, her sympathetic companion and partner along the adventurous paths of that dark underworld of secret diplomacy and political intrigue which, in his childhood, she had travelled alone. She looked for his support and his comradeship in the perils and excitements, the disappointments and the triumphs, of this murderous business of sovereignty; and in these first weeks of his reign she began boldly to take him into her confidence, initiating him little by little into the appalling secrets of her conception of statecraft, permitting him to see the ruthless striking power behind the virtuous calm of her outward appearance, believing that he would be a ready pupil.

But in this she was wholly mistaken: Nero shrank from her.

Suetonius makes it quite clear [13] that he was at this time, as has already been pointed out, an extremely simple and good-hearted young man, anxious to make his people happy, hating by nature to cause anybody pain, and trained by the humane Seneca to respect the lives and liberties of all men. He was, in fact, the true grandson of the large-hearted Germanicus, once the idol of the Roman people; and neither the pitilessness of his mother nor the brutality of his father were yet to be found in his character. He was shocked by the revelation of Agrippina's nature, and he was torn between love of her and horror at her deeds. Seneca and Burrhus, he knew, felt much as he did in regard to her; but even with their support, he could not blame her, knowing that all had been done for his sake, nor could he cease to pay her the highest filial respect in public. Yet he was conscious of a widening gulf between them, and of a sinking of his heart, a kind of dreadful dismay, as she showed more and more of her real character to him.

So, at least, I interpret the situation, bearing in mind the remark of Tacitus, that at this time "a constant struggle had to be maintained against the fiery spirit of Agrippina, who was burning with every lust of lawless dominion," and yet that Nero "heaped all kinds of honours upon her in public." [14] To make this view of the matter more obvious it will be as well, perhaps, to recount some of the young Emperor's actions which reveal the goodness of his nature, and which show the contrast between him and his mother.

He began his reign by recalling many people from exile, but no injury was done to any man, save to Narcissus and Silanus, both of whom, however, were attacked without his knowledge. He forgot no kindness rendered to him in his childhood, nor revenged himself in any way for past injuries. He applied to the Senate for an honour to be given to an old man, Asconius Labeo, who had once been one of his teachers; and he refused to prosecute a certain Julius Densus, who was accused of supporting the claims of Britannicus to the throne against his own. He was so anxious to prevent oppression that he tried, though without success, to introduce a sweeping reform, abolishing all indirect taxation throughout the Empire. He acted, indeed, with extraordinary mercy and generosity; and as an instance of his kindness it may be mentioned that he sent all the way to Egypt at his own expense for a certain doctor to attend a sick friend of his.

When a man named Antistius Sosianus was tried

by the Senate for having written some scurrilous and treasonable verses about him, he sent a message to the judges saying that he would be quite willing that the offender should be acquitted; and on other occasions he refused to punish his detractors. He reduced the payments given to informers, so that there should be less inducement to them to bring charges of treason against malcontents. He granted old age pensions to aged senators who were in reduced circumstances; and he was lavish in his gifts to the needy.

When he was first called upon to sign a criminal's death-warrant, he was nearly reduced to tears, and passionately exclaimed: "O, why was I ever taught to write?" He issued instructions that in the gladiatorial contests and other exhibitions in the arena, nobody was to be killed, not even criminals condemned, as an alternative to execution, to risk their lives in these combats; and during the whole of the first year of his rule not one life was thus lost—an astonishing innovation which had no support from the bloodthirsty Roman people. Once, as a child, he had been so concerned about an accident which had occurred to a slave, who had fallen from a chariot and had been dragged, that he had been sharply told that a gentleman should not show such pity for a servant.

Such being his nature it will be understood that the revelation of his mother's true character had the effect of arousing in him a bitter hostility to all that she stood for. He began to loathe that good repute which had been the ideal placed before him through his childhood; and, having in his nature a very notable quality of truth and sincerity, he displayed a growing repugnance to that hypocrisy which concealed a countenance of crime behind a mask of virtue. It had been dinned into his head that appearances and outward forms were everything, and that in order to present himself to the people in the guise which would make him acceptable to them, namely that of a Roman traditionist, he must cultivate an austere dignity, a pious concealment of weaknesses, a superficial restraint and self-suppression, so that he might appear to represent those virtues which were believed to have made his forefathers what they were.

He had been brought up with a rigour only maintained in the strictest of the conservative old families, and his friends were chosen for him from those same circles. He had been forced to walk in the footsteps of Augustus, and to accept his conventional interpretation of the duties of a Roman gentleman. He had been told that the arts he loved were for his patronage, not for his pursuit; and he had been everlastingly reminded that all things in the nature of free self-expression—his music, his poetry, his painting—were like minor sins, not to be indulged by the ruler of a militaristic empire save in secret. Even his outbursts of high spirits had been checked as unbecoming in a prince of the old school.

But now, suddenly, he made up his mind to have done with this infamous humbug: Nero should be himself.

In his revolt against decorum he sent for Terpnus, the most famous teacher of music and singing then in Rome, and began enthusiastically to take lessons in those arts, for he had been told that he had the makings of a great singer. Seneca may have smiled diplomatically, Burrhus may have shown his disapproval in so far as he dared, but Agrippina, one may suppose, was frankly shocked. Angrily she must have told her son not to be a fool; but, to her amazement, Nero, who was deeply in earnest about his music, stood up to her, saying, apparently, that he could no longer admit her right to interfere in his private life. It was a definite breach between them, and Agrippina was stunned by it.

But a further rebuff was in store for her. In the days of Nero's severe apprenticeship, as has been said, he had not been allowed to choose his own friends, and at his accession he neither knew nor was known by the young men and women of fashion in Rome. He had been kept away from the gay and up-to-date element in wealthy society—the set which modelled its life upon that of cultured Greece, and which deemed the Roman fatherland to be sadly behind the times. For many years, and particularly since the death of Messalina, Agrippina had ignored this group, having felt that the obtaining of the support of the old-fashioned aristocracy was more likely to bring Nero at last to the throne—a policy of which the wisdom had been fully proved.

Thus, in the first weeks of the reign, the leaders of that smart society which was by no means so much in eclipse as Agrippina seems to have thought, must have been curious to know what kind of youth their new Emperor might be. They believed that he was not at all one of themselves: he was apparently a pious young man, entirely under the thumb of his virtuous and puritanical mother. He was not at all fashionable; he had no idea of how to spend his money; the palace menage, than which he knew nothing better, was deplorably stodgy and inelegant: in a word, he was considered to be rather a country bumpkin, and probably a shocking Philistine. Yet Terpnus was now telling them, on the contrary, that he was by nature an artist, a poet and singer of merit, a lover of all things Greek, a romantic young fellow longing to break away from his humdrum life. The world of fashion was greatly intrigued, but it could do nothing: the gates of the palace had been closed to smart society ever since the disastrous occasion of the Bacchic orgy which had brought death to Messalina and most of her friends.

One may suppose it was Nero who made the first gesture of rapprochement, and soon he was shyly and diffidently making his début in that artistic and fashionable circle of which his mother was the declared opponent. Three elegant young men quickly attached themselves to him, and set about the task of educating him in what was comme-il-faut. There was the ambitious and charming Salvius Otho, [15] five years older than himself, recklessly daring yet something of a fop, a smiling full-faced young man, whose hair was prematurely thin, and whose chin was so beardless that people said he used a depilatory. There was Claudius Senecio, the son of a freedman who had acquired great wealth, a cultured and artistic youth, noted for his good looks. And then there was Petronius, called Arbiter because he was the recognized judge in all matters of taste—a bored and languid young man, a master of the art of good living, a connoisseur, in fact, in all the arts, and a satirical poet of high merit.

The red-haired, shy young Emperor, not at all sure of himself, but proud to be the friend of such brilliant and witty men, brought them to the palace in defiance of his mother's express wishes, and did his best to entertain them; and they, on their part, applied themselves to the amusing task of teaching him what was what, while Agrippina, deeply mortified, was obliged, I suppose, to swallow her pride and receive them with such grace as she could command. A story which is very enlightening is told of Otho's attempt to set Nero an example in the art of spending money, and to wean him from the parsimonious habits of Agrippina. At a dinner party at the palace, Nero produced a bottle of costly scent, and, conscious of its great value but wishing to prove his prodigality, lightly sprinkled a few of the precious drops upon Otho's clothes, remarking as he did so on the recklessness of the waste. Next day, when he was paying a return visit to Otho, his host caused the same scent to be showered over all the guests from a golden spray attached to the ceiling.[16] It cost him a fortune, but it taught the Emperor the desired lesson.

The results of Nero's introduction into smart and free-thinking society were profound. If he had begun to scorn the mock virtues with which his mother cloaked her evil deeds, he now vented his feelings by openly making fun of sham propriety. His new friends, for example, were always joking about the imbecilities of the late Emperor, and Nero, thrilled at the new experience of being allowed to laugh freely, was very ready to make a jest of his step-father's tenure of the throne, and particularly of his deification which had recently been pronounced. True, the death of Claudius had aroused a sudden pity in his heart, and he had treated his memory with the utmost respect; but Agrippina's exaggerated observance of the proprieties of widowhood had aroused in him a bitter sarcasm—for he knew well enough that she had been the foolish old man's actual or would-be murderess—and, anyway, all sentimental humbug about a man who had been the laughing-stock of Rome had left him at the moment when he had seen the people at the funeral hiding their smiles at his reference to the wisdom of Claudius.

The deification of the absurd old Emperor was the subject of mirth amongst all intelligent people, and the fact that Agrippina had just begun the building of a temple dedicated to his godhead, [17] was really too much to swallow. Ever since Julius Cæsar had learnt from Cleopatra the political advantage of the deification of royalty—the Pharaohs of Egypt having been accepted by their subjects as incarnate deities—the Julian and Claudian rulers had claimed divine honours. Julius Cæsar had been hailed everywhere as a god before he died; Augustus and Tiberius had been worshipped in Rome as gods after their deaths, and, in some parts of the empire, while they were still alive; Caligula had gone so far as to worship himself; and now Claudius, as a matter of form, had been deified.

But Nero, in his disillusionment, no longer believed in any gods at all, and he and his new friends laughed heartily at the thought of the doddering old Emperor being received into the astonished circle of the Olympians. Seneca at this time was amusing himself by writing plays, and Nero seems to have suggested to him that a ludicrous farce might be written around this subject. The festival of the Saturnalia—from December 17th to 24th—was approaching, and it was proposed to the philosopher that he should write this skit so that it might then be read, for the Saturnalia was a licenced occasion on which every man was free to joke with impunity upon any subject he chose.

The farce has come down to us,[18] and is one of the best pieces of satirical and malicious fun in Latin literature. Opening with a jibe against the old Emperor's casual bestowal of Roman citizenship upon foreign peoples, it shows him on his death-bed, while Clotho, the goddess who spins the fate of men, and Mercury stand at his side. Mercury asks Clotho why she hesitates to cut the thread of the Emperor's life, to which she replies with the sarcastic remark that there are still a few people in the world—Britons and such like—upon whom he has not yet bestowed the citizenship, and she is waiting for him to do so. However, at Mercury's bidding, she at last snips the thread, and immediately Claudius appears at the gates of Heaven, to the great dismay of the gods. They ask who this white-haired stranger can be, with his twitching head, his shuffling feet, and his stammering, unintelligible speech which sounds like the melancholy complaint of a walrus; and they tell Hercules to go and interview him. Though a great traveller, Hercules has seen nothing like him in all his wanderings, but, mastering a feeling almost of panic, he speaks to him in Greek, whereat Claudius smiles and nods with pleasure, for he has always contended that Greek is the language for scholars like himself.

He is about to ask if Hercules and the beings around him are acquainted with the historical works he has written, when Febris, goddess of Fever,[19] who has brought him from Rome, explains who he is. Claudius regards this as great impertinence and at once orders her to be put to death; but nobody pays any attention to him; indeed, they might all be freedmen of his for all the notice they take of him. Thereupon he realizes that his power is gone, and he attempts to make himself pleasant to Hercules, but to no purpose, for a meeting is held at which the deified Augustus protests that a creature like this, who cannot even say three words quickly, yet has wrongfully condemned scores of people to death, is not fit to be a god. "Who will worship him?" he scoffs. "Who will believe in him? If you make a thing like that a god, who will any longer believe that you yourselves are gods?" The celestial council thereupon tells Mercury to take him to Hell instead.

The road thither passes over the Forum in Rome, and, looking down, they notice the crowds showing every sign of happiness; and as soon as Claudius discovers that the cause of their rejoicing is nothing less than his own funeral, he realizes that he must indeed be dead. He pauses to listen to the song which the merry mourners are singing. "Weep for the hero," they chant, "who was always ready to listen to lawsuits, and to give judgment after hearing only one side of a case, or no side at all! Mourn, O minor poets!—for who will now read you? But lament, most of all, you gamblers who draw huge profits from the dice!"

Claudius is delighted and wants to hear more of his praises sung, but Mercury leads him on to Hell, whither Narcissus has gone ahead to make ready for him; and on their arrival the freedman runs up to fawn upon his old master, but Mercury hits him with his stick, and drives him away. They then descend into the infernal regions, with which the Emperor is quite charmed, until he sees Cerberus, the dog who guards the gates of Hades, for, it is explained, the black and shaggy creature is hardly a beast one would care to meet in the dark, especially as Claudius is used to a white poodle. However, the Emperor musters up his courage, and arrogantly shouts: "Claudius Cæsar comes!"—whereupon a laughing crowd gathers, and capers about in front of him.

Presently Messalina appears, followed by all the victims either of Narcissus or Claudius. "H'm!" mutters the Emperor. "Friends everywhere! How did you all get here?" At this an indignant spirit summons him to trial before Æacus, one of the three judges of the dead, and, to his great astonishment, he is prosecuted for the murder of thirty Senators, three hundred and fifteen gentlemen, and common people as the sands of the seashore. No defence is allowed, but although Claudius thinks this unjust, at least it is no novelty to him. He is condemned to play for ever with a bottomless dice-box; but just then Caligula appears, and asks to have him as a slave, reminding those in court that he used often to kick him when he was on earth. Claudius is therefore handed over to Caligula, who appoints him secretary to one of his freedmen.

The extant text ends here, but some passages seem to be missing, for Dion Cassius, [20] referring undoubtedly to the same farce, speaks of Claudius being turned into a pumpkin, his final end being, so to say, "pumpkinification" instead of deification.

It is hard to say what Agrippina's reaction to this wickedly amusing satire could have been. Viewed in one light it was a reflection also upon her, since she had been notoriously in control of affairs as the wife of Claudius, and had been responsible for many of his so-called murders. On the other hand it served to justify her in the eyes of those who believed she had poisoned him: and it certainly showed up her enemy, Narcissus, as an undesirable character. The fact, however, that it played havoc with imperial dignity, and heaped ridicule on the idea of an Emperor's divinity, must have offended her sense of fitness; and it may be supposed, therefore, that she took her son to task for this jest which she may well have described as being in execrable taste, while, as for Seneca, she probably never forgave him.

Meanwhile, Nero's behaviour in another regard was causing her equal anxiety for the reason that it did not conform to her idea of imperial dignity, nor, indeed, to anybody's. He had been brought up, it must be remembered, upon lugubrious stories of the noble acts of his ancestor, Augustus; but he had in his veins, also, the blood of the reckless Antony, whose life with Cleopatra at Alexandria was still the standard of social gaiety. Antony had been the enemy of Augustus; and Nero, bored with the latter's very name, eagerly emulated the doings of Antony's "Society of Inimitable Livers," an elegant club whose members behaved in a manner which always suggests the activities of those charmingly absurd creatures of our own times who are popularly known as the Bright Young Things.

Now, Nero had heard how the Inimitables used to disguise themselves at night, and roam about the city in search of adventure; and he and his new friends, who liked to think of themselves as having the light-hearted, care-free Greek spirit, and who enjoyed nothing so much as the shocking of Rome's dignified bores, decided to paint the town red, so to speak, in the unforgettable Antony manner. In false wigs or beards, and in the dress of townspeople or peasants, they wandered through the streets in the darkness, performing all kinds of silly pranks. Sometimes they would knock at the doors of the houses of respectable citizens, and then either run away or play some practical joke on those who answered the summons. Sometimes they would enter a low tavern, and make off with a bottle of wine or the sign-board outside the door. Again, they would creep into a private garden and set the fountains working, or steal their nozzles; or they would burgle a house and carry off some trophy in triumph. Sometimes they would seize upon some drunkard and toss him in a blanket, or again, they would accost people in the street, or bar their way, exasperating them into a free fight.

An ugly incident, however, brought this form of amusement to an end: it may be mentioned here, although it did not occur until A.D. 56. They had surrounded a young woman whom they had chanced to meet, and were paying their exaggerated respects to her, when her husband appeared, and put up such a furious fight that Nero had to go home to bed with a pair of black eyes. His friends told him that he ought to find the man and have him punished for his excessive violence; but Nero replied that, on the contrary, he ought to be commended for defending his wife from insult, since he did not know it was the Emperor he was thus battering.

The matter would have been forgotten had not the man himself, who proved to be a Senator named Julius Montanus, made the terrible error of writing to Nero, begging his pardon. "Oh, then he *did* know he was hitting the Emperor!" said Nero; and he let it be understood that that seemed to him to put a more serious complexion on the matter. Julius Montanus followed the old Roman code, and expiated his fault by committing suicide; and Nero, much upset, in the end abandoned his midnight adventures.

For the time being, however, these frolics continued, nor could Agrippina's scoldings check them. Nero was in open revolt against the austere principles for which she stood, and his love and awe of her no longer restrained him.

CHAPTER VIII

The Momentous January and February, A.D. 55—Nero's Love-Affair with Acte—The Dismissal of Pallas—Renewed Quarrels between Nero and his Mother—The Death of Britannicus.

Nero had celebrated his seventeenth birthday on December 15th, A.D. 54, and during the following week the whole country had been given up to the Saturnalia, the festivities of this particular year being memorable at the palace on account of the young Emperor's revolt against his mother's authority, as recorded in the preceding chapter, and the consequent venting of his long suppressed exuberance in an outburst of rollicking fun and indecorum, of which the most scandalous instance was the circulation and hilarious reading of Seneca's satire on the death of Claudius.

But this kicking of his heels caused him, of course, to neglect his official duties; and although Agrippina's control over his private life had been shaken by his discovery of her true character, her influence in affairs of state was strengthened rather than impaired by his behaviour. For so many years, during the reign of Claudius, she had exercised such boundless power that Nero would have found it difficult to relieve her of her now habitual functions; and the thought does not seem yet to have occurred to him that it was his business to apply himself to the details of government, and firmly to grasp the rudder of the ship of state instead of issuing a few general directions, or giving an occasional order. At present he was more concerned with the removal of his mother's paralyzing hand from his shoulder; and in the sudden liberty obtained by his success in this respect he was too excited to bother much about imperial affairs.

Moreover, the very fact of his breaking away from her made her so much the more anxious to assert herself; and it seems to me that the evidence of her high-handedness which has been thought to reveal her exultation at her new power as Regent, in reality shows that she felt her authority passing from her. Ignoring the Romans' rooted objection to female rule, she insisted that the Senate should meet in the Library of the palace, so that she might listen to their debates, although from behind a curtain; she demanded the right to be present at great military and other spectacles; she privately received foreign ambassadors and wrote letters to their sovereigns; and she even caused her head to be placed upon the coins beside that of Nero.

She was constantly scolding the excited young man, these days, and accusing him of ingratitude if he did not obey her wishes; but when Seneca and Burrhus attempted to defend him to her, and to explain that he was to be pardoned in view of the unbalancing suddenness of his discovery that he could do what he liked, she turned upon them and threatened them with dire punishments. In the stupidity of her inflexible sense of maternal right, she did not admit that he could do what he liked, and she would hear no excuses for him, certainly not from Seneca. She would listen to nobody but Pallas, and, indeed, the authorities are agreed that this Greek freedman, "whose insufferable arrogance moved the disgust of Nero,"[1] exercised, jointly with her, the chief power in the government.

As a matter of fact, Nero did his best to treat her with deference and to take care to show her every respect in public, even going so far as to walk on foot by her side when she was being carried through the streets in her litter; and it may well be that, having now successfully revolted from some part of her tutelage, he was anxious to compensate her in other ways, and to soothe her disquieted spirit by showing her that nothing could alter his fundamental love for her.

An instance of her imperiousness and his tact is preserved in history. One day, a deputation from Armenia, desiring to plead that country's cause, was to be received at the palace, and Agrippina announced her intention of being present beside her son on the imperial dais, so that she might tell him what to say, just as she had so often done in the case of Claudius. Now it was wholly against the etiquette of the time that a woman should take a public hand in such proceedings, and Agrippina had only done so without scandal in the days of Claudius because everybody feared that he would make a fool of himself unless his strong-minded wife were there to check him. Nero, however, had not the heart to offend her by telling her not to come: instead, at Seneca's suggestion, he went to the throne-room somewhat early, and received the deputation, but when Agrippina presently swept in, all dressed up in her cloth-of-gold and her jewels, he descended the steps, went to meet her, and affectionately led her out again, saying that he had postponed the audience.

In these first weeks of the reign the young Emperor was being closely watched, of course, by the public. The aristocratic families of the old school, who had approved of Agrippina's stern handling of Claudius, and had upheld her actions in sweeping the palace clear of the late Messalina's frivolous crowd, were now beginning to withdraw their support from her, partly because they were discovering that her outward virtues and pieties concealed a most criminal conception of statecraft, and partly because they were offended by her haughty assumption of power. They were glad, therefore, to observe that Nero was shaking himself loose from her; and though they hated to see him becoming mixed up with the free-thinking, luxury-loving, artistic and Hellenistic elements in society, they found no great fault with him for having his boyish fling, and, indeed, deemed it an indication of a spirited nature. The lower classes, meanwhile, had idolised him from the first, and in their eyes everything he did contributed to his popularity. They loved him for being so democratic; and his vivid personality, his modesty and even shyness, his sturdy figure, his striking red-gold hair which made them compare him to the young Apollo in his aspect as a sun-god, all served to endear him to them.

Mention has been made above of his many kind and

considerate acts which were already being enthusiastically talked about. The Senate now proposed that, in honour of his accession, the calendar year should in future begin with December, the month of his birth, instead of January; but Nero added to his laurels by refusing to agree to the change. Next, it was proposed to set up statues to him made of solid gold and silver; and this, again, he modestly disallowed. Another popular move of his was the appointment of Domitius Corbulo as commander of the Roman army which was to be sent to drive the Parthians out of Armenia, news of their invasion having reached Rome late in December. For so long it had been the custom to appoint as generals men of wealth and influence, regardless of their military talents, that when Nero chose this Corbulo, who was a plain and honest soldier of proven worth, beloved of the people, the crowd was wild with delight. The appointment, it may be mentioned, must have been a further cause of annoyance to Agrippina, for this general had been deliberately passed over by her and Claudius, apparently owing to personal dislike. Shortly afterwards, when news was received that the Parthians were withdrawing, the Senate begged Nero, but in vain, to make a progress through Rome, wearing the triumphal robes, and they asked permission to set up a statue in his honour in the temple of Mars the Avenger, as big as that of the god himself.

Nero enjoyed his popularity immensely; but still more he enjoyed his sudden freedom, and his introduction into the light-hearted and dazzling life of the younger set in Rome's most wealthy society, from which he had been kept away by Agrippina throughout his youth. He was thrilled to find that here, in this cultured atmosphere, his singing and his poetry were highly appreciated, and that his artistic talents in general were regarded as admirable qualities and not as misfortunes. He did not know yet that he was a genius in his way, but he was aware of that painful inner urge towards self-expression which is at once the happiness and the distress of the genius; and his enthusiastic young heart went out to his new friends who talked so appreciatively of those very interests which he had been taught to regard as effeminate and un-Roman.

In these new surroundings in which he found himself, he seems soon to have discovered that all the oddities of sensual indulgence into which human beings are led by desires intended by nature only to compel them to reproduce their kind, were not merely tolerated but admired as the concomitants of the artistic and cultured life. It was the custom, for example, for men of fashion to fall in love with beautiful youths, or for youths to entertain passionate attachments to men older than themselves. This curious eccentricity is, of course, and always has been, very prevalent in southern and eastern countries; and from time to time there are phases of it even in the west and north. Indeed, a great part of the Western World happens today to be passing through such a violent epidemic of this pathologically interesting aberration that, in looking back on ancient Rome, the eyes are quite accustomed to the spectacle presented thereby, and the outrage to masculine susceptibilities is not startlingly felt.

Nero, who was youthfully anxious to be a man of the world, did his best to be in the fashion in this respect, but without any real success: he was incorrigibly normal. It is true that there was in his nature that slightly feminine streak which is to be observed in the majority of artists; but it was not yet strong enough to divert the natural direction of his desires. Having no definite tendency towards the above-mentioned form of perversion, he does not appear to have been able to decide whether he wanted to be a young man attracted to some beautiful youth, or a beautiful youth attracted to some young man[2]; and in the end he revealed his rough and inelegant masculinity by seducing one of the Vestal Virgins.

Then, suddenly, some time in January, his normality proved to be his social undoing. He fell head over ears in love with a slave-girl named Acte. It was his first romance, and, like many first romances, it began, as has been said, soon after the lover's seventeenth birthday, it worked itself up to the protestations of lifelong devotion within a few weeks, and it was dead before he was twenty. We know hardly anything about Acte, except that she was of Greek extraction, came from Asia Minor, and was a modest and unassuming little girl, who gave nobody any trouble, not even when the Emperor ceased to care for her and her heart broke.

Nero, of course, had never pretended to feel affection for his official wife, Octavia, who was between fifteen and sixteen years of age; and it may be that he already detested her [3] as he certainly did a few years later. After all, there could hardly have been a basis even for mutual esteem, since he must have mistrusted her as the daughter of Messalina who had once tried to kill him; and Octavia must have been indignant with him for paying so little husbandly attention to her, and, recently, for making such fun of her father. Consequently, when he thus fell in love his first idea was to divorce Octavia, and to marry Acte; for his curiously frank and open nature, with its increasing disregard for aristocratic traditions, did not permit him to be satisfied that the girl he loved so passionately should merely be his mistress: gallantly he wanted her to be his wife and Empress.

Seneca and Burrhus were in his confidence in regard to this affair, as were his young friends, Marcus Otho and Claudius Senecio, though the cynical Petronius, who had no illusions, does not seem to have been admitted into the secret, which looks as though Nero were really shy of his bored superiority. Seneca, indeed, was delighted that Nero should thus have turned from experimental peccadillos and perversions to normal love, more especially since Acte was a girl of great sweetness and modesty; but when the ardent young man said that he wanted to marry her, the courtly philosopher, gasping for breath, must have pointed out that the Roman people would hardly accept a Greek born in slavery as their Emperor's official consort. Nero, of course, had given her her freedom at the very outset of the affair, and now he suborned some accommodating persons of consular rank to produce a pedigree showing that she was descended from Attalus, king of Pergamum; but Seneca then reminded him that Augustus had made a law forbidding a man of senatorial rank—and Nero was that, and more—to marry a woman who had not been born free. Augustus, again!—how Nero detested that pompous ancestor of his!

Seneca next suggested that, for the time being at any rate, the young Emperor should conceal his passion, and that his (Seneca's) great friend, Annæus Serenus,[4] should pretend to be Acte's lover, and the giver of all the presents—estates, slaves, furniture, jewels, and so forth—which Nero was now lavishing upon her. Matters were finally arranged thus, with the result that Acte became a great lady living in her own sumptuous house, wherein Nero secretly spent all his spare time, although the public, unaware of his visits, supposed that Serenus was the fond and generous gentleman-friend in the case.

The stratagem, however, did not deceive Agrippina. She had soon discovered her son's infatuation; she had heard that he even thought of marrying this low-born girl; and now she was well aware who had housed her in this splendid manner. She was beside herself with rage and anxiety; and one may suppose that she was consumed also by that jealousy which a mother often feels for the object of her boy's affections, more particularly in cases, such as this, where a very intimate and demonstratively loving relationship had existed in the past between them. She stormed at

Nero; she heaped abuse on Acte; she clasped Octavia to her bosom, and wept over this insult to Nero's legal wife. Octavia had always disliked her, as a matter of fact, and, since her childhood, had been very frightened of her[5]; but now Agrippina did her best to overcome this fear, for she wanted the girl's full co-operation at this crisis. Was an ex-slave, she asked, to be brought into competition with herself, the Empress-Mother, and perhaps to be her daughter-in-law? [6] She attacked Seneca and Burrhus for winking at the affair, and, supported in her tirades by Pallas, she split the imperial household into two factions—herself, Pallas, and Octavia on the one hand, with the young Britannicus following his sister; and, on the other hand, Nero, Seneca, and Burrhus, with Acte in the background.

For a few days a state of open hostility between these two parties seems to have existed at the palace, but at last Agrippina realized that her ends were not thus to be gained; and, suddenly changing her tactics, she made a great show of affection for her son, admitted that she had treated his love-affair too harshly, and even offered to place money at his disposal from her own private fortune, so that he might make further gifts to Acte, I suppose, without the fact being known to the officials of his treasury.

Nero was elated at this apparent end of their quarrel and the renewal of their former affectionate relationship; and during the first days of February it seems that he was demonstratively loving to her once more, fondly kissing her and holding her in his arms. The outcome of this situation is so nearly incredible to the modern mind that I hesitate to record it; and yet I suppose the duty of a biographer obliges me to do so. Tacitus states that, having plied him with wine, she took him to her bedroom day after day, and there attempted to change their relationship from that of mother and son to that of lovers. We are asked to suppose that—whether in her frenzy of jealousy of this other woman who had come into his life, in her terror of losing him, in her anxiety to be his all in all, or, alternatively, in sheer criminal licentiousness—she offered to become her own son's mistress.[7] We are asked by Tacitus to remember the terrible moral record of Agrippina, and he seems to leave us to judge for ourselves as to the truth of this monstrous story, which, he says, was generally believed; and I will therefore pass it by, only remarking that Nero does not appear to have accepted these overtures.

It was shortly after this that Pallas took some now forgotten step which aroused the young man's anger in an altogether unexpected degree. The powerful freedman had never dreamed that Nero would dare to punish him. He had thought that his intimate relationship with Agrippina would fully protect him: he had not supposed it possible that this youth of seventeen would have the heart or the hardihood to defy the Empress-Mother. Pallas, it must be remembered, was one of the proudest and richest men in the world, and, since the death of Narcissus, had regarded himself almost as the ruler of the Roman Empire. Even in the time of Claudius his power had been so great that Cornelius Scipio had asked the obsequious Senate "to tender a vote of public thanks to Pallas, for the reason that, although descended from the kings of Arcadia,[8] he had put his service to the state before his most ancient nobility, and had deigned to be numbered amongst the ministers of the Emperor." [9] His wealth, like that of Narcissus, had been acquired by such clever manipulation of markets under his control that once when Claudius had complained of the emptiness of his private treasury, somebody had replied that if only his two freedmen would take him into partnership with them his coffers would soon be full.[10]

When Nero now stood up to him, and ordered him to leave the palace, his amazement, and the amazement of Agrippina, must have been supreme. His exit was so sudden that he was unable to wind up his accounts, and he had to ask that they should be considered as balanced, to which Nero agreed; but as he swept out of the palace, followed by a train of his employees, Nero heard the muttered oaths which were rolling from his lips, and, shrugging his shoulders, remarked that the fallen minister was evidently swearing himself out of office.[11]

The dismissal of this mighty and arrogant personage, who was Agrippina's chief support in her movements along the lurid and devious ways of political and governmental intrigue, and who was at the same time her circumspect partner in the still desired intimacies of her bedchamber, led to a terrible scene between herself and her son, which becomes all the more horrible if we credit the above-mentioned story of her recent attempt to beguile the young man by the perverse use of her charms. But it would seem that he was not yet conscious of the murderous look which, there is warrant to suppose, came into her eyes as he thus defied her—that cold, snake-like look so reminiscent of her brother, Caligula; and had he been told that his life was thenceforth in danger he would not have believed it.

Soon, indeed, his heart was filled with remorse for his behaviour, for, after all, she, with all her crimes, was his mother, and it seems that he loved her in spite of the gulf these awful quarrels had opened between them. Longing to be reconciled to her, he hurried off to the wardrobe where the magnificent state-dresses and jewels worn by the Empresses were kept, and, selecting the most priceless set, sent it to Agrippina as a present. But his gesture had an unforeseen effect: she cried out that this was a deliberate insult, intended to remind her that the property of the Empresses was no longer hers by right. Her son was making her a selected gift, when actually everything in the wardrobe, everything in the palace, was hers.

Nero was distracted, and it is said that he went so far as to think of resigning his throne and its troubles, and of retiring to Rhodes, where in the congenial Greek atmosphere, he hoped to be able to live the quiet and unrestricted life of an artist. He could not overcome a feeling of awe of his mother, and, indeed, he still desired to do as she wished, in so far as that were possible. Their estrangement was due to obvious causes which surely could easily be removed. She would have to understand that he could not play the part of an Augustus—the rôle for which she had trained him—nor school himself to be superficially an old-fashioned Roman gentleman, patriotic to the exclusion of all things Greek or otherwise foreign, careful of the outward dignity of his position, and having an eye always on conventional society's approval. She would have to understand that he was an artist, an admirer of that taste and culture which the Greeks were teaching their Roman conquerors, a free-thinker, a hater of that piety which was a cloak of political immorality and murder.

It was his desire to live and let live; he wanted to have a good time, and to make everybody happy. He was quite willing that she should take her share of the government, but he was not going to allow anybody to be put to death by her orders in the ruthless old way to which she had become accustomed. He was no longer going to do just what he was told, like a good boy, especially now that he knew the kind of political criminality to which she desired him to be a party; nor was he going to be scolded and abused, called ungrateful, and made miserable by the reproaches of a mother whom he honestly loved, and to whom he had already shown that he wished every respect to be paid.

She, on her part, however, viewed the matter very differently. Throughout Nero's childhood she had fought and schemed for him, and had committed every sort of crime for his sake, believing, as has been said, that when he was Emperor he would, for many years to come, play the rôle of her junior-partner in the management of the world's government. As long as Claudius had been alive and a tool in her hands, her power had been supreme; and it was only because he had rebelled against her authority that she had been forced to desire a change in Emperors—from a once negligible husband to an obedient son. But the change had proved fatal to that supremacy which was as the breath of life to her, and she was bitterly chagrined. She had made a terrible mistake. The boy whom she had loved so fondly, and whom she had trained so diligently to be her intimate and understanding colleague in her difficult work, had turned upon her; and now he had given his heart to a silly little slave-girl who was, moreover, that abomination, a good woman. Nero was not worthy of the love she, his mother, had lavished upon him; and she began to see that she would have to steel herself to destroy that which she had nurtured. Already in these last hours she had grown almost to hate him, and now, for the first time, she allowed herself to consider the possible advantage of being rid of him.

In her fury, "she abandoned herself," says Tacitus, "to a system of terrorism and menace," [12] breathing threats against her son, and darkly suggesting that she would find means to raise the whole country against him. She glared at Burrhus, and swore at Seneca, calling him an ungrateful wretch who would still be an exile in Corsica had she not obtained his pardon; and at last she brought in the name of Britannicus, recklessly declaring that he would make a better Emperor than Nero.

Now, a very significant incident had recently occurred. Nero and his friends had one day been playing a game of forfeits, in which the elected "king" of the game had to order the others each to perform some particular act. Britannicus, now nearing his fourteenth birthday, was a member of the party, and, when his turn came, he was laughingly ordered to stand in the middle of the room and sing a song. It was expected that the boy, being shy and unused to jolly parties—which were considered too exciting for his nervous and epileptic constitution—would be embarrassed and would make a fool of himself; but, on the contrary, the pale and delicate youth, a tragic figure, old for his years, and embittered by his ill-health and his sense of orphanhood, picked up a harp, and, with perfect composure, sang a certain well-known lament in which he told of the sorrows of a parentless child, bereft of his rightful inheritance, unloved, unwanted and alone.[13] There was a painful silence when he ceased; the fun of the game was gone; and on all sides sympathetic references were made to the boy's unhappy fate.

Remembering this incident, and observing that Britannicus had lately been very moody, Nero began to wonder whether somebody had been reminding him of his supposed wrongs, and, making enquiries, he found, to his astonishment, that the culprit was his mother, the very person who had pushed the boy into obscurity. Shortly after this, on February 12th, the fourteenth birthday of Britannicus was celebrated, and Agrippina, who would hardly speak to Nero, showed marked attention to his cousin. Next day, Nero asked her to explain herself; and with that she rounded upon him, accusing him again of ingratitude, and telling him that she alone had made him Emperor, but that he was now using his power only to slight and insult her.

Then, her anger increasing to fury, "she heaped reproaches upon him with violent gesticulations," as Tacitus tells us,[14] "invoking the deified Claudius and the spirits of the Silani [15] in the regions below, and recounting the many crimes she had committed to no purpose. She declared that Britannicus was now growing up, and was the genuine issue and rightful heir of that imperial power of his father which Nero, a mere adopted son, now employed to trample upon his mother. She would not shrink, she said, from making public all the calamities of their unfortunate family, even her own incestuous marriage with Claudius, and her guilt in poisoning him. By the providence of the gods and her own foresight, however, one final resource remained to her—her stepson, Britannicus, was still alive. She would go with him to the barracks of the Prætorian Guard, and there they would assuredly listen to her, the daughter of Germanicus, as against the wretched Burrhus and that former exile, Seneca—one with a maimed hand and the other with the tongue of a pedant—who were pressing their claims to govern the world."

Nero could afford to smile at this absurd threat. He was immensely popular at this time, whereas his cousin was hardly known, was subject to fits of epilepsy, and was not yet old enough to hold office of any kind. At last, however, it began to dawn upon him that his mother would not hesitate to kill him if she were driven to it; and thenceforth the thought was ever present in his mind that his life was in danger at her hands. Yet, even so, his love for her was not destroyed, and, in a desperate attempt to calm her dangerous fury, he managed to patch up the quarrel so far as to enable them to dine together that evening, when Britannicus, Octavia, and a few friends, were also present. It was the custom for the young people, at a meal such as this, to sit upright upon chairs at a table, while their elders reclined on their couches; and on this occasion Britannicus was seated at table with some companions of his own age, including the young Titus, who was afterwards Emperor,[16] while Nero lay on his couch, his mother on one side of him, Octavia on the other, and their guests round about.

Britannicus, it would seem, was not feeling well: he had celebrated his birthday, the previous day, a little too freely, perhaps, for one so young. The February night was warm and sticky, and the rain was coming down in torrents outside the overheated room. Towards the end of the meal a servant brought him a draught of hot wine; but it was too hot for him to drink, and a little cold water was added, after which he was able to drain the cup. No sooner had he done so, however, than he appeared to be bereft of breath and speech, and fell to the ground, striking his face upon the mosaic of the floor.

Servants carried the boy from the room, but Nero, as befitted a host, quieted the general commotion by remaining where he was, upon his couch, and by assuring his guests and the frightened boys at the table—

some of whom were running from the room—that Britannicus had had these epileptic seizures all his life, and that there was nothing to worry about. Octavia evidently thought likewise, for she showed no concern whatsoever about her brother; but Agrippina was alarmed, and had difficulty in hiding her anxiety. The dinner then proceeded, but presently it became known to Nero, Agrippina, and one or two others, that Britannicus was dead, and though, for politeness' sake, the meal had to be finished without disturbance, horrified eyes were fixed upon the Emperor, while in those of Agrippina, which never left his face, there was silent and terrible accusation.

As soon as dinner was over, and the guests dismissed, the news was made public. After a hasty consultation, Nero issued a statement saying that as it was the ancient custom at once to withdraw from sight the bodies of such as died prematurely, and not to lengthen the solemnities by speeches and processions, the funeral would be conducted immediately; and he added that having lost by the death of Britannicus the support of a brother, he now rested his hopes in the State, relying on the Senate to treat him with all the more consideration now that he was the sole male survivor of the imperial family.[17] Before dawn [18] the body was carried to the Campus Martius, where it was cremated as soon as a lessening of the rain permitted. The face of the dead boy had been terribly bruised by striking the floor, and those who prepared the corpse for the last rites concealed the discoloration by covering the marks with white chalk; but some of the little group of people who braved the darkness and the downpour to witness the cremation saw this chalk washed off by the rain, and, noticing the livid stains, passed the word around that they were evidence of poison.

The story later became current that Nero had caused the poison to be administered in the water with which the wine had been cooled; and Tacitus, Suetonius, Dion Cassius, and other writers accuse him of the crime. Some modern historians, however, exonerate him,[19] and, for my own part, I do not find anything in his character at this time to lead one to suppose that he was guilty. He was only seventeen, and for some years yet to come he was free from all taint of murder: indeed, it is doubtful whether he ever took the life of anybody by underhand means, having in a very marked degree the courage of his convictions, and the necessary effrontery to commit his crimes quite openly.

It is true that Tacitus and Suetonius give detailed stories of how Nero caused the poison to be prepared, employing the same old woman, Locusta, whom Agrippina is said to have used in the case of Claudius, but the two accounts differ, which indicates that they were based on hearsay; and, in view of the fact that any sudden death aroused in those days a suspicion which usually grew into a circumstantial tale of foul play, it is no more than rudimentary justice to give the young Emperor the benefit of the doubt. It is difficult to suppose that Britannicus was to be regarded as a serious rival; and indeed Suetonius feels so strongly the absence of a motive for the supposed crime that he suggests that Nero must have been jealous of the boy because he sang better than he, the Emperor, did.[20] Nero's behaviour, moreover, is consistent with that of innocence. He pointed out to those around him that had he desired his cousin's death, there would have been nothing to prevent him from openly ordering it, nor any reason why he should deny doing so. "Why should I be afraid of the law?" he asked, meaning that it could not be set in motion against himself. The treason of a close male relation was always regarded in the imperial family as full justification for his summary execution: nobody questioned Caligula's right to order the death of Gemellus, and nobody would have blamed Nero for putting Britannicus to instant death on learning that Agrippina was going to take him to the Prætorian barracks to obtain their support.

A few months later, Seneca, seeing that Nero was troubled by these rumours, wrote a treatise on the subject of mercy and addressed it to the Emperor. "You have always set before yourself a goal which no other prince has attained, namely Innocence of crime," he wrote; and he added, presently, "It would be hard for goodness such as yours to be feigned, and, indeed, it would be impossible for you to keep up the deception." [21] The philosopher's words have the ring of sincerity in them.

Agrippina, however, undoubtedly thought that he had killed the boy: she supposed that the murder was Nero's cynical answer to her threat to have Britannicus proclaimed Emperor; and the tragedy caused her unspeakable consternation and alarm. He knew that she believed him to be a murderer, and he may well have found in this belief a revelation of her own character. From that moment, too, his wife, Octavia, hated him with all the intensity of her brooding and violent nature: Agrippina had assured her that Nero had killed Britannicus, and nothing could shake the implanted conviction. If only she had had the courage she would have murdered him in revenge.[22]

CHAPTER IX

The Removal of Agrippina from the Palace, A.D. 55—The Supposed Plots against the Throne—The Beginning of Nero's Love for Poppæa, A.D. 58—The Banishment of Sulla, A.D. 58.

THE effect of the death of Britannicus upon public opinion was, apparently, the opposite of what might have been expected; for those who believed that Nero had caused him to be poisoned seem to have declared for the most part that the deed was perfectly justified. The young Emperor was so popular, in fact, that he held the people's sympathy even as the villain of the piece, and everybody tried to find excuses for him. They said that Agrippina was the mischief-maker who had brought matters to this pass; and soon the masses began to show their dislike of her by various means.

Her position at the palace, too, became very precarious, and in desperation she attempted to form a party around herself with the object of securing her safety, while her economies and her efforts to raise money in one way and another gave the widespread impression that she was trying to create a sort of reserve-fund. She pretended, with shallow guile, to make a great friend of the neglected and lonely Octavia, sympathising with her in her grief at the death of her brother, and in regard to Nero's passion for Acte. She showed particular condescension to members of the old-fashioned aristocracy who had lately been turning from her in disgust, but who were readily drawn back to her by the realization that they were fast losing their influence in Rome under an Emperor who treated the conventions with disdain. She attempted to win the adherence of military officers of importance; and it was clear that she was trying either to obtain the support, or else to undermine the position, of Burrhus, the commander of the Prætorian Guard, by winning the friendship of his subordinates.

So sinister, in fact, did her angry and revengeful presence become in the palace that at last Nero, now seriously considering the startling thought that she might try to murder him, decided to give her a residence of her own, and, in spite of her furious protests, removed her, sometime in A.D. 55, to the house of her late grandmother, Antonia, the daughter of Antony—an action which was tantamount to depriving her of her recognized position as the power behind the throne. At the same time, knowing how she was courting the Prætorian officers, he took away from her the large body of these troops which had been attached to her private service ever since the days of her supreme power under Claudius. "The populace," says Dion Cassius,[1] "seeing her now for the first time without her bodyguard of Prætorians, took care not to fall in with her even by accident, and if anyone did chance to meet her, he would hastily get out of the way without saying a word." Nero, however, tactfully attempted to counteract this feeling that she had been humiliated, by removing the troops also from other somewhat similar duties, explaining that he did not like this military display, and that soldiers ought to be employed only in strictly military matters. He no longer allowed the Prætorians to attend at public gatherings, and he removed the force which was supposed to keep order at the amphitheatre. He did this, as Tacitus points out,[2] to encourage a greater feeling of democratic liberty; but it is interesting to notice, as an example of the later misunderstanding of his motives, that Dion Cassius declares his object in removing the troops to have been the encouragement of the riots and free fights which he always enjoyed.

But although Nero, with undoubted wisdom, thus removed Agrippina's turbulent and dangerous influence from the palace, he made a point of showing his respect and consideration for her by frequently visiting her in her new home; yet he never stayed long, nor did he allow himself to be left alone with her. He used to pay these calls upon her surrounded by court officials and military officers; and after he had kissed her and had said a few words of no importance, he would hurry off again with much tramping of feet and clatter of arms echoing along her empty corridors. Moreover, he used to encourage her to go out of Rome from time to time to one of her villas in the country or by the sea: he hoped, in fact, that she would gradually forget her grievances, withdraw from political life, and settle down to a quiet middle age far from the tumult of the city.

Certainly there was for her much inducement to

do so, for she had become so unpopular that the majority of her former intimates had deserted her. Some of her women friends, it is true, used to drop in to console her, though whether from affection or hate is uncertain, as Tacitus dryly remarks[3]; but, apart from Pallas, only four or five men out of all the crowd which once paid her court, now visited her. She was, however, not so easily to be suppressed. She was not yet forty-one years of age, and, rightly or wrongly, she believed herself still able to win the male heart by her feminine beauty and charm.

Now, there was a cousin of hers, a young man of twenty, named Rubellius Plautus, whose mother, Julia, had been granddaughter of Tiberius and sister of the unfortunate Gemellus, the rival and victim of Caligula, and whose grandmother, Livia, had been sister of Claudius. This youth was an occasional visitor at Agrippina's house; and since he was at once great-grandson of the Emperor Tiberius, grand-nephew of the Emperor Claudius, and cousin of the Emperor Caligula, the story soon began to be circulated that she was trying to make something more than a friend of him in view of the fact that he would be the likeliest candidate for the imperial throne in the event of anything happening to Nero.

One night, a certain dancer and actor named Paris, who was a freedman of Nero's aunt Domitia, and who had been lent to him to amuse him in the evenings, came trembling and distraught into the room where the Emperor, a little heated by wine, was dining and making merry, and told him that he had just heard that Agrippina was about to marry this young Rubellius Plautus, that she was going to attempt to murder Nero and have Plautus acclaimed Emperor, and that Burrhus was a party to the plot.

Nero was frantic. He sent for Seneca and repeated to him what he had heard; but Seneca was quickly able to convince him that the loyalty of Burrhus, at any rate, was beyond question, whereupon he, too, was sent for. Being an honest and fearless man he risked an accusation of attempting to shield Agrippina, and when Nero, in his excitement, cried out that her murderous plots must be stopped, and that she ought to be put to death, he at once replied that she must first be given the opportunity to defend herself. After all, he said, it was now so late at night, and Nero and Paris and everybody else were so nearly drunk, that it would only be fair to wait till morning, when their heads were clear, before taking any drastic action; and he swore that if, upon examination, she were found to be guilty, he himself would undertake her instant execution. With that, the distracted Nero agreed to let the matter rest until the morrow.

In the morning Burrhus and Seneca, attended by a group of freedmen, went to Agrippina's house, and the former, looking very stern and menacing, accused her of this treason; but the defence which she put up, though somewhat femininely complicated, was delivered with such passionate and majestic fury that her innocence could not be doubted by mere men. She said that the whole story was the invention of that wicked enemy of hers, Junia Silana (the divorced wife of Caius

Silius, Messalina's lover), who, though for years her close friend, now bore her a grudge because when Junia had recently wanted to marry a certain youth, Sextius Africanus, Agrippina had told him that she was too old for him, and had also said that she was a lewd woman. In revenge, so Agrippina stormed, Junia had conspired with the horrible Domitia who also had a score to pay off, because, years ago, Agrippina had taken her husband, Passienus Crispus, from her, and later had put her sister, Domitia Lepida, to death. With the aid of Atimetus, Domitia's steward and lover, the two women had concocted this story, she said, and had then whispered it in the ear of Paris, knowing that the fool would repeat it to Nero.

"I don't wonder," she cried, "that Junia Silana, who never had a child, should know nothing about a mother's love: I suppose she thinks that a mother can as easily turn upon her son as an adulteress, such as she is, can dismiss her lovers. And as to Domitia, I would thank her for all her attacks on me, if I thought she were trying to outdo me in kindness to my Nero; but she cares nothing for him. All those years when I was struggling to have him adopted by Claudius and made his heir, what was she doing? Constructing fish-ponds at her house at Baiæ! And now, with the help of her paramour, Atimetus, and this play-actor, Paris, she is inventing these theatrical plots, which would do for the stage, but have no relation to real life. If Rubellius Plautus were to be made Emperor, or anybody else for that matter, would I stand a chance? If Britannicus had come to the throne, would I not have been put to death? In the passion of my love and anxiety I have certainly said things I did not mean, and nobody else but my Nero would have forgiven me: is it likely, then, that I should want to depose my own boy, and give somebody else the power to pass judgment on me?"[4]

The simple Burrhus was deeply affected by her words, and when, at length, she burst into tears, he and Seneca were far more concerned in calming her down than in sifting the evidence further; and presently they took her to Nero. Very wisely she did not repeat her defence, nor did she taunt him this time, with ingratitude for all that she had done for him. She simply demanded vengeance upon her accusers, and rewards for those who were loyal to her; and at this Nero showed such consideration for her that it is hardly possible to draw any other conclusion from his behaviour than that he still loved her deeply.

Having made enquiries he discovered at least this much, that Atimetus was a man of odious character, and that Junia Silana was not much better: he had the former tried and executed, and the latter banished from Rome with two of her supposed accomplices; but —whether to Agrippina's annoyance or relief, it would be hard to say—he took no steps against any of the others involved, not even against Rubellius Plautus, although he seems to have entertained a suspicion that the young man was not entirely guiltless of treason. At the same time, to please his mother, he gave high office to the four men who, with Pallas, had conspicuously continued to show their friendship for her—the

Governorship of Egypt to one, the Governorship of Syria to another, the Directorship of Public Entertainments to a third, and, to the last, the Controllership of the Food Supplies of Rome.

Perhaps at about this same time he gave the command of the metropolitan police to Sofonius Tigellinus,[5] the horse breeder who had been exiled by Caligula in A.D. 39 for improper relations with Agrippina,[6] but had been recalled by her when she became Empress, and now was one of her favourites.

Nero felt, however, that Paris had done his duty in reporting to him what he had heard, and he rewarded him by issuing a decree in his favour which declared that the circumstances of his parentage were such that he ought never to have been regarded as a slave in the first place, that a sum of money which he had paid to Domitia when she had manumitted him and made him a freedman must be returned to him by her, and that he was entitled to all the privileges of a free-born Roman citizen. The Emperor's action must have infuriated Domitia as much as it pleased his mother; but he was probably considering Paris himself rather than Agrippina, for Paris was a great actor, and the dramatic art seemed to Nero to deserve social recognition.

No sooner had the commotion caused by this supposed plot against Nero's throne and life subsided than another storm was aroused by the attempt of a certain Pætus, a disgraced treasury-official, to regain favour by accusing both Pallas and Burrhus of conspiring to raise Faustus Cornelius Sulla to the throne. This noble scion of the famous Sulla family was married to Antonia, half-sister of Octavia and Britannicus, and daughter of Claudius by his wife Ælia Pætina; and the accusation stated that, as son-in-law of the late Emperor, he had dared to dream of ousting Nero and reigning in his stead. The Emperor, however, did not fully credit the story, but went through the formality of trying the case, though he showed his sentiments towards Burrhus by allowing him a seat on the judge's bench while Pallas was being examined. Pallas haughtily denied the charge against him, and when he was asked if he had ever spoken to any of his freedmen in regard to Sulla he—himself an ex-slave—replied with great insolence that he never deigned to speak to any of his servants at all, but always signified his pleasure by a nod or motion of his hand, and gave all orders in writing. Nero acquitted him out of consideration for Agrippina, and sent his accuser into exile; but it is said that any gratification at the wealthy freedman's escape that was felt in Rome was not so apparent as the general disgust at his arrogance. As for Sulla, the young Emperor, though vaguely suspecting him, showed him the same consideration he had displayed towards Rubellius Plautus; he gave no outward sign of displeasure, and took no steps against him —a fact which is an indication of the exceptional leniency of his character at this time. Had one of the former Emperors been on the throne neither Plautus nor Sulla would have escaped with their lives.

At the time when Agrippina was transferred from the palace to a house of her own, Nero was seventeen years of age. In December of that year, A.D. 55, he celebrated his eighteenth birthday; and from then until after his twentieth birthday at the close of A.D. 57, he seems to have had continuous, though indefinite, trouble with his mother, whose unpopularity steadily grew. The masses could not forget the many murders and other crimes she had committed, and the fact that her manners were haughty and that she posed always as a virtuous woman, aroused popular indignation. People went so far, sometimes, as to shout insults at her under the windows of her residence, and disturb her sleep with cat-calls; while in the Roman law-courts small but irritating actions were brought against her by those who believed she had wronged them, and who saw in her downfall the opportunity of redress. Yet nothing could humble her, nor remove from her mind the fixed idea that as the Emperor's mother she should receive obedience from him. With an arrogance which amounted to sheer blindness she asserted and again asserted by word and action the fact of her mothership, as though Nero were still a child; and nothing could shake her conviction that she, not he, should be the ruler.

She, of course, continuously brooded over her troubles, but never saw their cause. She thought that Nero was deliberately responsible for all her annoyances, and her feelings towards him seem often to have been bitter with resentment not far removed from hatred. He, on his part, though estranged from her, and though strong-willed enough to assert himself, was always awed by her, and was bound to her by curiously intense and deeply-rooted filial sentiments.

It is evident that he did his best, with aching heart, to please her, and to spare her pain; and the public impression given by him during these years was that of an unnecessarily dutiful son, far too tenderly considerate to so dangerous and immoral a woman. People said that he dared not be alone with her for fear that she would attempt to appeal to the lowest in him so as to recover her influence over him, and to detach him from Acte who continued to hold his affections. Now that they knew the mockery of Agrippina's virtuous pose, they thought of her, in fact, as they would think of some middle-aged harlot, or procuress, or cut-throat keeper of a brothel, a woman ready to lead even her own son astray to gain her ends.

Nero, on the contrary, grew to manhood in the sunshine of popularity. Everybody except the old-fashioned aristocracy, the stern traditionists, admitted that he was a very promising Emperor in spite of his democratic leanings and his dislike of the restraint of the conventions. Smart society was perhaps a trifle disappointed in him, for ever since the arrival of the quiet little Acte on the scene, he had ceased to bother about being a man of fashion, and his progress in the art of sumptuous and elegant living had not been considerable. In the eyes of the fastidious members of the fast set he was still rather awkward and rough, rather unpolished, not quite a man of culture. He was laughed at for being untidy, and it was particularly noticed that he did not mind how badly his hair was cut. But the masses adored him.

If there were in his mentality a certain effeminacy,

such as is often to be observed in young men of genius, he counter-balanced this fault, in the opinion of the crowd, by his love of manly sports and particularly of those connected with horses. From childhood he had evinced a passion for horses. An eager desire to excel in all that he did was a characteristic of his nature; and the public, who as yet had heard little of his youthfully earnest efforts to sing, to play the harp, to act, and to write poems and plays, knew him as an enthusiastic racing-man and as a reckless chariot-driver, ready to risk his life to win the victory. They knew him, too, and loved him, as a high-spirited young rascal who went about the city at nights, playing the fool and getting himself into all manner of scrapes, as has already been described. Laughingly they told stories of how he had often been present, incognito, at the amphitheatre during the riotous fights between the different factions of the racing world, and how he had himself hit a magistrate on the head with a rotten egg, or something of the sort, deftly thrown.

But most they loved him for the goodness of his heart and the humanity of his government. The first five years of Nero's reign, the famous *Quinquennium Neronis,* are notorious in Roman history as the period of the best government the Empire had ever known. The Emperor Trajan, a man whose judgment is worthy of respect, often declared this to be so[7]; and practically all historians are agreed that at this time Nero certainly deserved his immense popularity. His efforts to do good were exceptional. He severely punished certain high officials for oppressing the people and extorting money from them, and he rewarded with generous annuities the services of those who had honourably served the State. In the first seven years of his reign twelve Governors of Provinces were tried for mal-administration, and six of them were found guilty. The admiral of the fleet at Ravenna was suspended for cruelty to his sailors, and only escaped punishment by committing suicide. He never forgot his two former nurses, Ecloge and Alexandra, but kept them in comfort at the palace.

Nero also introduced some wise legislation in regard to the food and water-supplies of Rome; and he prohibited the presentation of public shows and gladiatorial exhibitions at the private expense of candidates for office, as being a corrupt means of canvassing votes. When called upon to act as judge in legal proceedings, he did not follow the example of Claudius and give his judgment with haste or before all the evidence was heard, but always postponed sentence until the next day, so that he and his advisers might give a considered opinion in writing. He was intensely anxious to be just.

There can be no question whatsoever, in fact, that he was at this period growing up to be a man of the greatest promise, a second Germanicus. He was good-looking in his florid, red-haired, freckled and boisterously healthy way—a powerfully built young fellow, thick-necked, heavy-jawed, and having a youthful beard of red-gold hue which, according to the custom of the time, he had never yet shaved off. His muscles were like those of a prize-fighter; but he seems to have carried his heftiness with grace, in spite of a certain shyness of manner. Though accused in later years of vanity, he was now noticeably modest and not at all confident of himself[8]; and he beamed with pleasure when he was applauded for his singing, his skilful chariot-driving, or any other accomplishment.

He was excitable, emotional, and highly-strung, but the charge of cowardice made against him in after life cannot be substantiated: he appears, rather, to have been uncommonly brave, as judged by his breath-taking exploits on the chariot-racecourse, of which we shall presently hear. His determination, and even obstinacy, was becoming very marked; and his capacity for hard work was limitless. His manners were charming, and he easily won the love of his friends by his frankness and his unassuming ways. Moreover he possessed the truly royal gift of a good memory for faces and names, and he seldom had to be prompted. At this time he showed no signs of any cruel streak in his nature; and, indeed, his forbearance and consideration were constantly being shown; while his generosity was extravagant. In his habits he was temperate, according to the standards of his epoch; but though he did not often eat or drink too much, and, in consequence, hardly knew what it was to feel ill,[9] he was, as it were, intoxicated with life, and his every action was performed with an eager enthusiasm which played ducks and drakes with imperial dignity. For this the people loved him; but his mother, who had so long upheld the ancient Roman tradition of dignity and outward restraint, was shocked at his behaviour;

and the older aristocracy frowned upon him and menaced him with the shadows and the murmurs of its impotent complaint.

In A.D. 58, when he was twenty years of age, a change began to take place in his mode of life, owing, so it seems, to the fact that his youthful passion for Acte was fading away. Once more he was beguiled by the gaiety and elegance of fashionable society, and his visits to the house of his quiet and retiring mistress became less regular as his appearances at the entertainments of the smart set increased in frequency. Acte quickly observed the difference in his manner to her, and she was greatly troubled by it. She was evidently a simple and good woman, and she well knew that she had neither the education nor the intellect to maintain her place in that brilliant circle in which the Emperor was now anxious once again to shine.

She could not have understood him when he talked to her about art, literature, and those matters of æsthetic taste which he had been discussing with these cultured people; she only stared at him, one may suppose, with melancholy eyes when he spoke of the artist's need of self-expression, of the importance of being emancipated from tradition, and of the fallacy of existing ethical standards. She could not compete with the scintillating young women of the world of fashion, from meeting whom she had somehow managed to hold Nero back for so long. In her great distress she caused a little shrine to be erected in honour of Ceres—the Roman divinity corresponding to the Greek Demeter or "Mother Earth"—in the hope that the goddess would give back to her the abundance of Nero's devotion; and a brief inscription referring to the building is now to be seen in the Cathedral of Pisa[10]—a pathetic record of the dying of a youth's first love.

Of the brilliant ladies of fashion to whom the Emperor was now unfavourably comparing her, the most conspicuous was Poppæa Sabina; and it was she who gradually took possession of Nero's more mature affections. Her mother was a celebrated society beauty of the same name, who had vied with Messalina in licentiousness, and had committed suicide in A.D. 47 at that Empress's instigation. This unfortunate lady had married Titus Ollius (who died in A.D. 32), and their daughter, who inherited her mother's beauty but not very notably her easy virtue,[11] was born in A.D. 31. At an early age she had been married to a man named Rufus (?) Crispinus, to whom she had borne a son, Rufrius[12]; but they had been divorced, and she had recently married Otho, Nero's great friend. She was now in her twenty-seventh year, that is to say she was between six and seven years older than Nero; and in the mastery of that dazzling coalescence of artistic taste, culture, elegance, frivolity, and potential immorality which constituted the fashionable canons of the time, she was capable of standing to the youthful Emperor in the relationship of a high-priestess to a neophyte. She was a woman of great wealth and proud lineage; and her beauty was incomparable. Her hair was of a glorious amber-colour—apparently natural, although the chemical blonde was then almost as well-known as in our own day; her skin was so white that people said she bathed herself daily in the milk of five hundred asses; her figure was slim and almost boyish, if we may judge from the fact that a youth named Sporos, of whom we shall presently hear more, was said to resemble her closely. She does not seem to have been vain of her looks, but she knew their value; and it is related that once when she thought that she could detect a decline in her beauty, she cried out passionately "Let me die before it fades." She was clever and witty, strong-minded and forceful, passionate and seductive; yet Tacitus, who thinks that she was curiously wanting in the ability to make any distinction between her husbands and her lovers, admits that she was dignified and even modest in public, keeping her face partially veiled, though probably she did this, he supposes, because it became her. To say that she was a leader of the fashionable society of her time, and to add that she was a decent woman, may seem to be both a paradox and an anachronism; yet to call her wicked, as is the custom, is decidedly an overstatement.

When the Emperor was first attracted to her, she gave him permission to come to see her, and very soon she had him at her feet by telling him that she thought him the finest looking man she had ever seen, which delighted the shy and diffident youth; but after she had once allowed him the intimacy he desired, she pretended, as women often do, that she had surrendered in a regretted moment of aberration, and that she hoped it would never happen again—an attitude nicely calculated to rekindle the interest which quick success is proverbially thought to endanger. Nero, however, required no such careful handling: after these years of fidelity to the easy and artless Acte, he was enthralled by the experienced and fastidious love-making of this brilliant and exquisite creature who knew so much more than he did about the finesse of these matters. He was overwhelmed, and, being an extremely honest young man, he at once told Otho of the state of his feelings, and asked him to be so good as to regard Poppæa in future as a wife only in name.[13]

Otho's feelings appear to have been mingled. He had sown his wild oats, and was so satiate that his attitude to Poppæa was one of artistic admiration rather than love. Moreover, he was ambitious for a career, and he was prepared to give up even so dazzling a wife in exchange for Nero's patronage. On the other hand, he could not overcome a painful sensation of jealousy; and when the Emperor told him that he had asked Poppæa to come to spend a night or two at the palace, Otho gloomily declared that it would be better for his peace of mind and his dignity for him to leave Rome. At this Nero gratefully offered him the governorship of Lusitania (the modern Portugal), which he at once accepted, taking his departure with thoughts torn between ambition and chagrin as he heard these lines of a wit at court:—

Why is it Otho lives an exile's life?
Because he dared to sleep with his own wife.[14]

Before he left, however, he had the satisfaction of seeing the Emperor mercilessly snubbed and teased by

Poppæa. After her first night's visit to the rather shoddy and uncomfortable old palace, where Nero had done his best to entertain her magnificently, she declared that really she could not think of abandoning her husband for a boy so rough and inexperienced in the art of love, and so little acquainted with the elegancies of wealthy and fashionable life. "After all," she said, "I am married to a man whose taste and whose mode of living nobody can equal. He is magnificent in his ideas and in his style of life, and everything one sees in his house is worthy of the admiration of the most exalted favourites of fortune. But you, Nero, seem to be satisfied with a second-rate menage: I suppose it is because you have become inured to all this inelegance and discomfort by living with Acte, who, being a slave, does not know any better."[15] Octavia, Nero's legal wife, it is to be observed, was hardly to be considered at all.

At length, however, Poppæa began to see the advantages to herself of encouraging the artistic development of this ardent youth by approving of, and not jeering at, his efforts to be worthy of her, and soon she had transformed both him and his palace. It is a question whether she was ever really in love with him, but there can be no doubt that she devoted herself to him, and that the splendour, the perfection of luxury, and the consequent extravagance, for which his court soon became famous, were due to her rather than to him. He was a ready pupil, and in the matter of spending money he soon left his teacher behind; and, when once his eyes were opened to the deficiencies of the palace, he was quick to make the necessary changes.

Agrippina was outraged at this new love-affair, more especially because Poppæa represented the fast society of Rome which laughed at the old order, and dared to be Greek, to be cosmopolitan, to be modern—dared to make fun of the revered memory of Augustus and to emulate the style of living and the deeds of his rivals, Antony and Cleopatra. At the first opportunity she attacked Nero once more, working upon his feelings and telling him how disappointed she was in him; and when he awkwardly replied that this time he intended really to divorce Octavia, so that he might marry Poppæa, she lost her temper, and, it seems, repeated her threats to bring about his dethronement. She might be living in retirement, her actual power might be broken, but it must not be forgotten that Nero's consideration for her had enabled her to secure high office for those who had shown their friendship for her, others being thus encouraged to do her service. Her ability to intrigue and to plot was increasing; and her dominating attitude towards her son, which had never diminished, was again becoming so pronounced that, as Tacitus says,[16] she was at this time a constant oppression and nightmare to him.

Poppæa soon found out that Agrippina was the greatest obstacle to her own power which she had to contend with. It was Agrippina who objected to his un-Roman mode of life; it was Agrippina who scoffed at his efforts to beautify the palace and to make the imperial menage a model of elegance; it was Agrippina who was warning him that Poppæa was actuated not by love of him but by ambition; it was Agrippina who was encouraging Rome to respect and honour Octavia and who was spreading such tales of her dignity under insult that the masses were gradually taking her to their heart.

At length, one day towards the close of A.D. 58, Poppæa threw down the gauntlet, and told Nero that she was not prepared to continue to be his mistress if she was for ever to be thwarted in all she did for him by his mother's secret and subtle opposition. "You are nothing but a schoolboy," she exclaimed, "tied to your mother's apron-strings, and instead of being able to act as Emperor you are actually a slave yourself. Why do you not marry me? Is it that you think I am not beautiful enough, or not your equal in birth—I, whose ancestors have held the highest honours in Rome? Do you fear, perhaps, that I would not bear you a son? Or do you doubt my love for you? No!—the truth is that you think, if I were your wife, I would expose your mother, tell the Senate what I know of her past intrigues against them, and bring down upon her the indignation of the people at her haughty and grasping ways. It is quite clear that she will never tolerate a daughter-in-law who loves you. She prefers one who, like Octavia, hates you: it suits her purpose better. . . . I think you had better send me back to Otho; for I would rather hear about your degradation than watch it taking place before my eyes. And, anyway, my life is not safe here, with your mother's hatred always directed against me."[17]

These words, says Tacitus, penetrated the very soul of Nero; nor did anyone to whom he spoke about his difficulties find fault with Poppæa's interpretation of the case, for all desired to see the influence of his mother removed. He asked Seneca and Burrhus what in heaven's name he should do to rid himself of Agrippina's continuous opposition to everything he did. All his life she had been trying to force him to be that kind of man he most hated; she had always refused to try to understand him and his particular temperament; and now she was grimly prepared to dethrone him, perhaps to murder him, rather than suffer him to live his own life in his own way, free from her dictation and her rebuke. As a child he must often have stamped his feet in impotent rage against her; and he still was unable to forget her former power over him: he dreaded her reproofs, and was made miserable by her bitter reproaches, at the same time that he was angered by her secret actions against him.

Both his old tutors sympathised with him, for, in their opinion, Agrippina was a far more serious menace to the Emperor even than he knew: they had seen the gleam of hatred in her eyes, and they felt that her son's life, and theirs also, might be exacted by her, the arch-murderess, at any moment. Both had sufficient evidence to justify a charge of treason being brought against her; but Nero could not bring himself to accuse his mother. Yet, now that the matter was being ventilated, he heard on all sides how she was calumniating him and Poppæa, and how she was threatening vengeance if they were to marry. The time would come, he knew, when he would be obliged to hand her over for trial. The public hated her; everybody knew that she was plotting against him; and the demand for her exile or death would in the end become insistent.

An incident then occurred which suggested once more that Agrippina was busy. Publius Suillius, who had been an agent of Messalina, and had played the infamous part of "informer" against those whom she had wished to destroy, was still alive, and was prepared to renew his activities whenever an opportunity occurred either of making money or of paying off old scores. There was no man he disliked more than Seneca, who had been instrumental in putting all such secret agents practically out of business; and now when Agrippina was known to be seething with anger, likewise, against Seneca who was aiding and abetting Nero in all he did, Suillius saw a possibility of revenging himself. History does not implicate Agrippina in the action which he took, but her complicity seems highly probable, since their hostility to the philosopher was mutual.

Suillius publicly attacked Seneca as the inveterate enemy of all the friends of the late Emperor Claudius, and as one who, while pretending to have a philosopher's contempt for riches, had lived the luxurious life of a courtier and had acquired a huge fortune by money-lending and other improper means. Seneca, of course, was always open to this kind of attack, for whereas his writings were imbued with sentiments which have been described as almost Christian in their unworldliness, his life was clearly that of a multi-millionaire—an inconsistency like that which so often troubles our minds today in noticing the wealth and apparent worldliness of some of the historic Princes of the Church who have lived in comfort in the name of the penniless Carpenter of Nazareth. He was not exactly a humbug, but he can hardly be said to have practised what he preached, unless we concede the point that by acquiring riches and maintaining a position at court he was enabled to exercise an influence for good quite beyond the power of any saintly pauper.

At any rate he defended himself warmly, and, in return, accused Suillius of having caused the deaths of various people, including the mother of Poppæa; to which Suillius replied that he had only acted under the complusion of the Emperor's orders. On hearing this Nero himself caused the Claudian archives to be searched, and personally testified that the prosecution of these persons had in no case been due to any such compulsion. In the end, Seneca was vindicated and Suillius was banished to the Balearic Isles, where he lived in great luxury and contentment for the remainder of his days, the mildness of his punishment providing an astonished Rome with another instance of Nero's leniency. But the impression left by the incident upon the minds of the court seems to have been one of anxiety and suspicion in regard to Agrippina.

Shortly after this, some time in A.D. 58, there was a more serious occurrence. It will be recalled that Sulla, the husband of Octavia's half-sister Antonia, had been accused of aspiring to the throne, but that Nero had allowed the matter to drop. Now, however, the charge was brought against him of having attempted the Emperor's life. Nero had one day been passing through the streets of Rome on his way to the palace, and had turned aside from his usual route in order to visit the gardens of Sallust on the Pincian Hill, but had taken only a small retinue with him, sending home the rest of his suite direct, in charge of a freedman named Graptus. The latter party was attacked by a band of ruffians; but after a free fight Graptus escaped and brought the startling report to the palace that an attempt on the life of Nero had evidently been intended, and that the attacking force was in the pay of Sulla. The evidence for this was not clear, and, indeed, Sulla was a man of such indolent and apathetic character that he could with difficulty be pictured by the Emperor as a serious rival. Yet he was very friendly with Agrippina and Octavia, and it was felt that he might have been persuaded by one or both of these ladies to try to gain the throne.

Nero, therefore, sent him away from Rome, obliging him to take up his residence at Massilia (Marseilles) and not to leave that city's precincts until further orders. Massilia was at that time one of the most important centres both of commerce and of culture and learning in the empire, and Sulla's fate was therefore by no means intolerable; but if this leniency to a suspected traitor suggested that Nero was taking no more than a precautionary measure against him, it none the less indicated that the palace was now definitely on its guard. People began to fear that their popular Emperor was really in danger, and angry looks were directed against Agrippina, who was thought to be the one real source of all the trouble. On all sides there were whispers, which came to the ears of Nero, hinting at the peril he ran by allowing his filial duty to override his common sense; but these warnings found him still unwilling to take any drastic measures against the mother he had once loved and of whom to this day he stood in awe.

Nothing seemed to be able to open her eyes to the stupidity of her continuous struggle against the existing fact of her son's independence of her. She demanded his obedience, and, since he would not give it, she threatened his throne. Nothing could check her blind and haughty advance towards a terrible and public doom; and the distracted Nero racked his brains in vain to find a means of saving her from her own folly. Over and over again he had made excuses for her, telling his friends that a mother's hasty temper ought always to be excused, and that it was better to soothe her than to reprimand her[18]; but he could not for ever make light of her threats. In the view of his advisers it was the dreaded scandal of the Empress-Mother caught plotting the death of her Emperor-son which had to be averted; but in Nero's view it was the distress of this mother of his, punished by the son she had loved, which somehow had to be prevented. He could not tolerate any longer the menace of her presence near him, yet he could not bring himself to hand her over to public vengeance.

Matters were in this pass when, in December, A.D. 58, he celebrated his twenty-first birthday; and the new year, A.D. 59, opened with every indication of approaching disaster either for him or for her.

CHAPTER X

Nero's Visit to Baiæ Early in A.D. 59—The Coming of his Mother to her Villa Nearby—The Death of Agrippina, March, A.D. 59—Nero's Return to Rome in the Autumn.

IN the early spring of A.D. 59 Nero went to stay at his palace at Baiæ on the Bay of Naples, an extremely fashionable resort where many of the leaders of Roman society had magnificent country-houses built on the wooded hills overlooking the bay, and where nearly everybody of standing owned some sort of villa, large or small, either on the high ground above the town or beside the beach, or even on artificial substructures projecting into the sea.[1] The place was close to Misenum, the naval port which stood near the promontory forming the northern horn of the bay; and on its other side was Bauli, a smaller and quieter resort, not far from the inlet known as the Lucrine lake, where Agrippina had a villa. Baiæ was famous for its hot springs, and the town was noted for its many bathing establishments which, in winter, were the centres of social life, while the sea-bathing was the great summer attraction.

The resort was notorious as the most luxurious and pleasure-seeking in all Italy; and Nero's sun-bathed palace, which seems to have stood on the headland west of the town, must have been the centre of that gay and brilliant social life of which Poppæa was teaching the Emperor to be the leader. She was probably there with him now, though it may be supposed that Octavia, his Empress, and Acte, his former mistress, were both in Rome, while Agrippina, it is known, was at the Ahenobarbi family seat at Antium. Seneca and Burrhus were both with the Emperor, though the former, in his capacity as a philosopher, had to pretend that he did not like the life there. "It is a place to be avoided," he wrote,[2] "because though it has certain natural advantages, luxury has claimed it for her own exclusive resort. . . . I do not care to live in a café, to see people wandering drunk about the beach and sailing-parties riotously fooling, and to hear songs shouted across the water." He speaks, too, of his boredom in a pleasure-palace, from the windows of which one must find occupation in counting the scandalous women sailing past in their boats, watching the many kinds of craft gaily painted in all sorts of colours, and looking at the roses floating about the surface of the water after a battle of flowers, while at night one has to listen to the songs of serenaders, and to the drunken brawls in the streets.

Others, however, found Baiæ entrancing. Martial, for instance, says of it,[3] "Though I were to praise Baiæ in a thousand verses, yet would Baiæ not be praised as it deserves—Baiæ, that kind gift of Nature who is proud of it." "Peerless Baiæ," "cloudless Baiæ," "indolent, charming Baiæ," other Roman writers call it; and Propertius,[4] writing to his mistress, Cynthia, warns her of its dangers, speaking of its immoral life, and declaring that "to many a loving couple have its beaches brought severance, beaches that have often proved the undoing of nice-minded girls."

Nero, however, could hardly have been happy, in spite of the gaiety of the life at the palace; for he must have been troubled about his mother and about the rumours of plots against himself which were always, in one way or another, connected with her. Now, a frequent guest at his parties was his freedman, Anicetus, who had been one of his tutors when he was a child, and was the Admiral of the Fleet stationed at Misenum. For some particular reason which has been forgotten this grim old man detested Agrippina, and one day, when Nero had been confiding to him his anxiety in regard to her, he remarked darkly that people sometimes made journeys by sea, and that travellers by sea were sometimes shipwrecked. He told the Emperor how easily a vessel might be constructed which, like the ships used in sham-fights and other aquatic entertainments, could be invisibly scuttled and sunk; and he went on, later, to say that if Agrippina were by any chance to come over to Baiæ to see the Emperor, he, Anicetus, would like to have the honour of taking her for a trip on a vessel specially prepared by him for her.

Nero understood his meaning, and a tremendous idea entered his head. If Agrippina were to be shipwrecked and drowned, he would be spared the misery of ordering her arrest and giving evidence against her. Her death was unavoidable now, for, as has been said, her intrigues were public property, and everybody was urging him to have her put out of the way before she should crown her career of crime by murdering her son. An accidental death: yes, that was the solution! She would never know then that he had condemned her: she would die without realizing that her own son had been the instrument of her destruction.

In spite of all she had done to stifle the spirit of youth within him, to oppose the kind of life he intended to live, to crush his artistic impulses which more and more insistently demanded expression, in spite of her cold-blooded resolve to dethrone him—the son who would not obey her—he was still unable to overcome his childhood's love for her and dread of her reproaches; and now, when Nemesis was upon her, when she could little longer escape the penalty of her misdeeds, he was almost happy, in a theatrical sort of way, that he was able to perform this last service for her, and thus spare her the ignominy and the pitiable distress of her inevitable conviction and condemnation. She should be shipwrecked here off the shores of Baiæ, so publicly, so openly, that no man would dare to say the disaster had been contrived! Death would come upon her suddenly, unexpectedly, mercifully; and at last he would be freed from this dread of having to hurt her which was now hanging over him like a dark cloud.

Thus I interpret the inception of the terrible deed which history regards as Nero's blackest crime, but which, I believe, he thought to be a sombre and dramatic act of mercy. We have to bear in mind the fact that his mother was, of her own accord, blindly courting death, for, in an age when life was cheap and family ties in the imperial house a danger rather than a protection, her stupid plots and intrigues were obviously carrying her straight to a public doom; and therefore, Nero, had he been actuated by hate, could well have waited, knowing that the law courts and the Senate would soon relieve him of the responsibility of condemning her. But his consideration for her feelings, as will have been seen, was always marked; and it is perfectly clear that there was something in him—whether love, pity, awe, or filial duty—which made him shrink from causing her the mental anguish of a trial for treason. It seems to me that the idea of her death did not in itself trouble him: if only he could feel that she would die believing that he loved her, her exit would be an unmitigated relief.

It can hardly be doubted that he discussed the project with Seneca and Burrhus [5]; and while Seneca may well have found in his stoic philosophy ample justification for mercifully destroying, as though by accident, this turbulent being who now menaced his own life, Burrhus must assuredly have been relieved to obtain exemption from that rôle of executioner which more than once he had very nearly been called upon to perform. Neither of them regarded it as murder any more than did Nero: it was like the final scene of a lofty Greek tragedy such as the ancient dramatists might have woven out of the threads of their dark and lurid imaginations; and it may be supposed that when Anicetus had been instructed to prepare a galley which could be quickly scuttled, they fortified themselves, while uncomfortably waiting the completion of the work, by reminding one another of the humanity and the nobility of their purpose.

Nero then sent his mother a letter saying how pleased he would be if she were to come to stay awhile at her villa at Bauli so that she might be near him, and take part with him in the celebration of the great annual festival of Minerva, which began on March 19th and lasted five days.[6] He told her that he wanted so much to be reconciled,[7] and to feel once more that there was only love between them; and, in my opinion, he wrote this with a kind of sincerity, for though his letter was primarily intended to disarm her, it is in keeping with his bizarre character that he should have honestly desired her last hours on earth to be marred by no unhappiness. She accepted the invitation at once, exulting in the thought that her headstrong son had come back at last to his filial allegiance, having found it wiser to have her as a friend than as an enemy; and she saw before her a triumphal return to power.

On the afternoon probably of March 18th, or, at any rate, just before the beginning of the festival, she set out from Antium on board the trireme, or galley with three banks of oars, which was permanently detached from the fleet for her service; and, passing down the coast, she arrived at Baiæ next morning. Nero met her on the quay, and, having affectionately greeted her, went with her to her villa, apparently by road. The house stood on the rocks at the edge of the water, and, moored to her private pier below its windows, she found a beautiful galley, richly ornamented, and having sails of many colours, while on the after deck stood an ornate and heavily-built pavilion furnished with couches, chairs, and tables. Nero told her that this gorgeous little vessel was his gift to her, and he said that he hoped she would use it in making her journeys to and from his palace. He then arranged for her to dine with him that evening, and so left her to her happy dreams of the renewal of their loving relationship. But when, some hours later, the time came for her to go to Baiæ, a sudden sense of foreboding caused her to hesitate as she was about to step on board the galley, and to decide to make the journey by road in her litter instead.

Her feeling of dread, however, soon left her as her son tenderly embraced her and presently led her to the place of honour at the banquet—the place usually occupied by himself. His manner to her was both deferential and affectionate; but while she, in that curious arrogance of her motherhood which has been so noticeable, supposed his attitude to be due to his contrition, he appears to have been actuated not so much by his desire to deceive her into trusting him as by a morbid and dramatic wish to re-create in his heart that tender emotion which her behaviour had dissipated, to recapture an hour or two of his childhood's love. She was jubilant, radiant, in the belief that her son had returned to his obedience; he was happy—but with a happiness of a strange and emotional character—because he thought of himself as about to render this final service to the mother who had once been his all-in-all.

During dinner, as Tacitus tells us, "he entertained her with a variety of conversation, at one time with the lightness natural to youth, at another time with an air of gravity, pretending to consult with her upon serious topics." [8] He made her laugh with him over incidents of his early life which he brought back to her memory; he put his arm around her, yearning to recall the lost emotions of other days. His heart, it seems, was bursting with the terror, the pathos, and the exalted tragedy of the situation; yet he did not forget to ply her with wine, and when, some time after midnight, she rose to depart, she was not quite sober.[9]

Seneca, Burrhus, and Anicetus, who were in the plot, had been present at the banquet, and they now followed Nero as he led his mother down the steps to the quay, where the galley he had given her was moored, having been rowed over from Bauli to meet her. No longer did she feel any suspicion; and, under the influence of the wine she had drunk, she was happy to anticipate a comfortable return journey by sea, reclining upon the couch in the deck-pavilion, rather than by road in a jolting litter. Only Anicetus and two or three of his men knew of the contrivance by which the ship could be sunk; and he must now have glanced at Nero with the unspoken question as to whether the deed should be done at once or postponed until another night.[10] The Emperor gave him the signal as Agrippina was about to cross the gangway, and, having thus committed his mother to death, he clasped her passionately to his heart, covering her face, her hands, and her bosom with his kisses. There can be no possible doubt that this demonstration was entirely sincere: it was his farewell to her. She was at this time a woman of forty-four, still good-looking, her clear-cut, aquiline features being softened by her thick hair; and in her triumphant happiness at this wonderful reconciliation with her son, the somewhat weary and haggard look which her statues of this period reveal must have wholly vanished. Nero could not take his eyes from her face.

The night was warm and starry, and the sea dead calm. Agrippina took her place in the pavilion, her lady-in-waiting, Acerronia Polla, being with her, while her freedman, Crepercius Gallus, stood at the back of the structure, near the helmsman. Anicetus, grim as Fate itself, was in command of the vessel; and when he was still some distance from Bauli, and two or three hundred yards from the shore, he gave his confederates the order to open the sliding contrivance which he had invented, and let the water in.

But the ship did not sink immediately: it heeled over, and thereby caused the collapse of the pavilion. Gallus was knocked unconscious by a falling beam, and, tumbling into the sea, was drowned; but the Empress and Acerronia managed to crawl out from amidst the ruins, only to slide, however, down the sloping deck and into the water. Agrippina, whose shoulder had been hurt, began to swim painfully about amidst the wreckage, and in the inky blackness of the night presently became separated from the rest of the ship's company; but Acerronia, clutching at the vessel's side in the darkness, made the mistake of crying out for help, whereupon somebody immediately hit her on the head, and she sank.

As luck would have it Agrippina, who seems to

have been quite unaware that the shipwreck was not accidental, chanced to elude Anicetus and the men in his confidence, who must have been swimming about, frantically hunting for her so as to make sure that she died; and at last, when she was nearly exhausted, she was picked up by a small fishing-boat and was rowed at once to her villa.

Her first act was to send her freedman, Lucius Agerinus, at top speed to Nero to tell him of the wreck, and of her safety, to beg him not to worry about her, and to say that she was going to try to sleep and would rather that he did not come to see her until the morning. Tacitus thinks that she had now begun to suspect that the ship had been scuttled, but had realized that the wisest course would be to pretend that she had no such suspicion. Personally, however, I think that this loyal freedman of hers, Lucius Agerinus, was the only one who harboured such thoughts, and that even in his case they were directed against the admiral, Anicetus, and not against Nero. The Empress may well have supposed that the new and untried vessel had sprung a leak, and, owing to the weight of the deck-pavilion, had proved top-heavy.

She then went to bed, where her bruises were treated, and hot fomentations were applied to her shoulder. With her usual avarice she ordered Acerronia's will to be brought to her, for she guessed that she had been drowned; and having found herself to be the chief beneficiary under it, she gave instructions that the unfortunate woman's effects should be listed and locked up—an action which clearly indicates, I think, that she had no expectation of death.

Meanwhile Anicetus had swum ashore, or had been rescued by prearrangement with some trusted boatman, and had hastened back to Nero, who was pacing to and fro in an agony of mind. In great excitement the dripping admiral told him that, so far as he knew, Agrippina had escaped and was now back at her villa, and that she was probably well aware that an attempt had been made to drown her. At this, Nero lost his head. With indescribable horror, he realized that she would now be thinking of him as her would-be murderer, and that the deed which he had conceived in mercy would appear to her to be one of perfidious and cold-blooded infamy. Moreover, he knew that she would attempt to rouse the country against him. Even now she might be preparing to set out by road for Rome to claim, as daughter of Germanicus, the protection of the Prætorian Guard; and she and they together would perhaps be able to turn the Senate against him.

He instantly summoned Seneca and Burrhus, who were waiting in another room, and who, on hearing the news, realized that there was now no chance of both Agrippina and Nero surviving the disaster: one or the other would be killed.[11] Seneca, we are told, fixed his eyes on Burrhus, and said, "What will happen if you give orders to the soldiers here to put her to death?" Burrhus replied that the Prætorians were so attached to the whole family of the Cæsars, and so reverenced the memory of Germanicus, that the detachment on duty here at Baiæ could not be trusted to carry out such an order. "Anicetus undertook to do it," he said; "let him finish the work."

It was at this moment that Agrippina's messenger, Lucius Agerinus, arrived. This man, already suspicious of Anicetus, quickly found in the admiral's demeanour the proof of his guilt; and, in sudden fury, drew his dagger and sprang forward. There was a scuffle, and, a moment later, the assailant was overpowered by the three of them, and the dagger fell to the ground.[12] The guards were called in, and, thinking that an attempt to assassinate the Emperor had been made, dragged the man from the room; and soon the whole place was in an uproar. Nero himself did not doubt that his mother had sent her freedman to revenge her by killing him; and when Anicetus cried out that he would give measure for measure, and would go at once and finish the work he had begun, neither Nero, nor Seneca, nor Burrhus raised a finger to stop him as he rushed from the room. Taking Herculeus and Oloaritus, two naval officers, and some sailors with him, he set out at once for Agrippina's villa.

By now a crowd of people, many carrying torches, had collected on the beach near which the supposed accident had taken place, while a number of boats had gone to the rescue of those who had not been able to swim ashore and who were clinging to the wreckage. When it was learnt that the Empress was safe, some of the crowd made their way to the villa; but at the gates they were turned back by the sailors who had just arrived with Anicetus, and were on guard there.

Agrippina, attended by a maid, was lying on the bed, a single lamp burning at her side, when suddenly the doors of her room were flung open, and Anicetus, sword in hand, and followed by the two officers, appeared before her, at which the maid fled through the opposite entrance. Instantly, Agrippina sprang to her feet. "If you have come from the Emperor to enquire after my health," she said, nervously staring at the admiral, "you may say that I am well."

In silence Anicetus approached her, and at this, knowing that her hour had come, she proudly drew herself up. "If you are going to kill me," she whispered, glaring at him, "I tell you that it is not my son who has sent you to do so. He would never order his own mother to be put to death . . ."

The words died upon her lips. Suddenly her eyes were opened, and in a flash she saw that the shipwreck had been planned, and that, having escaped, she was to be executed here and now at the command of her son. In a frenzy of rage and hate she tore open her dress. "Strike here!" she cried, pointing to the lower part of her body. "Strike here, at the womb which bore Nero!"

Her executioners hesitated, and it seems that she attempted to forestall them by snatching up her own dagger and stabbing herself. Almost at the same moment one of the officers hit her on the head from behind, and a moment later Anicetus drove his sword into her heart.

When Nero received the news that she was dead he was at first bewildered and incredulous. Then he began to tremble, and presently, collapsing upon a chair, he sat staring in front of him with wide, unblinking eyes. After a while he sprang to his feet, looking about him in a sort of amazement, and at length he burst into tears. To soothe him Seneca reminded him that he had acted out of motives of mercy; and Burrhus brought in to him some of the officers of the Guard, who pressed his hand and told him how near he had been to assassination.

Though Tacitus says that the point was widely denied, both Suetonius and Dion Cassius state that the Emperor then insisted on going to see his mother's body. When he was led into the room where she lay, if the story be true, he looked fixedly at her, staring in horror at her wounds, and then, turning away, perhaps overcome with faintness, called for some water to drink; after which, gazing once more at the body, he murmured, "I did not know that she was so beautiful." [13] He then gave orders that the funeral ceremonies and cremation should take place at once; and soon after he had returned to his palace, the people of Bauli heard the chanting of the priests and saw the flames shoot up in the midst of the garden of the villa as the body of the Empress was burnt to ashes upon the hastily built pyre. Her favourite freedman, Mnester, perhaps thinking that his complicity in some of his mistress's plots against Nero's throne would now come to light, killed himself as the fire died down.

Back once more at the palace, Nero "waited the approach of dawn in a state of distraction and despair," as Tacitus tells us; but he must have been somewhat eased in his mind when, at sunrise, he was told that people were flocking to the temples to render thanks that Agrippina was dead, and to praise the gods for having preserved Nero all these years from her murderous hands.

Seneca then drew up a letter for the Emperor to send to the Senate, in which Agrippina was accused of an appalling series of crimes and murders. It was she, he said, who was the cause of all the atrocities of the last years of Claudius. She had tried ruthlessly to gain absolute power by plotting against Rome's most distinguished citizens; she had endeavoured to obtain an oath of loyalty from the Prætorian Guard, and, on failing to do so, had opposed a proposed increase of their pay. "What labour it has cost me," Nero added, "to defeat her design of assuming a seat in the Senate itself, and of receiving foreign ambassadors!" He then described how she had been accidentally shipwrecked, and, believing that it had been an attempt on her life, had sent her freedman to assassinate him; and how, at the moment of her arrest, she had stabbed herself. At the end of the letter Nero wrote: "I can hardly believe that I am now safe from her, nor do I feel any pleasure in the fact." [14]

So great was the hatred in which Agrippina had been held that the Senate at once sent their congratulations to him, and decreed that the day of her death should be signalised for ever by thanksgiving, and her birthday marked in the calendar as a day of ill-omen; that the festival of Minerva, during which she had died, should be particularly celebrated by annual entertainments; and that a statue of that protecting goddess, and one of the Emperor, both made of gold, should be placed side by side in the Senate-house.

But Nero would not be comforted. "He appeared grief-stricken and dejected," says Tacitus, "seeming to be unhappy at his own preservation, and continually mourning for his mother." His sleep was beset by terrible dreams from which he would start up, calling upon her name, and whispering tender expressions of love for her; and he declared many times that he had seen her ghost, and had heard her voice wailing over the hills behind her villa. Unable any longer to endure the scenes connected with the tragedy, he went to Naples, and later wandered from place to place, refusing to go back to Rome. He tried once to invoke Agrippina's spirit at a kind of *séance,* but the experiment was not successful.

Thus he spent the whole summer, and gradually his gloom began to be dissipated as he realized that now he was free from restraint. "At last I am Emperor," he said, grimly, "thanks to Anicetus." And as a token of his new liberty of action he recalled from exile various persons whose banishment had been due to his mother, including Junia Calvina, who had been falsely accused of incest with her brother Lucius Silanus, and Calpurnia, the lady who had been admired by Claudius. He also ordered the ashes of the murdered Lollia Paulina to be brought home, and a sepulchral monument erected over them.

Throughout these months he received messages from Rome, begging him to return to the capital to receive the welcome which the people desired to accord him. He was told, to use the words of Tacitus,[15] "that the very name of Agrippina was detested, and that by her death the love of the people towards him had been fanned into flames; and they begged him to come in person to receive proof of this popular adoration." But it was not until the autumn that he returned there, receiving, however, such an ovation when he did so that even those who had expected an outburst of public affection were astonished. All along his route through the city tiers of seats had been erected, and these were occupied by wildly enthusiastic crowds, whole families being everywhere present with troops of women and children. All the Senators were there in their robes of state; and at the close of the procession Nero was conducted to the Capitol, where he returned public thanks to the gods for having rid the Empire of the mother who bore him.

CHAPTER XI

The "Festivals of Youth," A.D. 59—The Shaving of the Emperor's Beard—The "Neronia" Contests, A.D. 60—The Banishment of Plautus—The Disaster in Britain, A.D. 61.

It is a question whether Poppæa had been with Nero in his distracted wanderings during the late spring and summer of the year 59, but probably she was close at hand most of the time. If, however, she had thought that the death of Agrippina would be followed by the Emperor's divorce from Octavia and marriage to herself, she must have suffered a great disappointment. Nero appears to have pointed out to her that Octavia was much liked by the people, who, very naturally, were sorry for her—her father, mother, and brother dead, her half-sister Antonia far away in Marseilles, and her husband, himself, estranged from her. If he were to divorce her he would arouse public indignation, and just now when the people had treated him so handsomely in regard to Agrippina's death, it would be foolish to jeopardize their unexpected good-will.

I think he must have told Poppæa that the only cause for divorce which could be put forward without any danger of his being thought to have faked up a case against her, would be that of her barrenness. She was now twenty years of age; and either because of the infrequency of their conjugal meetings, or because their dislike of one another had kept them entirely apart,[1] or else because of his or her actual infertility, she had never shown the least sign of becoming a mother. In due course this would provide grounds for divorce, and Octavia could be honourably discharged with popular approval; but the time had hardly yet come. Poppæa would have to wait, and, indeed, the delay would be all for the best, since Nero's marriage to her now would inevitably suggest that she had had a hand in the death of Agrippina—who was known to have opposed Octavia's divorce—and would thus call in question the accepted motives for Nero's action against his mother. It may be added that Poppæa, of course, was still married to Otho; but this was a tie which could be broken at any time, and would best remain as it was until Nero was free of Octavia.

Roman society in that age fully recognized the polygamous tendencies of its male members, and while the law allowed a man only one wife, public opinion permitted him at least one official mistress and an unlimited number of casual companions of the night. Thus, Nero's behaviour in this respect was quite approved: Octavia, his wife and Empress, was hostess at ceremonious banquets, and was to some extent the controller of the imperial menage; Poppæa was established in a house of her own near the palace, and was his recognized companion in all his lighter entertainments; Acte, in another house, received visits from him in decreasing frequency; and occasionally some other lady took his passing fancy. But in spite of all that was later said to the contrary, Nero was not conspicuously a libertine, and at this time there can be little doubt that he was in love with the beautiful Poppæa, and looked only to her in his troubles and anxieties.

One fact above all others contributed to the recovery of his good spirits, namely that he was free from the curb with which his mother had always attempted to check the development of his artistic talents. He knew now that music and poetry were the most important things in his life, and with the zest of one suddenly released from bondage he determined, before all else, to become a great singer and a great poet. Everybody had told him that he had a beautiful voice, and, since his life seemed to him to be beset with majestic tragedy, his sentimental heart longed to be able to pour out its sorrows in song which should shake the world. He had lately found himself very successful in stirring his guests by singing to them after dinner, accompanying himself upon a harp. Tacitus says that people who heard about it thought it very scandalous that an Emperor should thus behave as though he were a common musician; but Nero pointed out that the kings and heroes of old were wont to burst into bardic song, and that singing was an art sacred to Apollo.

Encouraged by the general praise of his voice, and feeling the truth of the Greek proverb which he often quoted—that there was no value in music unheard—he excitedly made up his mind to sing to a larger audience than that constituted by his guests. He knew, however, that he would have to fight the bitter prejudice of the old-fashioned elements in Roman society who deemed it so very vulgar to sing; but he felt that he had the support of the younger set, amongst which the art-loving ideals of the Greeks were in vogue.

Towards the close of this same year, A.D. 59, therefore, he instituted a new kind of society entertainment, musical and dramatic, which he named the *Ludi Juvenalium,* or "Festivals of Youth," and by keeping these affairs socially exclusive [2] he was enabled to take part in them personally, providing himself with a large audience without, however, risking an offence to popular opinion by making an appearance on the platform before the general public. He invited everybody in society to take part in these festivals, "neither noble descent, nor age, nor the holding of honourable office, preventing them from practising the arts of mere persons on the stage," as Tacitus [3] remarks with horror. He was determined to break down this prejudice against artistic accomplishment; he was determined that the genius of the singer, the musician, and the actor should be socially recognized in Rome as it was in Greece; and both because he himself felt the passionate need to express himself in song, and also because he was ashamed to think that the aristocratic tradition of Rome should regard such means of self-expression as ungentlemanly, he was determined to stand up on the stage—himself, the Emperor—and sing his songs to Roman society, thus giving them an example and a lead. Having killed Agrippina he was bent on killing also the social bigotry for which she had stood.

Across the Tiber there was a charming little park which had been laid out by Augustus around an artificial lake, and here amongst the trees and flower-beds Nero caused a stage and auditorium to be constructed, while round about were restaurants, and stalls for the sale of objects of art and luxury. Winding paths led to lovers' bowers concealed amidst the shrubs and bushes; and it may be supposed that there were pleasure-boats upon the lake. The whole concern was lavishly financed by Nero himself, and the festivals must have been much like the private garden-fêtes organised by the millionaires of today, particularly in respect to the entertainments upon the stage, where the leading members of society acted, danced, played, and sang to an audience drawn from their own walk in life. Fashionable society was delighted: everybody began to learn to sing, dance, or act, and schools for the teaching of these accomplishments sprang up on all sides, and were patronised by old and young. Everybody wanted to go on the stage, and at these "Festivals of Youth" elderly ladies and gentlemen were proud even to have a place in the chorus, while one old soul of eighty, a certain Ælia Catella, offered to perform a dance, and did so.

Thus Nero obtained the wider hearing he so much desired, and it is said that daily and nightly he stood there upon the stage, surrounded by his companions, and by his bodyguard of Prætorians with its officers, even the stern old Burrhus himself being at his side, listening with outward pleasure but with inward misgiving to his Emperor's voice. Nero was always nervous on these occasions, and tuned his harp with excessive care before beginning to sing, and he was a pleased as a child at the applause he received. The traditionists were, of course, horrified on hearing that the Emperor had donned the dress of a professional musician, and had even used the conventional form of address of a paid singer to his audience—"My lords, of your kindness give me your attention." But smart society thought it all most amusing. A society of young patricians was formed, the members calling themselves the Augustani, their business being to applaud the Emperor and to encourage him in all his attempts, personal or otherwise, to promote the musical and dramatic arts. They were dedicated to the improvement of Roman delicacy and culture, and they were prepared to knock anybody down who said that the Emperor ought not to sing.

At the same time, Nero gathered around him all the young poets in Rome, encouraging them to write for the stage, and also shyly asking them to criticise and correct his own attempts to do so. He was at this time very doubtful and diffident about his talents, and just as his great pleasure in singing was often spoilt for him by his nervousness, so his joy in writing verse was marred by a youthful dread that he was making technical mistakes. Tacitus, who can never see any good in him, says that these poet-friends of his used to help him to the extent of patching their own lines onto his; but Suetonius denies this. "He had a natural turn for poetry," declares the latter, "and composed verses with equal pleasure and ability, nor did he, as some think, publish the lines of other writers as his own. Several little pocketbooks and loose sheets have come into my possession, which contain well-known verses in his own handwriting, and these are written in such a manner that it is evident, from the erasures and additions, that they had not been copied from another manuscript, nor dictated by somebody else, but had been actually composed by him." [4]

Being assured by his admirers—and at this time admirers crowded around him—that his verses were really good, he was induced at length to recite them to select audiences at the theatre; and since the declaiming of poetry was, like oratory, regarded as quite a patrician proceeding by those of the old school who considered singing, harp-playing and acting as ungentlemanly, he was enthusiastically acclaimed on this account. "He recited verses of his own composition not only at home but in the theatre," says Suetonius, "and his hearers so much enjoyed it that public prayers of thanksgiving were ordered by them to be returned to the gods on that account, and the verses which had thus been declaimed were inscribed in letters of gold and consecrated to Jupiter Capitolinus." [5]

Unfortunately only ten lines of Nero's poetry have come down to us, and these do not owe their preservation to their beauty but to their chance quotation by other writers. For example, one of Nero's verses had referred to some subterranean disturbance such as an earthquake, and the young poet Lucan, on hearing the abdominal rumblings of a friend, is said to have quoted the Emperor's line *Sub terris tonuisse putes,* "One might suppose that it was thundering underground"—a piece of fun which Suetonius happens to mention in his brief *Life of Lucan.*[6] Nevertheless, these fragments are quite workmanlike, and, indeed, there is much reason to suppose that Nero was a poet of merit if not an actual genius in this respect.

Representatives of all the arts were now to be found around him—writers, painters, sculptors, singers, musicians, actors, and so forth; nor were the sciences neglected, for Nero was eager to show the world that his conception of the imperial office was like that of an Antony, not like that of an Augustus. He wanted to be worthy of the fashionably cultured society of which Poppæa was one of the leading lights; and he was still young enough to enjoy the feeling that he belonged to the intelligentsia. It thrilled him to think of his palace as the center of the Empire's artistic and intellectual life, not merely the center of its proud and militaristic government; and thus we find that the place was overrun also with philosophers, who were permitted to debate with one another after dinner, the Emperor playing the part of a sort of referee. Tacitus grudgingly admits that even saintly and ascetic thinkers—men in mean attire and with grave, austere faces—gladly came, and were gladly welcomed, at these dinner-parties.[7]

On December 15th of this year 59 Nero celebrated his twenty-second birthday, the occasion, it would seem, being marked by the shaving of his beard for the first time.[8] A young man's first shave was regarded by the Romans as an occasion for rejoicing, but the age at which the operation was performed seems to have varied: Caligula, for instance, was first shaved at twenty, Augustus at twenty-five. In the case of Nero, the hair was carefully collected into a golden box studded with pearls, and was consecrated to Jupiter Capitolinus. An anecdote in this connection is told of the Emperor which is supposed to illustrate his brutality, but which actually reveals only his characteristic honesty. Soon after his return to Rome, he paid a visit to his wealthy aunt Domitia, his mother's surviving sister, from whom he had great expectations, she being the owner of beautiful estates at Baiæ and elsewhere, and the possessor, it may be supposed, of many coveted works of art. She was critically ill; and as he bent down to kiss her, she stroked his soft and youthful beard, saying, "I am determined to live to see the day when this is shaved off for the first time: then I shall die happy." Nero turned to his friends who were with him, and, with a wink, whispered, "I'll get shaved at once." When she died, many people said that he had poisoned her—a silly accusation, having no foundation whatsoever.

A few months later, in the summer of A.D. 60, he instituted games or contests in the Greek manner, which he named "Neronia," and which were to be given in Rome every five years. Music and poetry, wrestling and certain other athletics, and chariot-racing were the three fields of endeavour in which trials of skill were held thereat, for the Greeks always associated music with athletics, and athletics were closely connected with chariot-driving. For these games he had caused a new amphitheatre to be constructed on the Campus Martius: it was a wooden structure, and it may be mentioned that less than three years later it was struck by lightning and burnt to the ground. Attached to it was a magnificent bath-house, and it seems that this part of the building was finished first; for it was at its dedication, presumably on his birthday, that the ceremony of the Emperor's first shave was celebrated.

These new games were hailed by fashionable society as a great advance on the gladiatorial shows and other primitive amusements of the Romans; but the traditionists considered them to be foreign and far too refined. Tacitus, their spokesman, regards them as degenerate, and he says [9] that the very fact of their being held in a permanent theatre, furnished with built seats, was degrading. In the good old days, he points out, the audience had to stand, and thus had no inducement to idle long hours away in the theatre; and in more recent times a temporary stage and a few benches were considered good enough. It is true, he admits, that Pompey, a century and more ago, had erected a proper amphitheatre of this sort, but he had been very much censured for it, and the experiment ought not to have been repeated. It was bound to lead to the corruption of manners; and he bewails "the degeneration from the virtues of ancestral times revealed by this introduction of foreign customs, which habituated people to mere athletics, and thence to softness, and so to love-making," and all that sort of thing. And then again "under the pretence of encouraging poetry and music, the best people of Rome were exposed to the degradation of the stage, and stage-scenery!" How, he asks, could men who were content to witness or take part in these mild Greek contests instead of military exercises, ever hope to become good soldiers? How could they hope to become stern officials of the State after "listening with critical ear to the languishing tones and the melodious inflexions of the voice" of people on the stage? And then, again, he says, these performances often continued into the night, with the result that young men and women in the auditorium flirted with one another without any modesty. It was disgraceful that such wickedness should have been patronized by the Emperor.

Tacitus here reveals plainly enough to us the prejudices which led him to regard Nero as a monster of iniquity, and we can clearly see how an Emperor who did not feel "the degradation of stage-scenery" came to be vilified in later years. Tacitus, as a matter of fact, admits that "to many these dissolute pastimes were congenial." Such persons, he says, argued that a permanent theatre was more economical than one built for each occasion and afterwards torn down. They declared that contests in artistic achievement would tend to cultivate genius; and as to the supposed immorality after dark, who could possibly misbehave himself or herself when the place was all lit up by lamps and torches? At any rate, the puritanical historian confesses, the contests "passed off without any particular violation of decorum." The crown for the best performance in Latin prose and verse, for which several persons of the highest merit contended, was unanimously given to Nero; but when the crowd had insisted upon him also playing the harp, although he had been "too modest" to do so,[10] and the crown for this contest was likewise awarded to him by the judges, the Emperor received it as though it were something sacred, and, as a reproof to those who considered musical accomplishments to be vulgar, ordered it to be laid before the statue of the deified Augustus. He took the whole affair extremely seriously, and, regarding the contests as worthy of the most impeccable patronage, even invited the Vestal Virgins to attend the wrestling matches, thereby following the Greek custom at Olympia, where these competitions were always considered to be so proper that the priestesses of Demeter were allowed to be present. One may question whether these Vestal nuns, vowed by their parents to perpetual celibacy, and buried alive if they broke those vows, derived any benefit from watching the wrestling of naked men; but the dignity of the contests was certainly enhanced by their presence, and that was the main consideration.

It does not appear that Nero competed in any but the musical contests on this particular occasion; yet he certainly practised wrestling, for, a few years later, he wanted to take on Rome's champions at this sport, believing himself capable, at any rate, of making a fair show, since his physical strength was enormous. He was so skillful in this and other athletics, in fact, that he did not mind performing his daily exercises on the Campus Martius in view of the public. Chariot-racing, too, as has been said, was a sport in which he was intensely interested; and already his skill as a driver was so great that he was willing, again, to allow the public to watch him at practice on his own private course—a circus laid out by Caligula on the site where now stands the church of St. Peter, and finished by Nero in A.D. 59. Tacitus admits with sorrowful surprise that "this public exhibition of his shame did not produce disgust in the people, but actual encouragement. They cheered him on with their acclamations, rejoicing that the inclinations of their Emperor pointed in this direction." [11]

Seneca and Burrhus are both stated to have supported Nero in his enthusiasm for the races, knowing that it made him so popular with the masses; and if they did not so readily approve of his appearances on the stage, they at least waved their gowns about and beat time with their hands when he was singing, as though they were enjoying it.[12] As for Nero, he was tremendously elated at finding himself able to indulge these propensities which his mother had striven so hard to suppress in him, and which, out of consideration for her, he had felt himself obliged to restrain so long as she was alive. He was doing now what he had always wanted to do; and, supported by the approval both of the masses and of the progressive elements in smart society, he cared little that he was deeply offending the old-fashioned aristocracy whose point of view is so constantly placed before us by Tacitus.

Nevertheless this opposing faction was not altogether silent, and a secret and sinuous little undercurrent of hostility to him made itself apparent in Rome. Somebody hung the lash of a whip on one of his statues to indicate that he ought to be thrashed. The most obvious method of attack was that of calling him the murderer of his mother; and one day a baby was found abandoned in the Forum, with a notice hanging round its neck, reading: "I will not bring you up for fear that you, also, may kill your mother." Many of the statues of Agrippina had been removed before Nero's return to the capital, and of those which still remained the most conspicuous were shrouded from sight by linen covers; and on one of these veiled figures an inscription was found, reading: "*I* hide my face for shame, but *you* are unabashed."

These things were reported to Nero, and he was told that people were making treasonable remarks about him; but he treated the matter "with utter contempt," [13] and refused to take action. During the holding of the Neronia, however, a comet appeared in the sky and was seen for many weeks; and since this was generally regarded as a sign of a coming change of rulers, Nero's ill-wishers spread the rumour that he was about to be deposed, thus working on public feeling to such an extent that discussions as to who would be the next Emperor presently came to be ordinary topics of conversation. The name on everybody's lips was that of Rubellius Plautus, Nero's cousin, who had once before been thought to be aiming at the throne. He was a strict traditionist, and it was widely thought that the old-fashioned patricians were urging him to lead a rebellion against Nero in order to put an end to a state of affairs which, they believed, was undermining the ancient institutions of Rome.

Now, the paternal ancestors of Rubellius Plautus hailed from Tibur (Tivoli), a few miles from Rome; and it so happened that one day when Nero was sheltering from a thunderstorm in an open pavilion in the grounds of the imperial villa in that neighbourhood, and was eating an alfresco meal, a flash of lightning struck the polished metal dishes before him, scattering the food and upsetting the table. The story at once spread that the ancestral deities of the Plautus family had thus signified the coming overthrow of Nero; and on all sides the expectation of an imminent rebellion was excitedly discussed.

Without fear of contradiction it may be stated that any one of the previous Emperors would have instantly safeguarded himself by ordering the death of his rival, as also Agrippina would have done. But Nero behaved with a restraint and an absence of panic which has forced an approving comment from many historians. He wrote a letter to Rubellius Plautus diplomatically advising him, for the sake of the peace of Rome, to withdraw himself from those who were wickedly accusing him of disloyalty, and to retire to Asia Minor, where he possessed hereditary estates and where he might pass the rest of his days in security and comfort.[14] The advice was promptly taken, and thus, without bloodshed, Nero rid himself of a most serious menace to his throne and life, thereafter being enabled to go his own unconventional way without hindrance.

But while Rome was thus discussing the merits and demerits of this burly, red-haired athlete and artist, whose government, after more than five years of his unconventional rule, was still the best that the Empire had ever known,[15] news of a terrible disaster to the Roman cause in Britain shook the nation and turned its angry attention upon Seneca who, as will be seen, was blamed for the catastrophe.

Britain had been annexed by the Roman Empire in A.D. 43, under the Emperor Claudius; but some of its local kings still held their thrones under the supervision of Roman military officers and civil officials. At this time, Prasutagus, King of the Iceni—the nation which inhabited the modern Norfolk and Suffolk[16]—had recently died, and his country was ruled by his widow, Queen Boudicca, the famous Boadicea of romance and legend, who bitterly resented the presence of these Romans and their control of her affairs. In some heated quarrel with one of them she appears to have been smacked or roughly handled in some way—actually beaten, says Tacitus, but that is highly unlikely—and she declared that her two daughters had been outraged, which, perhaps, was another way of saying that these young ladies had found the elegant Roman military officers quite irresistible.

Now, Seneca had lent a huge sum of money to King Prasutagus, it being not unusual for wealthy Romans to make loans at high interest to petty rulers, though it must be admitted that a philosopher turned money-lender was something quite out of the ordinary. But on the King's death, Seneca called in the loan,[17] whereupon, in A.D. 61, Boudicca revolted.[18] Her tribesmen swooped down on the Roman colony at Colchester and massacred it; and then in turn they destroyed St. Albans and London, putting tens of thousands of Romans and Romanized Britons to the sword. The Ninth Legion, at this time on duty between Lincoln and York, hurried South, only to be wiped out by the rebels; but the Fourteenth Legion and part of the Twentieth marched down from Chester, came up with Boudicca outside London, and crushed the rebellion, the Queen thereat taking poison.

The trouble, however, is said to have cost the lives of some seventy thousand Romans or persons loyal to Rome; and, in my opinion, there is little doubt that Seneca's position at court was greatly shaken by the fact that his money-lending was the main cause of the slaughter. The sneers and jests at his expense, as a man who miraculously combined the sentiments of a plutocrat with those of a stoic philosopher, evidently worried him; and, being now over sixty years of age, he began to turn over in his mind the advisability of retiring from public office so as to devote the remainder of his days to the writing of moral discourses on such subjects as the charm of the simple life and the vanity of riches. Nero, however, would not at first consider the suggestion, for he was genuinely fond of his old friend and mentor, even though, just now, he seems to have realized that the courtly philosopher had more to explain away than his philosophy could be stretched or twisted into explaining.

CHAPTER XII

Octavia's Resentment Against Nero—The Death of Burrhus, A.D. 62—The Appointment of Tigellinus as Commander of the Guard—The Retirement of Seneca—The Execution of Sulla and Plautus, A.D. 62—The Decision to Divorce Octavia, May, A.D. 62—Seneca's Interview with Nero.

By the close of A.D. 61 the best part of three years had elapsed since the death of Agrippina; and at about this time Poppæa, tired of her anomalous position, began vigorously to renew her demands that Nero should divorce the odd and brooding Octavia, for she felt that public opinion was ready to admit that the Empress was barren and that the Emperor ought to have a wife who would present him with an heir. Poppæa herself, it is true, had not had a baby during these years of their life together; but, birth-control being at that time quite effectively practised, the fact is more likely to have been due to her desire to preserve her looks than to her inability to become a mother. But now she was getting on for thirty-one years of age; and she was doubtless beginning to feel that she ought to try to have a child, since Nero, who was just twenty-four, would be more easily softened by the expectation of her coming motherhood than by the enjoyment of her departing beauty. Yet she need not have worried: he was still in love with her, and still thought her the most bewitching of women.

He declined, however, to divorce Octavia. He was certainly eager to please Poppæa; he was certainly harassed by the presence of Octavia in the palace, who sullenly hated him as the supposed murderer of her brother Britannicus, and, as though devoured by that hatred, grew daily thinner, more pale, and more menacing; yet he would not consent to divorce her, even though, in refusing, he ran the risk of losing the love of the woman he adored, and possibly of receiving Octavia's dagger in his back as well. A hint of his reason is perhaps revealed by the statement of Dion Cassius that when the suggested divorce was mentioned to the blunt and honest Burrhus, he replied, "Very well, but give her back her dowry," meaning thereby her contribution to Nero's right to the throne.[1]

In this regard it must be explained that the whole conception of imperial sovereignty in Rome, in my opinion, was strongly influenced by the ideas of female inheritance which had prevailed in Egypt at the time of Julius Cæsar's intimacy with Cleopatra, she being the representative of the only really great and important royal line then existing in the civilized world—a Greek royal line, moreover, and the best available model for Rome. Cæsar had thought of making himself sovereign of a united Græco-Roman world with the Greek Queen Cleopatra [2] as his consort, and Antony had entertained similar hopes; and when Augustus was made Emperor, the fact that he had already been accepted as Pharaoh of Egypt must have influenced his conception of his rulership. In the Egyptian royal house the hereditary right was vested in the female line, the Pharaoh's eldest daughter being heiress of the kingdom and conveying the crown to her husband; and Augustus had been the more ready to adopt this view since he himself was Cæsar's heir through the female line. The imperial office, of course, was not really hereditary, but in so far as its hereditary right was considered at all, it seems to me that the memory of the Egyptian matriarchal system undoubtedly influenced that consideration. The second Emperor, Tiberius, was only related to Augustus through the female line; the third Emperor, Caligula, was the son of the daughter of the daughter of Augustus; and the fourth Emperor, Claudius, was the son of the daughter of the sister of Augustus. Caligula had definitely adopted the Egyptian system by regarding his sister, Drusilla, as heiress of the Empire; and now in the case of Octavia there seems to have been a general if undefined feeling that, as Burrhus had said, she had conveyed to Nero from her father Claudius the right to the throne. Thus, if she were to be divorced, and were to marry somebody else, that other personage might become a serious rival to Nero—Rubellius Plautus, for instance: what more easy than for him to divorce his own wife, marry Octavia, and claim the throne in right of that dowry of hers to which Burrhus had referred?

Octavia's unbalanced state of mind at this time is startlingly revealed in the drama *Octavia,* a vivid piece of work traditionally attributed to Seneca, but, in my opinion, more probably written by Curiatius Maternus, or some other author of the period following Nero's death, who had access to the journals or papers left by Seneca, or who was familiar with his account of the events of this part of the reign. The drama opens with a dialogue between the smouldering Octavia, at this time twenty-two years of age, and her anxious old nurse; and though the conversation is not to be regarded, of course, as precisely historical, much of it may well have been actually spoken and afterwards repeated to Seneca by the nurse, and certainly reflects the sentiments which the historical narrative leads us to expect.

Octavia, we are told, traced all her misfortunes back to her mother, Messalina, whose misbehaviour, she said, was a constant source of tears to her. Messalina had been made mad, she declared, and in her mad folly had married another man, regardless of law, and forgetful of her husband. And her death had left Octavia at the mercy of the tyranny of a cruel step-mother, Agrippina, who, at heart, had always been hostile to her, and, as a girl, had often terrified her. It was this Agrippina, she reminded her nurse, who had killed her poor father, Claudius, and it was Agrippina's son, Nero, who, she was convinced, had murdered her beloved brother, Britannicus. And still this Nero was her husband, although she and he hated one another.

Her nurse sadly agreed that Octavia always seemed to recoil from him; and she made the comment that Octavia's indignation against him had already got the better of her sanity, and that she seemed positively to draw strength from her grievances. Octavia replied that she had good reason to recoil from him. For fear of his temper, she said, she was always afraid to mention in his presence the name of her father or her brother—her brother who had been the solace of all her sorrows; and, indeed, ever since the boy's death she had known that nothing but the grave would end her misery.

At this her nurse, having some sympathy, evidently, for Nero, sharply told her that, instead of brooding sullenly upon her wrongs, she would be far wiser to try to win her husband back by kindness and gentleness; but Octavia revealed the depths of her hate by retorting with heat that it would be easier to win the heart of a raging lion than that of a man such as Nero.

The nurse begged her to try to control her temper, but she only bewailed the more her lot, and poured out her woes in a flood of words. The light of day, she said, brought no joy to her, crushed as she was by her misery—her father murdered, her mother executed, her brother taken from her, and her husband setting her lower even than that slave-girl, Acte. She was always trembling, she cried, not from fear of death itself, but from dread of all this bad feeling. It was worse than death to have to look into Nero's face, always scowling at her, these days; yet, in her own smarting anger, she could not endure to show him any civility, since she always thought of him as the usurper of her brother's throne. She was always dreaming about her brother; she was always seeing his wretched ghost raising its feeble hands to strike at Nero's eyes or face in a futile effort to be revenged, and then flying in terror to her bedroom, gibbering and clinging to her as Nero pursued him, or murdered them both.

And now, added to all this, Poppæa had come—this proud mistress of Nero, wearing the family jewels which, no doubt, he killed his mother to obtain. If ever there had been any chance of reconciliation, what hope was there now? The triumphant Poppæa was threatening her position as Nero's wife, blazing with hate of her, and, as a reward of her adultery, demanding her very life. O, if only the spirit of her father would come to her aid, she cried!

Bitterly her nurse replied that it was no good looking for help from the deified Claudius, for it was he who had preferred Nero to his own son, Britannicus, after taking his own brother's daughter, Agrippina, to wife—from which disgusting and incestuous marriage sprang a whole train of crimes. First, the unhappy Silanus, who had been betrothed to Octavia, was charged with incest, of which he was innocent, she declared, and was done to death for fear that he might become too strong—a monstrous crime of Agrippina's. Then Nero was married to Octavia against her will—Nero, a youth of abnormal character,[3] fertile in sin, whose love for her, if it ever existed, was something merely fanned into flame by his mother, all because Agrippina dared aspire to the awful empire of the world, and had been mounting the ladder rung by rung, helped by every sort of crime and intrigue. Next, Britannicus was killed—Britannicus, the world's star, the pillar of the imperial house. Even the stony-hearted Agrippina wept when she gave the body of

Britannicus to be burnt on the pyre. "Let Nero destroy me also," Octavia burst out, "lest by my hand he die, this hand made strong by anguish, anger, sorrow, wretchedness, grief . . .!"

"Hush!" whispered her nurse. "You should try to win your husband's love, so that you may remain unharmed, and may present him with the son and heir he so much wants. After all, the people are fond of you."

"Nero is mightier than the people," Octavia replied.

"Well, Nero himself treats you with respect," the nurse reminded her.

"He would if Poppæa let him," said Octavia.

"Poppæa!" scoffed her nurse. "She's disliked by everybody."

"Nero loves her," Octavia answered, "and he would like to make her his wife."

"It is only a passing passion," said the nurse; "but you have something more enduring to give him."

"Even Acte is afraid of Poppæa's hate," Octavia added. "Acte is very humble these days, and shows signs of her great dread."

"Can you not forget your anger against him?" the nurse pleaded.

"Never!" Octavia cried. "Sooner shall the sea unite with the stars, water with fire, light with darkness, day with night, than shall my soul, ever brooding on my brother's death, unite with the impious soul of my husband, Nero, this scourge, this enemy of gods and decent men, who has driven out the virtues from their seats and good citizens from their homes, and has killed

Britannicus and his own mother; Nero, this usurper, this son of Ahenobarbus, this tyrant over a world he burdens with his shameful yoke, and with vulgar behaviour pollutes the name of Augustus!"

"Hush, hush!" her nurse begged her again. "How can you expect not to arouse your fiery-tempered husband's anger, when you go on like this?"

The drama then passes to other scenes, from which further quotations will presently be made. But, to return to the historical narrative, the extraordinary fact is that Octavia's attitude towards Nero did not alter his resolve that he would not divorce her. At last, however, he decided to send her to live in a house of her own,[4] or, more probably, in a particular part of the palace, so that her presence should no longer give Poppæa cause for complaint. Octavia, of course, was enraged at this enforced removal, and her anger was increased when Nero told her she ought to be satisfied that she was still his wife and Empress.[5] She was not, however, alone in her sequestration. Apparently at the same time he agreed, also, to give up his occasional visits to the sad little Acte; and he sent her out of Rome to a beautiful villa near the town of Velitræ (Veletri), overlooking the Pomptine Marshes and the sea beyond—the home of the paternal ancestors of Augustus.

It was shortly after this, in A.D. 62, that Nero lost the most loyal friend he ever had—the worthy Burrhus, his old tutor and Commander of the Prætorian Guard. He became ill with an affection of the throat—probably quinsy—which, at his age, was extremely dangerous. Nero went to visit him, but the brave old soldier, panting for breath, turned his face away, and, to all the Emperor's enquiries, only replied, "I'm all right—I tell you, I'm all right." He had always been curt and uncommunicative. It is said that on one occasion, when Nero had asked him more than once for his opinion on certain matters, he had sharply replied, "When I have said my say about anything, don't ask me to repeat it"; and now as he lay dying, he refused to discuss his ailment.

When he died there was the usual crop of rumours that Nero had poisoned him; but Tacitus says that "the fact that his throat gradually swelled up internally so that the air-passage was at last choked, indicated that his death was due to a natural malady"[6]; and no modern historian, of course, supposes that Nero had anything to do with the matter.

Previous to the appointment of Burrhus as commander of the Guard, that post had been held jointly by two officers, and now Nero reverted to this dual command, appointing Fenius Rufus, one of the late Agrippina's particular friends, and Sofonius Tigellinus, the man, it will be remembered, who had been exiled by Caligula in A.D. 39 on the charge of being Agrippina's lover, and had been recalled by her as soon as she had the power to do so. Tigellinus was a Sicilian, born at Agrigentum, who had first been a fisherman, and then had taken to horse-breeding in the Calabrian hills. The latter business had brought him to Rome, and to the court, and his handsome figure had commended itself to Agrippina and her sister, who made a friend of him with the above-mentioned result. Later,

Nero, to please his mother, had given him the command of the city guards or police; but now in promoting him to this higher office the Emperor seems to have been guided partly by his personal liking for the man and partly by the fact that the step from the command of the police to the command of the Prætorians was a natural one. It is curious, however, that two of the late Agrippina's friends should thus have been honoured together, and it may be that Nero was beginning to feel some desire to pay respect to her memory now that time was dulling the sharpness of his quarrel with her; or it may be that the Prætorian Guard, which had always been loyal to her as the daughter of their hero, Germanicus, needed to be conciliated by being shown that Nero bore no grudge against those who had served his mother. In this connection it is significant that Dion Cassius refers to some sort of religious sacrifices which, at about this time, were made in honour of her memory.[7]

The death of Burrhus was a terrible blow to Seneca, who had worked with him so happily for so many years; and it was not long before he asked Nero to allow him to retire. He was troubled by the attacks which were being made upon his character, and he was aware that tales were being told against him, which, even though they were not believed, were a cause of worry to the Emperor. Seneca, who had perhaps grown somewhat vain and critical, had evidently offended some of the ardent young people who regarded Nero as a genius and a superman, and who, nowadays, were always clustering around their somewhat bewildered hero, telling him how wonderful he was, or following him about with adoring looks.

Their accusations against Seneca are recorded by Tacitus[8] in a passage which may be quoted in full. "They assailed him," he writes, "with various imputations, namely, that he had already made an enormous fortune, far greater than was right in a private citizen; that he was trying to alienate from the Emperor, and divert to himself, the admiration of the people; that he was endeavouring to out-do his sovereign in the beauty of his gardens and the splendour of his houses; that he was claiming a monopoly in the art of eloquence; that ever since Nero had taken seriously to writing poetry, Seneca had himself done the same with unwonted diligence, because he was an open enemy to the Emperor's gifts, belittling his vocal powers when he sang, or disparaging his skill in driving his racing-chariots, always with the object of showing the whole nation that nothing was praiseworthy except his own talents. Surely, they said, Nero was now past the age of correction and had arrived at the prime of his youth, and therefore he ought to discard this pedagogue and rely on those most accomplished of instructors—the gifts with which he had been born."

Nero refused to listen to these accusations, and seems to have been genuinely reluctant to part with the pleasant and courtly old philosopher, although the general criticism of his wealth and, particularly, his usury had made a retirement from office desirable, especially since Tigellinus, the successor of Burrhus, did not get on very well with him. Seneca put the proposition to the Emperor in the following manner.[9] He said that Nero had showered such honours and riches upon him that he simply did not know what to do with them; and what had he done in return for Nero except help him somewhat in his studies? Yet Nero had enriched him to such an extent that he could only ask himself how it all happened, and how his upstart name had come to rank amongst the great. As a philosopher professing to be satisfied with scanty means, was it right for him to walk majestically through magnificent houses and gardens, and to handle untold riches, putting out vast sums at interest? His only excuse was that he could not politely have refused Nero's gifts.

"But now," he went on, "both of us have filled up our measure: you, of all that the bounty of a sovereign could confer upon his friend; I, of all that a friend could accept from the bounty of his Emperor. Every addition can only furnish fresh materials for envy; and though envy, like all earthly things, lies prostrate beneath your towering greatness, it weighs heavily on me. I need your help. I am tired. I am unable any longer to sustain the weight of my riches. I want your protection. Tell your stewards to take over the management of my fortune, and annex it to your own. Don't think that I shall thereby be plunged into poverty; for, having rid myself of those things which expose me to envy, I shall be able to apply once more to the cultivation of my mind that time which I now waste in the care of my houses and gardens. Do this for me, and it will redound to your glory that you had elevated to the highest rank one who can be content with the lowest."

To this earnest appeal—earnest because he was truly troubled, and longed for his lost peace of mind—Nero modestly replied that the memory of the favours Seneca had bestowed upon him would never perish while life remained. What were the gifts of riches, estates and houses, he asked, as compared with those Seneca had conferred by his teaching and his never-failing friendship and advice? "I am ashamed," said the Emperor, "to be able to instance mere freedmen who were more greatly enriched than you have been; and, indeed, I have cause to blush that a man who holds the highest place in my esteem does not as yet transcend all others in the gifts made to him. And," he added, bitterly, "if you give back your wealth to me it will not be upon your sacrifice and your retirement that the tongues of all men will be employed, but upon my supposed greed and cruelty. Your behaviour will certainly form the theme of public applause, but it will hardly reflect any honour upon your character to reap a harvest of glory for yourself from an action which will bring infamy upon me, your friend." [10]

Tacitus, of course, treats these imperial sentiments as sheer hypocrisy; and when he adds that Nero then tenderly put his arm around his old friend and kissed him, he says that the Emperor was trained by habit to hide his hatred under the guise of honeyed words. But Nero did not hate Seneca: he loved him—the fact is perfectly apparent; and he refused to allow him to retire. All that he would concede was that Seneca should in future give more time to his philosophic studies, and should abandon the outward symbols of power—the train of attendants and the holding of audiences—on the pretended score of ill-health. "Have no fear of calumny," he said in bringing the interview to a close; "I would rather die than harm you." [11]

The philosopher's partial retirement was followed by a sharp action on Nero's part. Tigellinus, anxious to prove his devotion in his new office, reported to the Emperor that Sulla—husband of Antonia, Octavia's half-sister—who had twice before been accused of treason, and had been banished to Marseilles as already recorded, was again plotting a rebellion, and was in close touch with the troops in Gaul. Nero had always suspected Sulla, but until now had been content to leave him alone. At this news, however, he took sudden fright: Sulla was so closely related to Octavia; and Octavia, he was well aware, was seething with rage against him for having sent her away from the palace. Moreover, his wife Antonia, being the elder daughter of the late Emperor, may well have been felt to confer upon him a certain right to the throne. Sulla's name, he was told, carried the utmost weight in Gaul; and the fact that his fortune had been dissipated, was reason enough, apart from anything else, to induce him to rebel.

Nero took swift action: he told Tigellinus to send men at once to Marseilles to put the traitor to death. In six days they reached the exile's house, immediately called him from the dinner he was eating, and executed him upon the spot, thereafter bringing his head back to Nero, as was customary in the case of a man beheaded for treason. Nero stared uncomfortably at the head, commented on his premature greyness, and then, looking closer, remarked: "Oh, I didn't know he had such a big nose," accenting the last word as though to imply that he would have spared him had he been aware of the fact beforehand.[12] It was one of his curious, grotesque jokes, recalling the remark he made at the sickbed of his aunt Domitia; and if we observe that life was cheap then, and severed heads a usual sight, we shall have said all that there is to be said in excuse.

This execution was followed at once by that of Nero's other close relation and rival, Rubellius Plautus, who, it will be recalled, had been ordered to retire to his estates in Asia Minor. It was Tigellinus, again, who opened Nero's eyes to the danger of a rebellion in that quarter; and though this new Commander of the Guard ultimately proved to be such a scoundrel that any villainy may well be believed of him, there is no reason to suppose that he had trumped up this charge against the exile. Tacitus [13] says that Rome was full of rumours of an insurrection, the report being that Plautus was conspiring with Corbulo, the Commander-in-chief of the great Roman army in the East, and that the troops and populace were about to take up arms against the Emperor; and Tigellinus, in this case, only did his duty in warning Nero of his peril.

Though Plautus is described as an arrogant and rather degenerate idler, [14] he was admired by the conventional elements in aristocratic Roman society as one who conformed to the strict patrician etiquette [15] which

Nero so often outraged; and he was earnestly desired by them as Emperor, if only because he did not sing. His mother Julia, widow of Caligula's eldest brother, Nero, was daughter of Drusus and Livia, this Drusus being the son of the Emperor Tiberius. Thus, in view of the tendency in the imperial family of Rome to pay particular respect to the female line of descent, Plautus had a real claim to the throne; and Nero had every reason to be afraid of him. Again and again this dangerous young man—now some twenty-eight years of age—had been accused of treason. It had once been thought, the reader will recall, that Agrippina was going to marry him in spite of his youth, and try to make him Emperor in place of her disobedient son; and later the rumours of his activities had obliged Nero to ask him to leave Rome. In Asia Minor, however, he had lived with his wife, Antistia Pollitta (or Pollutia), in the greatest luxury and state, being enormously wealthy; and now the information placed before Nero stated that he was boasting that he was the only hope of the old aristocratic party.

Tigellinus was therefore instructed to send sixty men by sea to arrest and execute him, taking with them a certain court chamberlain, named Pelago, to see that the sentence was properly carried out. The father-in-law of Plautus, however, heard of the sentence of death, and dispatched his freedman in a faster vessel to warn him, and to tell him that if he were to act promptly and raise a rebellion he would find plenty of men in Rome ready to espouse his cause. Plautus, however, refused to take any action, being encouraged, some people thought, to await his fate with quiet dignity by two Stoic philosophers, one of whom, Musonius Rufus, afterwards became celebrated and was the teacher of the great Epictetus. It is possible, of course, that Plautus was in love with his wife, and knew that an attempt upon the throne would mean that he would have to divorce her and marry Octavia as soon as he could dispose of Nero, in order to improve his claims to the imperial office.

The troops sent by Nero, at any rate, found him, one noon, stripped and unconcernedly doing his daily exercises; and he was instantly butchered, in the presence of his wife, who flung herself upon the body, her clothes being drenched with his blood. These clothes she afterwards preserved as a memorial of the tragedy, and thenceforth she never ate more food than would keep the breath in her body, and, taking the blood-stained garments with her wherever she went, "devoted the remainder of her life to unrelenting sorrow," [16] and, it may be supposed, to undying hatred of Nero.

The Emperor then sent a letter to the Senate, stating that both Sulla and Plautus had been proved to be traitors, and remarking what a terrible business it was to preserve peace in the Empire. The Senate thereupon deleted the names of the two men from its roll of honour, decreed public thanksgiving for Nero's safety, and organised a grand procession through the streets of Rome to mark their joy at the removal of these turbulent personages. Tacitus, of course, says that this was sheer mockery; but I fancy that the danger had been very real and that for some time past these harassed statesmen had been nervously discussing the chances of civil war and its menace to their lives should they happen to back the wrong horse.

Tigellinus, who had quickly pushed his colleague, Fenius Rufus, into the background, had made himself indispensable to Nero by having helped him to nip these two rebellions in the bud, and he seems to have told his master that sharp and drastic action of this sort was incumbent upon a ruler. Soon he made Nero see that the throne was surrounded by lurking dangers, and that a firm hand was required in ruling so vast an Empire. It was all very well to spare people's lives and to behave as mildly as a Seneca or a Burrhus would have had him behave; but there was more to be said for being feared.

The new rôle of tyrant rather appealed to Nero at the moment. Perhaps Poppæa had told him that he was too soft-hearted, too spiritless, in fact—especially in regard to the matter of the divorce of Octavia. Why should he not boldly divorce her, and marry the woman he loved, he asked himself? Was he not lord of the earth, able to do whatsoever he wished? His subjects should learn that, artist though he might be, and a hater of bloodshed, he was nevertheless a man not to be trifled with. Tigellinus was right: an Emperor must be feared as well as loved. It was to him a new conception of his position and of himself; and though he proved to be unable to live up to so ruthless an ideal, and soon slipped back to clemency, his dramatic heart just now was stirred by it. He would sternly look into Octavia's private life, he told himself, and, should he find anything traitorous in it, he would cast her off.

Tigellinus, excitedly helped by Poppæa, at once undertook this secret enquiry; but the result of their investigations proved a surprise to all concerned. Octavia had always been supposed to be morally above reproach; but now one of her ladies gave information that the Empress had a lover, an Egyptian flute-player named Eucerus; and that she had once been made pregnant by him, but had managed to produce an abortion.[17] At this, Tigellinus cross questioned all her household, putting some of them actually to torture. One of his victims, a woman named Pythias, to whom torture was being applied, spat in his face, and uttered a remark which became famous in Roman history,[18] but which, owing to the greater decency of our own times, cannot now be repeated save in so far as one may convey its significance in the paraphrase: "My mistress's body is a great deal cleaner than your speech, Tigellinus!"

It was now the month of April (A.D. 62); and the evidence against Octavia being insufficient to act upon, Nero called off the enquiry prior to leaving Rome for the summer. Poppæa was in despair; her marriage was still as far distant as ever, and her youth was passing. But now, as though in answer to her prayers, nature intervened. In the first days of May she became certain that she was going to have a baby; and no sooner had Nero learnt the fact than he threw all caution to the winds, and, in the wildest excitement, prepared to divorce Octavia, not on the ground of a problematic unfaithfulness for which, in any case, he could hardly blame her, but on the kindlier charge of barrenness, which carried with it no moral stigma. He was thrilled at the thought that he would soon be a father. He had longed for a son to be his heir; and perhaps he was beginning to wonder whether there were something wrong with him, since neither Octavia, nor Acte, nor Poppæa, nor any other woman with whom he had had such relations, had ever become enceinte.[19]

Tigellinus and most of his other intimates were all for the divorce; and they seem to have told him that if Octavia were to resist she might justifiably be banished or executed for treason, since her ungoverned hatred of Nero was unconcealed and she had gone so far as to threaten to kill him. Seneca, however, was opposed to the plan, for he was afraid of its effect on public opinion; and, indeed, he was troubled by Nero's new impetuousness and severity. He had been shocked by the summary executions of Sulla and Plautus: he did not recognize this new Nero, who was so different from the gentle youth he had once guided. He did not know what had happened to him.

Yet what had happened is quite plain. Nero had discovered that the advice of Tigellinus was more effective than that of Seneca in clearing the air of its thunderclouds. He had been exasperated by the repeated rumours of rebellion against him, and had found that the drastic action which Tigellinus advocated had seemed to remove the menace much more thoroughly than the earlier clemency had done, and had removed it, moreover, to the applause of Poppæa. It had surprised and delighted him to find a new admiration for him in her eyes—that admiration by which women have throughout the ages inspired men to deeds of savagery. It had astonished him to notice how those sections of society which were opposed to him had hastened to show their loyalty since the execution of Sulla and Plautus, and how they had suddenly ceased to pay court to Octavia. For the first time in his reign he had realized both his power and the importance of a wholesome fear of him in maintaining that power; and he was determined that never again would he allow treason to go unpunished, nor rumours of treason to trouble his mind. In future he would strike quickly and ruthlessly. He had more than himself to think of now: he had to protect Poppæa and her unborn child.

Seneca discussed the whole matter with him, and in the tragedy *Octavia,* there is a conversation between them which may be recorded here, since, as has already been pointed out, this drama seems to have been based upon Seneca's recollection of what was actually said and done.

The philosopher had begged Nero not to proceed rashly in his new rôle of tyrant, but to submit all cases to the judgment of the courts; and to this the Emperor replied, "It is easy to be just when the heart is free of fear"—a remark which went at once to the root of the matter.

"Well, is not clemency the best cure for fear?" asked Seneca.

"Yes, but to destroy the enemies of peace is a ruler's first duty," Nero answered.

"To respect the lives of the citizens is a higher duty," said Seneca.

"It seems to me," replied Nero, "that a mild man is only fit to teach schoolboys."

"All the same, it is necessary to control the fiery impulses of youth."

"Thanks; at my age I have some sense."

"Well, I hope that all you do will be pleasing to the gods," Seneca sighed.

"The gods!" Nero laughed. "It would be silly to be afraid of the gods, since I myself make them." He was referring, of course, to the deification of the late Emperor Claudius.

"Fear them the more that they have given you so great a power," responded Seneca. "You often say that your luck will never fail you; but, I beg you, be more cautious in your trust in your luck. Fortune is a fickle goddess."

"It is stupid not to know what one may do," remarked Nero, thereby giving Seneca the opening for the philosophic reply, "It is right to do not what one may but what one ought."

"That may be, but I have learnt that the man who lies down, the crowd tramples upon," said the Emperor.

"No, it is he whom they hate that they crush," Seneca corrected. "You have been saying lately that the sword must protect an Emperor; but I think devotion protects him better. A Cæsar should be feared, of course, but more be loved."

"Yet men must be made to fear him."

"That which is compelled is always burdensome.

If you would have them respect your orders, give just orders."

"That is my own business," Nero retorted. "The sword will force respect."

"Heaven forbid!" Seneca exclaimed.

At this Nero turned upon him. "Shall I go on allowing people to seek my blood, then," he burst out, "so that, unavenged and despised, I may suddenly perish? Exile did not break Plautus and Sulla. Though they were far away their persistent hostility induced their agents to attempt to work my death; and even in their absence they commanded a great following in Rome. No!—let the sword remove those whom I suspect of treason. If Octavia hates me, let her die: let her follow the brother she loves! Those who are aiming at my power, whoever they may be, let them fall."

Seneca attempted to calm him by reminding him that the Senate and Roman society were devoted to him; but Nero replied scornfully that the Senate, at any rate, only showed affection to him through fear. "Why, your revered Augustus," he said with perfect truth, "killed so many people that the Forum reeked with blood. *He* maintained his power by fear: why should not *I?* But I am going to do more than that: I am going to provide a son of my own to succeed me"—which Augustus failed to do.

"I hope so," said Seneca, not yet knowing that Poppæa was with child. "Octavia will give you children of the Claudian race."

"Oh, will she!" Nero smiled. "You forget that her

mother, Messalina, was a harlot, a fact which puts her parentage in doubt; and, any way, the temperament of my wife was never compatible with mine."

"Have patience with her," Seneca begged. "When a girl is young, love is rarely shown, for modesty hides it."

"That was what I once hoped," said Nero, "but her hatred of me was soon revealed in her unloving manner, and in her face; and at length my hot resentment made me resolved to be revenged. And then I found a woman worthy of my love in birth and beauty, Poppæa, to whom Venus herself would yield, outshone."

"But, it is not beauty, it is honour, faithfulness, virtue, and modesty which should please a husband," Seneca replied. "It is only these things that abide: beauty's flower each passing day despoils. . . ."

Nero stopped him. "God has bestowed all charms upon one woman, and fate has decreed that thus was she born for me."

"Don't be too confident," Seneca warned him. "Love may depart from you."

"What!" cried Nero. "Why, man, I regard this love as the chief source of life to me, whence all happiness has its birth. It is a deathless thing. All I want is that the god of Love shall bring about our marriage, and with his fire join Poppæa to me for ever."

Seneca wrung his hands. "The people's disappointment will scarcely be able to endure such a marriage," he declared.

"Shall I alone be forbidden to do what all may do—marry for love?" Nero protested.

"The State always exacts the greatest from the highest," said the philosopher. "Bow quietly to your people's will."

"A nice government it would be in which the people governed their ruler!" Nero remarked.

"When their wishes are of no avail," Seneca told him, "people naturally become restless."

"Well, is it right to extort by force what their wishes cannot obtain?"

"It would be harsh to refuse them."

"It would be an outrage to force the Emperor."

"He should himself give way," said Seneca.

"Then gossip would say he had been conquered," replied Nero.

"Gossip is a trivial thing," Seneca declared.

"Oh, *is* it!" Nero answered, thinking of the philosopher's own dread of it. "It brings disgrace on many."

"It fears to touch the exalted."

"But it maligns them, all the same."

"It can easily be stopped," said Seneca. "Let Octavia's youth, and her faithfulness, break down your opposition."

"Oh, have done!" Nero exclaimed. "Your persistence makes me tired. Permit me to do what Seneca disapproves. I have long enough kept Poppæa waiting, for in her womb she bears a pledge and a part of me!"

At this news Seneca was staggered; and he saw that there was nothing further to be done. The worst had happened. Nero would divorce Octavia and marry Poppæa, and then there would be a revolution; for the people, for some unknown reason, if it were other than pity, had taken the strange and sullen Octavia to their hearts, and they disliked Poppæa as a woman older than Nero, and not of the imperial blood, who was trying to oust her. In great dejection the philosopher returned to the seclusion of his literary studies.

CHAPTER XIII

The Divorce of Octavia, A.D. 62—The Marriage of Nero and Poppæa—The Death of Octavia, June, A.D. 62—The Birth and Death of Poppæa's Daughter, A.D. 63—Nero's Public Appearance as a Singer, A.D. 64.

OCTAVIA was divorced, probably in the first week of May, A.D. 62, on the grounds of her sterility; and Nero, to mitigate her vexation, presented her with the vast wealth confiscated from Rubellius Plautus and with the house which had been occupied by Burrhus, and which, as the residence of that mighty personage, Commander of the Prætorian Guard, had become, one may suppose, a place of dignity and renown. There was perhaps a little irony in the gift; for, before the execution of Plautus, rumour had said that if Octavia were divorced she would marry him and attempt to make him Emperor; and, as to Burrhus, everybody knew that he had tried to induce Nero to keep her at the palace at any rate as nominal Empress.

Twelve days later, about the third week in May, Nero and Poppæa were married. Smart society was delighted, for Poppæa was its acknowledged queen; but the old-fashioned aristocracy and the common people were united in their annoyance, the former because of Poppæa's advanced views and go-ahead ideas as compared with Octavia's conservatism as a Claudian princess and a woman of seeming chastity, and the latter because Octavia had aroused their sympathy and Poppæa their dislike. On the day of the wedding the mob surged around Octavia's house, shouting their condolences; whereat she addressed them out of the depths of her hatred, skilfully inflaming them by telling them to go away, lest their love for her should arouse the anger of Nero and lead to their punishment. All she asked, she said, was that she might be spared a fearful death.[1]

On hearing of this commotion Nero took fright. He was not a coward by any means, but he was highly-strung, excitable, and inclined to make a great to-do about matters upon which his imagination had been at work. He therefore deemed it best to send her out of Rome to one of his villas in Campania, in the neighbourhood of the Bay of Naples, and, so that there should be no renewal of the disorders, he despatched a strong guard of soldiers with her. But the Roman mob made such trouble that presently he changed his mind, and, thinking it better to fight the matter out, allowed her to return to the capital. It was the end of May when she came back.

On hearing of her arrival at the house which had been assigned to her, the crowds were overjoyed, for, in these last few days, they had made a heroine and a martyr of her. They swarmed up to the Capitol, carrying figures of Octavia, wreathed in flowers, and placed them there and in the Forum. Some of them marched to the palace to thank the Emperor for acceding to their wishes in recalling her; but others, incited, it was believed, by Octavia, made their way thither for the purpose of booing Nero's new wife, and soon a wild riot had developed in which statues of Poppæa standing in the imperial gardens were overthrown and rolled in the dust.

Poppæa was terrified. According to the tragedy, *Octavia,* from which quotations have been made in the previous chapter, she was found by some of her ladies weeping and trying to hide. She said she knew that something terrible was going to happen, for she had had a dream in which, as she was holding her dear Nero in her arms, the room seemed to be filled suddenly with mourners, and Agrippina appeared, threatening her. Then Poppæa's first husband came to her rescue and kissed her, at which Nero sprang at him and killed him.

After describing this dream she wept again, and begged her ladies to join with her in prayer that her marriage might endure; and it was while they were praying that the scared servants burst into the room saying that the mob was attacking the palace in earnest, and that the soldiers who had been sent out to quell the riot had been driven back. This mob, it was said, was in the mood for any crime: the people were shouting that Octavia must be restored, and were cursing the name of Poppæa, saying that if their wishes were not granted they would burn down the palace.

According to Tacitus,[2] Poppæa rushed to Nero, and clung to his knees. "I am not in a position to argue about the rights and wrongs of our marriage," she cried. "I only know that it is dearer to me than my life; but that life is now threatened by these people out there.

who pretend to be townsmen, but are really Octavia's own slaves and dependents. They only want a leader, and they will overwhelm us. If they are unsuccessful now, and see that they cannot make you take her back, they will find another husband for her, and attack your throne itself under his leadership. They want my life. What crime have I committed? Whom have I hurt? Is it because I am about to give a son and heir to the family of the Cæsars? Do the people prefer that a child of Octavia's adultery with her Egyptian flute-player should be palmed off one day as yours?"

Nero was frantic. The sanctity of his imperial position had never been thus outraged before: he had hardly known what it was to be anything but a hero. He was furious that Poppæa should have been given this shock, lest it should ruin her hope of becoming a mother; and though reinforcements hastily brought up by Tigellinus at last drove back the attackers and restored quiet, his rage was fearful to behold. "This is treason!" he told Tigellinus. [3] "These people shall suffer for their sacrilege, and Octavia, who has incited them, shall pay for it with her life." It was evident, he declared, that the people were utterly ungrateful for all his acts of kindness to them, and were indifferent to the peace and prosperity he had given them. "They shall be made to suffer," he cried, "for having dared to lift their hands against Poppæa, my wife, and for having tried to drag her from my bed. Justice demands the head of Octavia!"

"But what proof is there of her guilt?" asked Tigellinus.

"The people's anger is the proof," Nero replied, and, so far as one can see, he spoke the truth.

"Could anybody have stopped their madness?" Tigellinus questioned.

"Octavia could," said Nero, striking his breast. "She must die, so that this terror at my heart may be stilled."

Next day, however, when his anger had cooled, he decided to spare her life, but to banish her to the little island of Pandataria (Ventotene), some thirty-five miles off the coast of Campania. Strabo tells us that the island, though small, was well-peopled; and the fact that it was due east of Baiæ and the great naval port of Misenum, and was within sight of the popular island of Ænaria, caused it to be well in touch with civilization. Upon it stood the villa once occupied by Julia, Nero's great-grandmother, daughter of Augustus, when she had been exiled by that Emperor; and here, too, the elder Agrippina, Nero's grandmother, had lived in banishment at the command of Tiberius. The last imperial occupant of the house had been Julia Livilla, sister of Nero's mother, who had been sent there by Claudius.

Probably at dead of night Octavia was arrested, and, surrounded by soldiers, was placed in a carriage and driven off along the Appian Way. The port of Misenum was the destination, and on the party's arriving there some time next day, letters were delivered to the admiral, Anicetus, Agrippina's executioner, who was still in command of the fleet, ordering him personally to conduct Octavia to the island and to see to her proper housing there.

This he did on about the second or third day of

June; but when, afterwards, he went to Rome to report, he brought Nero an amazing story which Tacitus, of course, believes to have been a prearranged lie, but which I see no reason to doubt. He said that during the night-voyage from Misenum to Pandataria, Octavia, who had always been friendly with him, had made such passionate overtures to him, after they had dined and drunk together in her cabin, that he, being still but human if no longer young, had availed himself of her unchastity, only to find, next morning, that what she desired was not his grizzled love but his veteran help in raising a rebellion in the fleet.

Nero could do no otherwise than order Anicetus instantly to be deprived of his honours and banished to the island of Sardinia, and it is this fact which makes it unlikely that the accusation had been arranged beforehand. It is true that Anicetus lived the rest of his days in unmolested contentment, Sardinia being quite possibly a place in which he had no objection to spending the evening of his life; but it is highly improbable that he would have voluntarily accepted disgrace, exile, and his Emperor's "exceptional detestation of him," as Tacitus tells us, so that a false charge of adultery might be brought against Octavia, especially since the all-sufficient accusation of treason, of inciting the fleet to mutiny, was one upon which alone Nero could quite well proceed against her.

The wretched affair is all too apparent. Octavia, daughter of the passionate Messalina, and herself a little queer in her head, was not the chaste and virtuous woman described by those who afterwards idealised her memory so as to vilify Nero's; and when, in the extremity of her anger and fear, she found herself in the custody of an old friend, Anicetus, she inevitably employed those methods to win him which her mother, Messalina, her stepmother, Agrippina, and many another imperial lady, to her knowledge, had used to gain their ends. She knew that half Rome was on her side: if only she could induce Anicetus to espouse her cause, there might be hope of dethroning Nero. Or, failing that, it was at any rate within the admiral's power to make her lot upon the island of Pandataria very much more comfortable than it would otherwise be. Therefore she made him drink with her, and, excited by her last desperate hope, drew him to her, and enfolded him in her trembling arms. And when Anicetus, impelled by his duty, reported to Nero her verbal efforts to win his support, the story led him on to relate also her actions; and, suddenly, unintentionally, he inculpated himself, and saw Nero freeze before him into a jealous upholder of the honour of the imperial house.

The Emperor at once issued an edict stating that though he had divorced Octavia on account of her barrenness, he had since discovered that once—while he was absent from her, I suppose—she had found herself about to have a child by a lover—the reference apparently being to the Egyptian flute-player—and had produced abortion; and that now she had corrupted Anicetus in the hopes of engaging the fleet in a conspiracy against the throne. It was then the seventh of June, and that same day he sent messengers to Octavia to tell her, as her mother Messalina had been told before her, that death was the only escape from dishonour, and that, as wife of the Emperor, convicted of adultery and conspiracy, suicide in the traditional manner was incumbent upon her.

These messengers arrived at the island on June 9th. When they told Octavia that she must kill herself she cried out that she was no longer Nero's wife but only his sister[4]; and as such, she could not be accused of unfaithfulness— an argument which suggests an admission of guilt. She appealed to the spirit of Germanicus to save her; she invoked the name of Agrippina, saying: "If you had lived you might have made my married life a misery, but you would not have doomed me to destruction." Then, screaming and half fainting, she was forced to lie down while a doctor opened her veins; and, to prevent her struggles to rise, she was presently bound hand and foot. But in her cold and fainting condition, the blood did not flow freely, and, as was customary in such cases, she was carried into the sweating-room of the baths, where the heat and lack of air accelerated her death. Her head was then cut off and brought back to Rome, that being the gruesome custom of the time. It was shown to Poppæa, who, being a woman, had no objection to seeing the severed head of a rival; but Nero did not care to look at it. The Senate, as usual, sent its congratulations, and thank-offerings were made in the temples for the Emperor's safety and for the prevention of the incipient rebellion; but the people murmured, and the popularity of Nero, until these last few weeks unassailed, suffered a temporary collapse.

Shortly after this died Pallas, once the lover of Agrippina and the most powerful man in the Empire; and rumour of course said that Nero had poisoned him, but the charge is quite unfounded. He was also believed by some to have poisoned off his freedman and secretary, Doryphorus, at about this time, because he had opposed his master's marriage to Poppæa; but such accusations were easy to make in that age of medical ignorance, and no notice need be taken of them except in so far as they reveal the trend of public opinion. Suetonius,[5] it may be mentioned, states that this Doryphorus was Nero's elder partner in his early experiments in homosexual vice, and records a certain incident to prove it[6]; but this is the kind of story in which Suetonius delights, and all that need be said is that, if the gossip were true, a dose of poison might have been the only suitable gift from one who had long since developed into a normal and manly lover.

Poppæa's baby was born on January 21st, A.D. 63, at the family seat of the Ahenobarbi at Antium, the house in which the Emperor himself had first seen the light. Nero at this time had just passed his twenty-fifth birthday, and Poppæa was nearly thirty-two. The child proved to be a girl, and was named Claudia in honour of the Claudian house to which Nero belonged as grandson of Germanicus and adopted son of Claudius. He does not seem to have been in the least disappointed that it was not a boy, for Tacitus says that his joy and excitement exceeded anything known to have been experienced by man.[7] He was, in fact, quite off his head with delight. He at once conferred the title of

Augusta both on the baby and on its mother. He gave orders for the building of a temple to Fecunditas; he instructed the goldsmiths to make two images of Fortuna, a goddess particularly associated with Antium, which were to be placed upon the throne of Jupiter Capitolinus; he instituted games and contests in honour of the Claudian and Ahenobarban families; and so forth. The Senate, which had already placed the womb of Poppæa by prayers and vows under the protection of the gods, came down to Antium in a body to offer its congratulations; and everywhere there were festivities and fêtes.

A fortnight later, on February 5th, however, a disaster occurred in Campania which seemed to presage misfortune for the imperial house. A violent earthquake partly destroyed the towns of Pompeii and Herculaneum, shook Nero's villa at Baiæ, and was perhaps felt as far north as Antium.[8] This, of course, was not the convulsion which finally destroyed these cities, that being sixteen years later, in A.D. 79; but it was sufficiently serious to cast a gloom over the whole country. At about the same time the amphitheatre constructed by Nero in the summer of A.D. 60 for his "Neronia" games, was struck by lightning and burnt to the ground; and the metal statue of the Emperor which stood therein was melted into a shapeless mass. Shortly after this came news that the Roman arms had suffered great reverses in Armenia, and that while Corbulo, the popular general appointed by Nero, was otherwise engaged, and was covering himself with glory, another general, the cowardly Cæsennius Pætus, had been obliged to retire. This latter personage arrived back in Rome in the early spring, expecting nothing but a court-martial and death; but Nero, whose anger seems seldom to have been directed against any but traitors, freely pardoned the miserable man, saying, with a smile, "I do so at once, because, knowing your timidity, I am afraid that if I keep you in suspense, you will die of fright." [9] The incident is a clear indication that, even in his new rôle of tyrant, Nero was unable to overcome his incorrigible good-nature.

The Emperor and Empress, with their baby, returned to Rome on April 10th; but in the middle of May the little Claudia Augusta died, and Nero's grief is said to have been as immoderate as had been his joy at her birth. The baby was deified and enrolled amongst the company of the gods; but utter gloom descended upon the imperial household here on earth, and for a long time there was no sign of the old gaiety at the palace. At length Nero turned for relief to his music and his poetry, just as he had done in the troubled times which had followed the death of Agrippina; and soon he was hard at work, composing long poems and setting them to music, studying his dramatic effects, practising his harp-playing, and sparing no pains to improve his voice. More than ever these arts took possession of him, and during the next months he thought of little else. He worked with his teacher, Terpnus, for hours on end; he lay on his back, doing breathing-exercises, with a heavy lead weight balanced upon his chest; he consumed quantities of onions and oil in the belief that they were good for his voice, and, indeed, before singing to his friends he ate nothing else.

It will be as well to consider here the question of his abilities as a singer. Tacitus, writing about fifty years after Nero's death, says that his voice was so powerful that the garden-theatre where he sang at his "Festivals of Youth" was too confined for it[10]; and this may well be believed, for he was a most powerfully built man, with a mighty chest and a neck like a bull's. The same author admits, too, that his audiences appeared to be enraptured by his singing.[11] Suetonius, however, writing a few years later, says that his voice was "naturally neither loud nor clear"; but he, too, admits that he was "prodigiously applauded."[12] Dion Cassius, a century and a half after the time of Nero, says that "according to tradition he had but a slight and indistinct voice," and that his audiences were inclined to laugh at him;[13] and Philostratus, still later, makes fun of his abilities, and declares that though he was a poor singer, he was a better singer than emperor.[14]

These later authors, however, are not to be regarded as authoritative in this matter; for in their day Nero had become, in the view of the aristocracy, almost a mythical figure, half criminal and half buffoon. After all, it is hard to believe that the enthusiasm his singing aroused when at last, as we shall presently read, he appeared on the stage before a public audience, was merely due to a desire to flatter. The Romans were pretty outspoken, and did not hesitate to express their disapproval even when their lives were endangered by so doing. For example, when Caligula, the most fearful of tyrants, gave his patronage to unpopular competitors in the races, the public howled him out of his box, and showed their annoyance by refusing to attend the next events; and the Emperor Claudius knew what it was to be booed by the crowd. Thus, it is almost inconceivable that the public would have applauded so wildly had Nero's abilities not been exceptionally great; and when we find, as will be related in the following chapters, that during the last two years of his life he was singing nearly every day to enthusiastic Greek audiences, and was being hailed throughout Greece as the very god of music, and that, after his death, people still talked about "the songs of the Master," the conclusion can hardly be avoided that he was, indeed, a great artist.

During the autumn and winter of A.D. 63, that is to say when time had dulled the edge of his sorrows, he constantly sang to his friends at those "Festivals of Youth" at which the fashionable young votaries of the Arts entertained one another, and made their elders do likewise, in Nero's private theatre. But soon he was encouraged by them to seek a still larger audience, and at length, in the spring of A.D. 64, came the day when, in an agony of nervousness, he made his public début.

For this momentous event he selected the annual musical festival in the city of Naples, because the population there was largely Greek, and he had always felt that he had more in common with the warm, artistic Greek temperament than with the repressed and conventional Roman. His plan was to go over to Greece, after this festival, in the hope "of winning some of the crowns (i.e. diplomas) which conferred such signal honour and were traditionally held sacred, so that, with this accession of fame, he might win the favour of Rome."[15]

It may be contended that the audience at Naples consisted partly of his friends and followers, or that it was controlled by soldiers ready to cuff anybody over the head who did not applaud; but the fact remains that the performance was a tremendous success. Refusing to make use of his imperial status in this world of Art, Nero, Emperor of the Earth, came onto the stage wearing the ordinary garb of a professional musician, and, like a paid singer, addressed the audience in the prescribed manner, bending his knee and humbly requesting them of their kindness to give him their attention. The conservative-minded Romans gasped; but the democratic and understanding Greeks went wild with enthusiasm, and, after he had sung through his appointed programme, they called him back again and again.

On the subsequent days of the festival he sang for hours on end: in fact, he could hardly be dragged from the theatre even to go to bed, and in the mornings he was back again long before the appointed time. When the interval for dinner was announced each day he would not leave the building, but had some refreshments brought to him in the orchestra; nor could he refrain from calling out to those of the audience who were still in their seats, telling them that as soon as he had had a bite, and something to drink, he would give them a tune which would really please them. On the last day an earthquake rocked the theatre during one of his songs;

but Nero, who was lost to the world, continued to sing, and, his artistic ecstasy being mistaken for bravery, he received a renewed ovation. No sooner, however, had the audience left the building than the whole theatre collapsed. Fortunately, nobody was hurt, and Nero spent the next day in composing a poem of thanks to the gods on this account, which he set to music and sang to his friends.

A fleet of ships from Alexandria, the capital of Egypt, happened to be in the harbour during the festival; and the officers and men, eager to see the Emperor who was also their hereditary Pharaoh, had swarmed into the theatre, and had applauded his songs in their own peculiar style—a rhythmic clapping and stamping, and a kind of organized chanting somewhat in the manner of a modern college yell. Nero was so thrilled by it that he made them teach his own people how to do it; and he instituted a body of applauders, said to have been five thousand strong, divided into local groups, who, combining the Alexandrian method with the Roman, practised three kinds of applause in particular, known as the *bombi,* or "humming," the *imbrices,* or "tapping" (like hail on a roof), and the *testæ,* or "banging" (like utensils clashed together). The members of this body were chosen for their physique, and were remarkable for their fine heads of hair. They were extremely well dressed, and wore rings on their left hands; and their leaders or trainers received large salaries.

From Naples Nero set out for Brindisi (Brundisium), where he was to embark for Greece; but he broke his journey at Benevento (Beneventum), an important city standing on the Appian Way—the high-road from Rome to the south—about a day's march back from Naples. This happened to be the home of Vatinius, the court fool, a deformed little cobbler, whose wit had won him not only wealth but the power to do an immense amount of harm by acting as a sort of secret agent for his master. He was now giving a gladiatorial show at his own expense in his native city, and Nero honoured the exhibition with his presence; but Vatinius, it seems, took the opportunity to report to the Emperor some details of a conspiracy of which he had got wind.

It will be remembered that Lucius Silanus, Nero's cousin, who had been betrothed to Octavia, killed himself when Agrippina broke off the engagement in A.D. 49, accusing him of immorality; and that his brother, Marcus Junius Silanus, was poisoned by her immediately after Nero's accession in A.D. 54, for fear that he would attempt to claim the throne, his mother being Æmilia Lepida, granddaughter of Julia, the daughter of Augustus. There remained a third brother, Decius Junius Silanus, called Torquatus, who had lately been closely watched, since the traditionists had been paying him court as a possible leader of a revolution. With the exception of Nero himself, Torquatus and his nephew, the son of the murdered Marcus, were the only male representatives of the Julian house; and now that Rubellius Plautus and Sulla were dead, Torquatus was the recognized claimant to the throne should anything happen to its present occupant.

No sooner had Nero decided to sail for Greece than

a plot was hatched for his dethronement; and Torquatus was reported as having all his plans ready for a coup. He had given away huge sums as bribes to his supporters; he had staked his last penny on his chances of success; and he had even nominated his cabinet and had trained his household officials to assume immediately their imperial duties.

The shock of the news brought Nero suddenly and painfully back to earth from his artistic flights; and he was obliged to abandon his trip to Greece. For some months past he had quite forgotten to sustain the character of a tyrant feared by all. He had been too much occupied with his music to trouble about the rod of iron which Tigellinus had thrust into his hand; and it was with evident distaste that he resumed the rôle, and ordered the arrest of some of the small-fry in the conspiracy, so that they might be cross-questioned. Torquatus, learning that the plot was discovered, at once committed suicide by opening the veins of his wrists in the usual manner; but on hearing of his death Nero, who, for the ten years of his reign, had left him unmolested and had even seemed to like him, sadly remarked: "However guilty, however justly hopeless of clearing himself, he might have been, I should have let him live, had he waited for my clemency." [16] Tacitus, of course, supposes that that was a lie: perhaps it was, but even so it indicates that Nero's desire to be feared and dreaded had given place once more to a wish to be loved. The plaudits of his audiences were still ringing in his ears, and the camaraderie of the theatre seemed now to be a finer thing than the awful isolation of a tyrant's throne.

He then returned to Rome, angry at being thwarted in his musical career, longing to be acclaimed, and worried by these continuous and upsetting plots against him; but soon his friends and admirers diverted his mind from his troubles by urging him to devote himself to his art. Nero therefore announced that he would sing at his garden-theatre across the Tiber, and that "those who desired to hear him" might come there. But at this everybody made such a rush to secure admission, so as "to listen to his heavenly voice," [17] that there was soon found to be no chance of accommodating them. Then, strange to say, the soldiers of the Prætorian Guard, perhaps prompted by their commander, Tigellinus, begged him to hold immediately, and to sing thereat, a second "Neronia"—the musical contest he had instituted in A.D. 60 as a quinquennial festival, and which was not due to be repeated until the following year.

To this Nero at once agreed, and, the contest being announced, he entered his name upon the list of musicians who proposed to contend, but insisted that the time of his appearance should be put to the ballot as would be done in the case of the others—so tremendously was he in earnest, so eager to be judged on his merits alone in this sphere of Art, which he regarded as so much grander than that of material dominion. He was almost prostrated with nervousness at the thought of this first appearance before the Roman public; for whereas in Naples he had sung to a friendly and easy-going Greek audience, in this Roman contest he would have to abide by the strict rules of the competition, and would have to sing before a bench of professional judges. The rules were very exacting: no singer was allowed while on the stage to clear his throat, blow his nose, or use a handkerchief to wipe the perspiration from his face; and the marks were assigned according to the clarity of the voice, its power and sweetness, and the absence of exertion in producing it. Not only this: he would also have to compete in the solo performances of classical epics, wherein the singer, in the manner of our Grand Opera, had to act a part. Fortunately for him, his popularity had recently revived; and he was encouraged by many proofs of public approval.

There is nothing in Nero's life which brings him before us so sympathetically as his diffidence and anxiety over this and his other public appearances as a vocalist. Was his voice really "divine"? he kept on asking himself. Was it true that there had been nothing so moving heard before? Would Rome confirm the opinion of Naples? One pictures the red-headed young man, handsome, herculean, deep-chested, bull-necked, feverishly practising his scales and his breathing-exercises, memorizing his lines and studying his dramatic gestures, as he rehearsed such epics as "Canace in Childbirth," "The Blinding of Œdipus," "Niobe," and "The Frenzy of Hercules." At a rehearsal of the last-named, a young Prætorian recruit suddenly seeing his Emperor bound in chains, as the rôle required, dashed to his rescue and nearly killed the actors who were pretending to guard their prisoner. On another occasion, when Nero, dressed as a woman, was groaning in the rôle of

Canace, a bewildered soldier whispered to his officer: "Good God!—what's the Emperor doing?" "Ssh!" was the reply. "He's having a baby."

When the day of the contest arrived he was shaking with fright. His turn came in the late afternoon. He stepped upon the stage attended by some officers of the Prætorian Guard, one of whom carried his harp, and by a group of his intimate friends; and he addressed the judges in the most deferential terms, saying that he had done all he could to perfect his voice, but that accidental mistakes were bound to occur, which he hoped they would overlook, and that the issue was in the hands of fortune. Some of the judges, therefore, seeing his nervousness, told him to be of good heart; but others, not knowing what to say, remained silent, whereat Nero whispered anxiously to his friends that he was afraid they were going to be hard on him. He then told a certain Cluvius Rufus, a man of high rank, to announce that he would begin by singing the story of "Niobe," which, apparently, was the longest item in his repertoire. He did not finish it until nearly ten o'clock at night, and then was so dissatisfied with his performance that he asked for a postponement of the contest so that he might accustom himself a little more to public appearances.

In the ensuing weeks he gave a series of recitals, and even sang at entertainments and musical-competitions got up by private people. "He always observed the rules of a competition most scrupulously," says Suetonius, [18] "never daring to spit, or wipe the perspiration from his forehead in any other way than with his sleeve.

Once, during the performance of a tragic song, he dropped the sceptre he was carrying, and, not quickly recovering it, was in a great fright lest he should be disqualified for the accident, and his confidence was only restored when his accompanist swore that it had not been noticed owing to the acclamations and enthusiasm of the audience." Whenever the prize was adjudged to him, he was so excited that he used to rush onto the stage and announce his victory himself, panting and smiling, and nearly in tears.

The time came, however, when the less enthusiastic elements in the Roman audiences grew to be somewhat bored with the Emperor's performances, which were so frequently repeated, and which became something of an ordeal, particularly to the unmusical, owing to the fact that Nero, elated by the applause, could not be induced to stop giving encores. His strength was inexhaustible, his memory prodigious, and his repertoire enormous; and when he had sung all the classics, he used to sing his own compositions, some of which were very lengthy. His particular group of friends and followers, being hero-worshippers, never wearied of listening to him; and the common people, also, maintained their enthusiasm. But to those persons who feared to stay at home lest they should seem disrespectful and yet found nothing to stir them in these musical performances, the tedium must have been almost insupportable.

At last the flagging interest had to be whipped up by soldiers stationed about the theatre, and by his trained bands of applauders; and the doors were closed so that no one should leave the theatre until Nero had retired, which he generally did with the promise that he would be with his dear public again at the earliest opportunity. This locking of the doors resulted in the most astonishing situations. People compelled to leave the theatre by necessities which need not be specified, bore their discomfort as long as they could, and then either dropped quietly over the walls at the back of the tiers of seats, or pretended to faint so that they might be carried out; and on one occasion a man, bored to distraction, feigned death and was conveyed from the auditorium as though for immediate burial. Once, too, a woman escaped by saying that she was going to have a baby there and then.

In these recitals and contests, Suetonius tells us,[19] "Nero's nervousness and anxiety, his keen desire to win the prize, and his awe of the judges, can hardly be credited." As if the other competitors were of exactly the same station in life as himself, he would watch them narrowly as they sang, try to gain their friendship, or disparage them behind their backs, or even quarrel with them when he met them, in the well-known manner of professional singers.

Meanwhile the whole court continued to pursue his favour by attending classes to learn music, singing, dancing, and acting. Society people thought it very smart to appear on the stage in the chorus, or to play an instrument in the orchestra; and even elderly men and women went in for acting or dramatic dancing as a means of entertaining their guests. One clever diplomat, who was about to give an important party, offered Nero a huge fee if he would sing at it; and by ranking the Emperor thus as a successful professional, whose voice was worth big money, paid him a highly appreciated compliment. Indeed, the astonishing fact begins to be apparent that Nero thought it far grander, far more praiseworthy, to be a great singer than a great Emperor; and, in view of this opinion of his, I do not feel that there can be any doubt that he was temperamentally an artist—a man deeply in earnest in regard to his art, having something within himself to express, something to tell mankind through the medium of music, which he deemed to be more important than empire. He used often to say that he would abdicate and retire to some Greek city, and there devote himself to his singing and earn his living thereby.

But if, then, he was truly an artist—highly-strung, dramatic, emotional, full of the importance of his calling, short-tempered and impatient of interruption, as artists invariably are—he must elude any judgment by an ethical rule of thumb. No jury of "twelve good men and true" can understand an artist.

CHAPTER XIV

The Palace as the Intellectual and Artistic Centre of the Empire—Nero's Proposed Journey to Egypt Postponed—The Great Fire of Rome, July, A.D. 64—The Persecution of the Christians.

THE court over which Nero and Poppæa presided was now the artistic and intellectual centre of the world; and, as has already been stated, the palace was overrun with artists and thinkers of all kinds. The Emperor himself had developed into a knowledgeable connoisseur, and was also a man of considerable reading and scholarship. Besides giving hours a day to practising his singing, he now devoted a great deal of his time to the writing of poetry, and it is said that his poems displayed his learning. It seems that his most famous composition was a long epic called the *Troica,* dealing with the fall of Troy[1]; but the work is now lost, as is another important poem named *Luscio.* It may be mentioned, too, that he is known to have written some excellent verses on the subject of Poppæa's golden hair.

In spite of his objection to the social traditions of an earlier age when applied to the circumstances of his own more enlightened day, he had a great love of the antique, and the glamour of Roman history thrilled him.

He began an immense work which was to include the whole story of Rome in a vast epic; but he was discouraged by the philosopher, Annæus Cornutus, who told him frankly that nobody would wade through it.

The Emperor was clearly a man of vast industry; and what with his singing-exercises, his gymnastics, his wrestling, his chariot-driving, his poetry-writing, his studies, and his official duties, there could hardly have been an idle hour in his hectic life. Himself an amateur sculptor of merit, he filled the palace with masterpieces in stone and metal, his love of the genius of the ancient Greeks being instanced by the fact that the statuette of an Amazon, the work of Strongylion, the famous Greek sculptor of the Fifth Century B.C. was carried about with him wherever he went. The beautiful Apollo Belvedere, and the Fighting Gladiator were found in his house at Antium, and the famous Laocoon comes from his palace in Rome. He greatly admired, too, a statue of Alexander the Great by the celebrated Greek sculptor, Lysippos, and in accordance with the fashion of the time he had it gilded over; in which regard it may be mentioned that this was an age of gilding and gold, of strong colours, and ornate decoration.

Being also a talented painter, he patronised that art, and gave important commissions, among others, to Dorotheus, the best mural decorator of the time. The fashion then was to depict huge figures and groups upon the walls of the main rooms and halls of important buildings; and in a palace in the Lamian Gardens on the Esquiline there was a painting of Nero no less than 120 feet in height. Tapestries were also very popular, and Nero paid a vast price for some such hangings from Babylonia, which Cato, a hundred years earlier, had purchased for a fifth of that price. Delicate vases and other *objets d'art* were bought by the Emperor for fabulous sums; and his plate and jewels were astounding in their beauty and intrinsic value.

Being eager to rid Rome of its unfortunate reputation for philistinism, and to make it the revered mother of the arts instead of culture's laughing stock, Nero encouraged the bringing of the world's artistic treasures to the city; and soon the palace and the great houses of the wealthy became veritable museums and art-galleries. There were many ancient temples and other buildings in the city which were worthy of admiration, and possessed the romantic charm of historic association; and of these Nero was immensely proud. He wished the capital to be also the world's throne of learning, and into its libraries he collected books from far and wide. Rome should be the new Athens, a second Alexandria; and to prove its right to that position he made the most of its history and its antiquities.

The luxury of the court, thanks to Poppæa, was unparalleled. When Nero moved abroad, hundreds of state carriages drawn by horses and mules shod with silver, driven by men dressed in scarlet, filled the road for miles; and the procession was headed by troops of picturesque African cavalry. The public entertainments given by the Emperor to the people were more magnificent than ever before; and it was his habit to fling to the crowd little balls each marked with a number which, when presented at his treasury, entitled the holders to presents ranging from a small piece of money to a mansion and estate, and including such gifts as food, clothes, jewels, pictures, slaves, animals, ships, and so-forth. The curious story that he used a large emerald as a kind of eyeglass through which to watch the performances at the theatre has never been explained.

When he first met Poppæa, it will be remembered, he was still under the influence of his thrifty mother: the palace was poorly furnished, the pennies were counted, and Nero deemed it a breath-taking extravagance to sprinkle a few drops of expensive perfume upon his friend, Otho. Now, however, he had learnt from Poppæa and her friends how to live recklessly, and his artist's heart had responded to the training so fully that no man on earth could rival him in his gifts and his expenditure. "He now thought," says Suetonius,[2] "that there was no other use for money than to spend it lavishly, and he regarded those who kept their expenses within bounds as mean and sordid, while he extolled as noble and generous those who squandered all they possessed. He praised his uncle Caligula because he had in so short a time run through the vast fortune left him by Tiberius; and he himself was lavish beyond all bounds." He rewarded talent with enormous gifts: to Menecrates, a musician, he gave a house and estate worthy of the greatest in the land[3]; and to Spicillus, a skilful gladiator, he made a similar present. When he gambled he staked huge fortunes on the throw of the dice.

The description of a fête organized for him in Rome by Tigellinus one night in the early summer of this year, A.D. 64, has come down to us. In the lake of Agrippa, near the Pantheon, he constructed a raft, carpeted with purple, upon which a gorgeous banquet was served, while vessels "striped with gold and ivory" towed it gently about. Along one shore of the lake pavilions were erected, where those guests who were not with the Emperor upon the raft were entertained. On the opposite shore were booths in front of which nude dancing-girls and musicians entertained the company. During the evening many of the guests, both men and women, strolled round to these booths and talked to the girls, with the result that some improper incidents occurred; and the fraternizing of the richly dressed women of fashion with these naked little hussies who made a business of what the society ladies regarded as an amusement, led to much scandalous gossip.[4]

It will be recalled that after the musical festival at Naples Nero had wished to go over to Greece, but had been prevented by the great danger of a revolution in his absence. At Naples, however, he had met a number of Egyptians, as has been recorded; and it seems that some of these had asked him to come to Egypt to sing to the Alexandrians. He now made up his mind, therefore, to make the journey, taking advantage of the calmness of the Mediterranean at this time of year. The route usually chosen was that which, from Brindisi, passed across to Greece, and thence southwards along the Greek coast to Crete, being almost all the way thus far in sight of land. From Crete to the coast of North Africa about 150 miles of open sea had to be crossed, after which the route followed the coastline eastwards to Alexandria. It was not a perilous journey at this time of year, and one of the big triremes with three banks of oars could accomplish it in a fortnight.

Nero's mind was more easy now about leaving Rome, for his popularity in the capital seemed to be re-established. The acclamations of the audiences before whom he had sung had given him a feeling of confidence, and his own friends at court had idolised him to such an extent that, diffident though he was by nature, he believed himself to be enthroned in the hearts of his people high above the turmoil of politics and the whispers of sedition. He therefore issued an edict assuring the citizens that his absence would not be of long duration, and that while he was away the State would continue in its wonted peace and prosperity; after which he fixed the day of his departure, and, on its eve, paid a formal visit to the temples to pray the gods for their protection upon his travels.

But while he was in the temple of Vesta he happened to seat himself upon a bench, and, when he got up, the skirt of his robe became caught—a very bad omen—while at the same time a fit of dizziness, due, no doubt, to indigestion or a touch of the sun, caused him a momentary dimness of vision. The unusual sensation scared him, for he had hardly known any illness in his life; and, suddenly thinking that it was a warning from heaven of some peril before him, he began to wonder whether he was wise in going away.

The more he thought of it the more troubled he became, and at last, a few hours later, he abandoned the whole project.[5] He then issued a second edict stating that since every other consideration with him was overruled by his love for his country; since he had noticed the anxiety of the citizens in regard to his long journey and had remembered that they had complained even at his short absences, accustomed as they were to turn to him in all their troubles; and since the people of Rome were to him like his family circle whose wishes had to be considered, he had decided to give up his journey and remain near them.

At this, to the surprise of Tacitus who records the fact, the people were obviously relieved and delighted; and this historian attributes their sentiments to their fear lest in his absence there might be mismanagement and a scarcity of food, or something of that sort, as well as the inevitable cessation of the usual gaieties of the city. These, no doubt, were the chief reasons for their rejoicing; but it is clear that amongst the masses at this time Nero was still beloved by the majority and tolerated by the others, and that his proposed absence was genuinely regretted. He had now reigned nearly ten years, and was twenty-six years of age; and thus far, it will be agreed, there had been little to suggest that he was to become in history the most hated of men. The divorce and death of Octavia had certainly made him temporarily unpopular, but he had re-established himself, and public opinion seems to have decided that Octavia, obsessed by hatred, had been quite as impossible as, formerly, Agrippina had been. Nero's government had been good, the people acknowledged; the country was prosperous; civil wars and rebellions had been frustrated by quick and drastic action; and the Emperor himself, if unconventional to the point of eccentricity, was, in their opinion, undoubtedly an extraordinary genius, a wonderful singer, a patron of the arts and sciences, an enthusiastic racing man and athlete, and, above all, a friend of the common people.

Thus far. . . . But now there occurred that terrible catastrophe, the burning of Rome,[6] as a consequence of which the whole picture of Nero was smudged over not only in his own time but in subsequent history. The Emperor was spending the height of the summer at his sea-side palace at Antium, thirty-five miles from the city, when, during the night of July 19th, A.D. 64, a conflagration broke out in the wooden sheds and small shops at the east end of the Circus Maximus, at the foot of the Palatine and Cælian Hills, where great quantities of oil and inflammable materials were stored; and the flames and sparks, carried by the south wind, soon set the circus itself alight, for, after a long period of hot and dry summer weather, the wooden seats and beams were like tinder. Thence the fire spread along the valley between the Palatine and Cælian Hills towards the Esquiline, and also along the wider valley between the Palatine and Aventine Hills; and in either direction the dry woodwork of the crowded houses provided fuel for the blaze. The narrowness of the streets allowed the flames to leap quickly from the burning buildings at one side across to those as yet unharmed on the other, while the intricate windings of the lanes and alleys carried the fire in unexpected directions.

For six days the city blazed; and then, when the catastrophe was thought to be over, the flames broke out again and continued their destruction for three days more. These nine days provided scenes of horror far transcending those when the smaller Rome of four and a half centuries earlier had been burnt by the Gauls, far transcending, also, those of the great fire of London in 1666 which lasted only four days. Panic soon took hold of the citizens, and during the first days of the disaster the confusion was appalling. The screams of the women and children, the cries and shouts of the men, were incessant; and the noise and smoke, the crashing of the buildings, and the heat and glare of the leaping flames, bereft the people of their senses. Distractedly they ran to and fro, often finding themselves hemmed in when they had waited too long in helping the aged or infirm to escape, or in salvaging their goods. In the sudden panics and rushes which occurred as street after street was attacked, scores of people were trampled underfoot or suffocated; scores more were burnt to death as they attempted to rescue their friends or relations or to save their belongings; and it is said that many went mad and flung themselves into the flames which had destroyed all they loved or possessed, or stood dumb and motionless while their retreat was cut off.

To add to the confusion, thieves were soon at work, assaulting and robbing the householders who were carrying their treasures into the streets; and Dion

Cassius states that soldiers and police, bent on plunder, were sometimes seen themselves to set fire to the houses of the wealthy so that they might steal the valuables which they were pretending to save.

The flames early began to move up the eastern and southern slopes of the Palatine Hill, on the summit of which stood that vast conglomeration of buildings of various ages which formed the straggling Palace of the Cæsars[7]; and when news was brought to Nero that the conflagration could not be extinguished, and that the palace with all its treasures and works of art, was in danger, he decided immediately to go back to the city and take command of the operations. The wind being from the south, clouds of smoke must have been blowing across the Palatine Hill from the fires which raged all around its southern slopes and which cut off the approaches to it on that side; and Nero, obliged to enter the city on the north-east, must have made his way to the undamaged Forum—which lay just under the north-west end of the Palatine—and thence up the steep incline to the palace, with the smoke beating into his face, and the scorching wind driving the smuts and sparks into his eyes.

The place was already doomed, and Nero, one may suppose, could do no more there than give orders about the removal of some of his works of art; and then, coughing and half choking, he seems to have returned to the Forum and to have made his way around the Capitoline Hill and across the Tiber to that part of the city which was south-west of the conflagration and therefore free of smoke. He appears to have made his headquarters there, in his pavilion in the gardens where his private theatre was situated, and where he used to hold his "Festivals of Youth"; and from its roof, during the following days of terror, he watched his palace go up in smoke and flame. The loss of hundreds of ancient books and documents of extreme value and interest, the destruction of paintings and works of art, appalled and infuriated him. One by one, he saw the famous buildings and monuments of antiquity, of which he had been so proud, devoured by the flames—the ancient temple of the Moon, on the northern slope of the Aventine, overlooking the Circus Maximus, built by King Servius Tullius in the early days of Rome's history; the temple and altar dedicated to Hercules by the mythical Evander the Arcadian, at the foot of the Aventine; the shrine supposed to have been built by Romulus himself, Rome's founder, to Jupiter Stator; the original temple of Vesta, on the Palatine, believed to have been erected by King Numa at the dawn of the city's history, and containing the Household Gods of Rome; the ancient palace of Numa, nearby, afterwards restored by Augustus: all these and many others were burnt.

Fortunately so much of the Forum and Capitol was built of stone, and protected by walls and open spaces, that these famous groups of buildings escaped; but the fire, licking the southern end of the Capitoline Hill, passed north-westwards into the Campus Martius, and there destroyed, amongst other buildings, the great amphitheatre of Statilius Taurus, erected about a century earlier. Meanwhile, however, the eastern wing of the conflagration was checked at the foot of the Esquiline—to the north-east of the Palatine—by the drastic destruction of the houses in this area, by Nero's orders, so that the fire should have nothing to feed upon; but, just when hopes were high that the end had come, the flames broke out in the area between the northern end of the Forum and the southern slopes of the Quirinal, where the house and gardens of Tigellinus were situated, and these, likewise, were burnt, together with all the surrounding buildings. It was not until July 28th that the fire was finally extinguished, and by that time about two-thirds of the city had been reduced to ruins and ashes, and the losses in human lives, in property, and in works of art and learning, were incalculable.

The measures which Nero took for the relief of the distress during the height of the blaze, and afterwards, were regarded by his contemporaries as very praiseworthy. He gathered the refugees together in that part of the Campus Martius which was free from danger, housing them in the Pantheon, the Baths of Agrippa and other large buildings there situated, and erecting temporary shelters for them in his own private gardens across the river, in the Vatican neighbourhood. As soon as the fire had passed from any area he placed guards there to protect the ruins on behalf of the owners of the property; and he instituted a search for the dead at his own expense. He brought up stores from Ostia and other towns to feed the homeless, and he reduced the price of corn to bring it within reach of those who, though impoverished, did not need to be fed by the State. During all these days of horror he worked with indefatigable energy, directing these operations and attempting to calm the terrified people; and although he had heard that those who had conspired against him on previous occasions were now taking advantage of the catastrophe to arouse hatred of him and to bring about his death by assassination, he went fearlessly about his business, appearing amongst the distracted people without guards or companions and showing himself everywhere, in the smoke-darkened daytime or in the flame-lit night, in complete contempt of danger. The loss of Rome's ancient treasures, and particularly the destruction of nearly everything he loved in his own palace, must have very nearly broken his heart; and he worked in rage and despair.

Standing one night on the roof of his pavilion beside his garden-theatre,[8] across the Tiber, where he had established his headquarters, Nero was so moved by the distant spectacle of the burning city that, in the manner of a professional mourner at a funeral, or one of the bards of old, he took his harp and began to sing a sort of dirge, a lament for Rome, likening the disaster to the burning of Troy; and his powerful voice, carried by the wind, came to the ears of the frenzied refugees gathered on the outskirts of the gardens, who soon spread the story that the Emperor, thrilled by the beauty of the conflagration, had dressed himself up as a professional musician, and was callously singing songs in his theatre.

The tale took hold of the unbalanced minds of the

people, and on all sides the question was asked whether Nero himself had fired the city in order to provide a dramatic setting for the singing of his own poem on the siege of Troy. Recalling the behaviour of the thieves who had set fire to houses, as has been recorded above, for the purposes of robbery, people declared that they must have been Nero's agents; and the fact that the wise measures taken against the spread of the fire had involved the apparently ruthless destruction of undamaged buildings gave colour to the ridiculous tale that the conflagration had been deliberately planned. Some said that Nero had wished to destroy the city so that it might be built again on a more elegant plan, others that he just wanted a big thrill; but, whatever might have been his supposed reason, the belief that he was the cause of the disaster gained ground. Maledictions were heaped upon him, or, rather, upon those who were thought to have set the city on fire at his orders, for, as Dio says, the actual name of the Emperor was not cursed; and the result, Tacitus tells us, was that all his exertions and all his deeds of bravery were overlooked. Somebody said that once when the Greek quotation "After I am dead let fire devour the world" had been uttered in Nero's hearing he had replied "No; let that happen while I am still alive." Somebody else declared that it had always been the Emperor's fixed purpose to make an end of Rome and of the Empire during his lifetime, and that he had often remarked that Priam of Troy was happy in that he had seen his city burnt up in the same hour in which his reign had ended.

The absurdity of supposing that Nero was responsible for the catastrophe is recognized, of course, by most modern historians[9]; but in ancient times only Tacitus, amongst our authorities, is bold enough to state that the Emperor's guilt "is not certain." Today, however, the picture of Nero as author of the disaster, standing upon the roof of his palace, and "fiddling while Rome burnt," is impressed upon the popular imagination, and will hardly be obliterated by the facts that he strove desperately to extinguish the blaze which was destroying all that he most valued, that his palace was in flames, and that his dirge was sung, elsewhere, to the accompaniment of a harp, not a fiddle.

Nero was cut to the quick by these accusations, the more especially because the evidence did certainly suggest that the fire, or rather, its spread, was not wholly accidental; and, eager to exonerate himself, he held an enquiry into its origin, as a result of which his agents brought an accusation against the Christians, at that time a rapidly increasing sect, under the intellectual leadership of Paul of Tarsus, whose members were largely drawn from the ranks of slaves and aliens.

This new sect, being wholly misunderstood, was held in the greatest odium throughout those parts of the Roman Empire where it was known,[10] the chief criticisms against it being that its doctrines were socialistic and anarchical, and were taught to slaves and to the scum of the earth, putting insubordinate ideas into their heads, and that its members were haters of the human race, who believed that the end of the world was at hand, and that all mankind, except themselves, were to go into perdition. Nero's agents knew little about the origin of the sect, but they understood that it had been founded by a man called Christus or Chrestus,[11] who had been executed in Judæa some thirty years ago; and that this personage had said that he would return in glory to judge the world, for which event the members of the sect were excitedly waiting, performing secret rites meanwhile, and shunning the society of other men, whose happy indifference pained them, and whose gods they cursed.

Their leader, Paul, a Jew but a Roman citizen, had appealed to Nero when accused of sedition in the provinces, and had been brought to Rome in about A.D. 61 or 62, where, there is reason to suppose, he was acquitted of the charges against him, but was later arrested again, after which he was permitted to live in his own hired house under the eye of a soldier, and was not forbidden to preach to the numerous Christians, many of whom were slaves in Nero's own household.[12] There was another man, Peter, also a Jew, who was one of the leading spirits amongst them. The Emperor Claudius, it was recalled, had banished the members of the sect from Rome, because they "were continually causing disturbances"[13]; but others had taken their place, and were now quite a multitude.

Enquiries seem to have shown that when the city was blazing these weirdly misanthropic persons had been in a state of ecstasy, crying out that the end was at hand, that Rome, like Babylon, was being destroyed by this Christus, who would at any moment appear above the smoke and flames of the conflagration to take the elect to heaven and to annihilate Nero and all his people; and it was said that when they were asked by their distracted fellowmen if, then, they were glad to see Rome burn, they had replied that this was heaven's fiery vengeance for which they were waiting, nor would they raise a hand to extinguish the flames.

There can be little doubt that this must have been their attitude, for our Lord's immediate return was, in actual fact, the mainspring then of the faith, the Second Coming being the supreme event which the elect were hourly expecting; and so great a disaster could not possibly have been thought by these fervent souls to be anything but the beginning of this tremendous advent for which they had yearned so long. Jesus was coming! The heavens would open now at any moment, and they would see Him riding upon the fiery clouds. These blazing houses, that stupendous bonfire upon the Palatine as Nero's palace was consumed, the mansions of the mighty belching smoke and flames, the temples of the old gods crashing in ruins, the shrieks of the panic-stricken crowds—all these things were just what their leaders had told them to expect at the approach of their divine Lord and Master.

When the behaviour of these Christians was reported to Nero it seemed to him almost certain that they had originated the fire, or, by their magic arts—for he believed in such arts—had called it down upon the people they hated. He himself was being cruelly accused of having burnt the city; but here, evidently, were the real culprits, who, apart from the general destruction, had deliberately burnt the two amphitheatres, the symbols of the pleasures of this world, then his palace, and then the house of Tigellinus, who was equally hated as the Emperor's chief agent. "These persons were commonly called Christians," says Tacitus, "and were hated for their enormities. The founder, whose name was Christus, had been punished as a criminal by Pontius Pilate in the reign of Tiberius, but the pernicious superstition, repressed for a time, broke out again not only throughout Judæa where the mischief originated, but in the city of Rome also, whither all things horrible and atrocious flow from all quarters, and where they are encouraged. Accordingly, first those were denounced who confessed; then, on their information, a large number were convicted, not so much on the charge of burning the city as of hating the human race."[14]

"Those were denounced who confessed." The phrase has been the subject of much argument. What was it that they confessed? That they had set Rome alight? This cannot be, for Tacitus is quite clear that, though guilty in general, they were *wrongly* accused of incendiarism. Simply, then, that they were Christians? This, too, is unlikely, for Tacitus makes it equally clear that they *were* accused, although wrongly, of incendiarism. It seems to me more probable that what they admitted was that they had made no attempt to extinguish the flames, because they had believed at the time that the conflagration was the signal of the coming of Christ in glory, and still believed that it was one of the signs of the beginning of the end. It is probable that they admitted their satisfaction at the disaster, and implored their accusers to turn from their earthly allegiances, and to enter the service of Christ, while yet there was time. These admissions, voluntarily made *before* arrest, as the words of Tacitus imply, were doubtless understood to be tantamount to confessions of guilt—brazen confessions, they seemed, accompanied by no feeling of shame, no sense of wrong-doing, but revealing a fervour, an exultation, which was sufficiently uncanny to suggest the influence of Magic—that dreaded power in which Nero and almost every other man firmly believed.

It is not known with certainty that St. Paul was at this time arrested and executed, but he is traditionally believed to have been one of the first to be put to death, probably by decapitation, and the evidence points to this conclusion.[15] Tacitus says that his followers were punished with terrible tortures, and that they were made the subjects of sport by the furious Romans, some of them being worried to death by dogs set upon them, others being lynched or crucified, and yet others being burnt as they were supposed to have burnt the victims of the fire. St. Clement, writing some thirty years after the event, adds that some of the accused women were fastened to wild bulls and dragged to death.[16]

Tacitus goes on to relate that the executions of certain of the condemned by retaliatory burning were carried out after dark in the Emperor's own gardens, so that the spectacle was like a display of nocturnal illuminations; and he says that Nero organized some chariot races on this occasion, and freely mixed with the people, who, however, were not pleased at his barbarous severity, and "felt pity for the victims, guilty though they were and deserving to be made examples of by capital punishment." This story, however, is not confirmed by Suetonius, who merely states with approval that "Nero inflicted punishments on the Christians, a sect of people who held a new and odious superstition"; and in the Apocalypse, which, as will be explained presently, was written four years later, there is no reference to these burnings, though the victims are said to have been beheaded.[17] The horror, however, may possibly be fact. Tigellinus, who acted for the Emperor, was probably beside himself with rage at the destruction of his beautiful mansion and gardens. Nero, too, was furious at the devastation of Rome and at the loss of his palace and its treasures; he was exasperated at being accused, himself, of having planned the conflagration; and he may have been determined both to let the people see what he thought of such criminality, and to give them an unforgettable lesson in retaliation. He had always been troubled by the thought that the vast number of the slaves living in Rome might give them courage to rise against their masters; and on one occasion, when there had been a mutiny in the house of a certain rich man who had, as a result, been killed, Nero had refused to intervene when all the slaves in that household were condemned, innocent and guilty alike. These Christians were largely slaves, and it was essential, he may have felt, to terrorize them. Arson, moreover, called for particularly severe punishment. Those who burnt property should themselves burn: there must be no pity for the incendiary.

The consequent executions were hardly as terrible as the burning of Christians by Christians in the Middle Ages; they were hardly as terrible as the punishments inflicted by the otherwise saintly Marcus Aurelius upon the Christians of his time, whom he flung wholesale to the wild beasts in the arena; but they were terrible enough, and one can no longer regard Nero as the mild and self-controlled ruler revealed by his previous record—a man who put to death only those who were actually conspiring against his life, but, with these exceptions, respected human life in a degree which is remarkable in his bloodthirsty age. His only excuse is his exasperation, his anxiety, and his nervousness in these days of disaster, when a fiendish plot seemed to him to have been afoot: with his own eyes he had seen men and women trapped in their houses and burnt to death, their shrieks were still ringing in his ears, and his heart had no pity for those whom he believed to have perpetrated this enormous and unspeakable atrocity in the name of this Christus who was said to have been the gentlest of men.

The punishment of the Christians—the persecution as we call it now—was short and sharp; and during the remainder of the summer the survivors, though living in terror, gradually came to realize that their danger was passing and that they were not to be exterminated. Paul, their beloved leader, and scores of their friends, were dead, but Peter was living, and was passionately encouraging them to hold fast to the faith, and to believe still that the Master would soon come now to take them to their heavenly home. Their disappointment was intense that the conflagration had failed to be the sign they had expected, and that He had not come; but still they hoped, still they gazed at the sky with longing eyes, daily watching and praying for the advent of their Lord.

It was at this time—in August or September, perhaps—that Peter wrote the epistle which is incorporated in the New Testament,[18] addressing it from "Babylon" —the contemptuous name by which Rome was now known to the little band of the faithful—to the Christians in other parts of the world, but intending it, no doubt, to be read also by the remnant of his immediate flock. The letter is a passionate appeal to them not to be frightened, and not to deny the name of Jesus Christ, though for a season they are heavy of heart and though their faith be tried with fire indeed. He begs them to create no disturbances, but to fear God and honour the Emperor, whom, therefore, he must have regarded as well-meaning, and no fiend; and he tells those who are slaves to submit themselves to their masters. "If ye suffer for righteousness' sake," he writes, "happy are ye; and be not afraid of this terror, neither be troubled. Be ready always to give an answer to every man that asketh you a reason of the hope that is in you, having a good conscience, that, whereas they speak evil of you, as of evildoers, they may be ashamed that falsely accuse you."

"The end of all things is at hand," he says, "therefore watch and pray. Beloved, think it not strange concerning the fiery trial which is to try you, as though some strange thing happened to you; but rejoice, inasmuch as ye are partakers of Christ's sufferings. If ye be reproached for the name of Christ, happy are ye; and if any man suffer as a Christian, let him not be ashamed. When the chief Shepherd shall appear, ye shall receive a crown of glory that fadeth not away. Humble yourselves therefore under the mighty hand of God, that he may exalt you in due time, casting all your cares upon him, for he careth for you. Be sober, be vigilant; because your adversary the devil, as a roaring lion, walketh about, seeking whom he may devour; whom resist, steadfast in the faith, knowing that the same afflictions are accomplished in your brethren that are in the world. But the God of grace, who hath called us unto his eternal glory by Christ Jesus, after ye have suffered a while, make you perfect, stablish, strengthen, and settle you."[19]

Peter did not long survive the writing of this letter. Tradition says that he was arrested and executed at about this time, and there is no reason to suppose otherwise.[20] It is said that on the day before his death he had the opportunity to escape, but that he did not avail himself of it, feeling that the Master perhaps needed, for the sake of the faith, "to be crucified a second time in his little servant."[21] He was bound to a cross, but, at his own request, he was placed ignominiously head-downwards, so that there should be in his death none of the sacramental majesty which was already attached to the uplifting of Jesus Christ upon the immemorially sacred tree.[22]

CHAPTER XV

The Rebuilding of Rome, A.D. 64—The Golden House—The Detection of the Great Conspiracy, April, A.D. 65—The Deaths of Piso, Seneca, Lucan, and other Conspirators.

DURING the autumn and winter of this year, A.D. 64, Nero was kept busy designing the new Rome, a task which must have interested his artistic mind intensely; and, indeed, so drastic were his alterations, so novel his plans, that they must have given colour to the belief that he had burnt the city in order to be able to effect these improvements. In the Rome that was no more, most of the streets had been extremely narrow, and many of the houses five and six storeys high; and thus very little sunlight ever penetrated into the lower rooms. But now Nero laid down broad streets, and limited the height of the houses to sixty or seventy feet,[1] so that the purifying sunshine should fall upon the roadway for some hours of each day—a fact to which the old-fashioned townspeople much objected, for they were used to the dim, evil-smelling warrens of the former city, and deemed the direct heat of the summer sun far more dangerous than the noisome obscurity of the ancient alleyways.

To meet this objection, it was arranged that there should be pillared colonnades along either side of the streets, and in front of every house, in order both to give the townspeople shady promenades and to lessen the danger of fire. These colonnades, which were a complete novelty in Rome, Nero built at his own expense. Space was left for numerous courtyards, gardens, and open squares in every street. Rows of houses, or even houses semi-detached, were ruled out: every house had to have its own four walls, and had to be separated from the next by a narrow passage-way. The lower part of every building had to be built of fire-proof stone, the upper storeys being supported upon masonry arches, no wooden beams being allowed below the second floor. Every house was to have its own back yard, and in this yard every householder would be obliged to keep all the necessaries for extinguishing outbreaks of fire, including, of course, a good supply of water. Water-conduits were laid down so that every house should be supplied; and a Water Board was instituted whose inspectors were to see that the flow was nowhere intercepted or otherwise diminished. The number of street fountains, also, was greatly increased.

The débris of the ruined houses was partly used to raise the level of certain low-lying areas, and partly shipped down the Tiber to Ostia, where it was distributed over the unhealthy marshland at the river's mouth. This clearance also was done at Nero's private expense, by way of compensation to the owners of city property for the loss of ground consequent upon the widening of the streets and the providing of open spaces. The Emperor then offered to give from his own treasury a sum of money to every landlord, proportionate to his standing and fortune, on the condition that the new buildings were finished by a certain date.

In the excitement of this creation of a new and beautiful Rome, Nero flung his money about like the reckless artist he was; and when he had exhausted the city's funds, he opened a subscription list to which the cities and communities throughout the Empire were invited to contribute. Meanwhile, he devoted his private fortune to the building of a palace which should be really worthy not only of the Cæsars but of himself, an artist; and so much ground did he appropriate for its park that he was jestingly charged with wishing to take in the whole of Rome and its suburbs, and to push the city ten miles out into the country. He was accused, of course, of having stolen the property of private owners in order to increase the size of this park; but there is every reason to suppose that he paid for what he took, and certainly the sums he spent from his own fortune on the rebuilding of Rome were unquestionably so vast that he is to be excused if he appropriated some land in return. The new palace, which he called the *Domus Aurea,* "The Golden House," was placed, as before, on the Palatine Hill; but on the eastern side of this hill the new park extended down the slope, across the valley, where later the Colosseum was built, and up the western side of the Esquiline and the northern spur of the Cælian.

This palace and park constituted an estate so original, so completely unlike anything Rome had ever seen before, that the citizens did not know what to make of it, and the Emperor Vespasian, a few years later, contemptuously swept the whole thing away. The gardens of that time were, as a rule, strictly formalized, clipped hedges, stiffly arranged trees, and architectural effects being in vogue; but Nero's park was laid out with a rural landscape as its motif, and, from its description, one cannot fail to see in it an ancient attempt at an æsthetic ideal of natural simplicity astonishingly out of keeping with the spirit of that age of heavy grandeur.

In the valley east of the Palatine, where once the dank and ramshackle houses of a slum built upon a marsh had stood, he dug a beautiful lake, one end of which was bordered by sylvan glades and reedy shallows where the wild duck nested, while on the opposite shores he erected picturesque groups of rural buildings designed, it would seem, to suggest the fortuitous growth of years. Behind these buildings were cornfields, vineyards, meadows and pastures; and beyond these again he planted thick woods, here and there relieved by areas carefully planned to look like natural wildernesses, rocky and overgrown with grasses and wild flowers. Into these woods and open spaces he introduced herds of deer and other wild animals, while flocks of sheep and goats, tended by flute-playing shepherds, wandered lazily about. In the meadows were cows and horses, and all the creatures of the farmyard were to be seen in the vicinity of the homesteads beside the lake.

He seems, in fact, to have wished to create a magical little world of rural and sylvan beauty here in the heart of the busy metropolis, a place of dreams and rustic quiet, a miniature Arcady, wherein he might roam about like a yeoman of old, pottering around his meadows and his farms, and where, sauntering into the woods, he might be alone with nature, or, in poetic mood, might listen to the notes of the birds and to the shepherds' songs in the distance, and, in imagination, might hear the pipes of Pan.

It was a most curious and, at that time, an entirely original conception of a palace park; and it suggests that, in spite of the magnificence of his ways, Nero had always yearned for a country life. Nobody but a poet would have thought of turning the center of imperial Rome into a Garden of Eden; and if the charm of the picture is for us a little diminished by its association with the affectations of certain "simple-life" movements, we must remember that an idea is always more arresting at its birth than in its dotage.

The palace itself seems to have been a strange mixture of simplicity and magnificence, and one must suppose that the north-western side of it, which overlooked the Forum, was designed with grandeur, while its eastern aspect, facing towards the park, was built in a style more suitable to the rural landscape. A triple colonnade, perhaps encircling the Palatine, provided shady promenades a mile in length, and the entrance hall was so vast that it was able to house a colossal bronze statue of the Emperor a hundred and twenty feet in height, [2] the work of Zenodorus, the leading sculptor of that period. Large areas of the building were "overlaid with gold and adorned with jewels and mother of pearl," says Suetonius; "and the banqueting halls were domed, and sections of the ceiling, inlaid with ivory, were made to revolve and scatter flowers, while other parts contained pipes which sprayed perfumes upon the guests." There was one dining-room which was circular, and its dome could be revolved so that its windows caught the sun all day long in winter time, or excluded it in summer.

Many of the walls of the rooms were decorated with paintings by Amulius, the greatest painter of his time; but, on the whole, the palace must have been much less ornate than was to be expected. It was probably characterized by a certain artistic bareness which permitted concentration upon some one particular feature; for Tacitus says that the ornamentation of the rooms was not so much an object of attraction as the view from the windows, and a few years later the wife of the Emperor Vitellius scoffed at the small amount of decoration and at the scantiness of the furniture.[3] Vast numbers of works of art, however, were collected from Greece and other parts of the Empire, and brought to Rome for the embellishment of the palace and the city; and it is said that Nero's seizure of famous statues was bitterly resented by the municipalities from which they were taken. A commission of art-experts literally pillaged the cities of Greece; but if we are to censure Nero on this account we must also pass adverse judgment on those who gathered together the art treasures in the Louvre, the British Museum, and other European galleries. Nero's public and private expenditure on the rebuilding of the city and the palace was, as has been said, enormous; and his donations to those who had suffered by the fire, and also to poets, musicians, painters, sculptors, actors, athletes, charioteers, servants, and friends who, both now and at other times, had seemed to him to merit reward, were rapidly emptying his coffers. Before he died he had given away, out of his own fortune, 2,200,000,000—nearly two and a quarter billion—*sesterces,* the value of which can best be estimated by recalling the fact that the entire fortune of Pallas, reputed to be the richest man in Rome, was three hundred million *sesterces,* or about a seventh part of Nero's *gifts* alone.[4] He thoroughly enjoyed spending his money; and the gratitude of those who had been enriched by his generosity went far to re-establish his popularity.

But the traditionists still hated him, and found in this reckless expenditure justifiable cause for anxiety. If he were allowed to go on throwing his money about in this insane fashion, they said, he would soon be bankrupt and would begin to pillage private fortunes and the public Treasuries. Something must be done quickly. Moreover, he was now singing again in public, and thereby bringing disgrace upon the imperial office. His building-plans, too, were converting Rome into the likeness of one of those artistic Greek cities which they so greatly despised. These white, colonnaded streets, these squares and public gardens, these tinkling fountains, were corrupting the morale of the people, softening them, making them luxurious and un-Roman. Yes, indeed, something must be done quickly.

But these traditionists were not the only people who were hostile to Nero. In the Emperor's immediate circle there were many persons whom he had offended or annoyed, or whom Poppæa had irritated, if only by her good fortune. When a man is idolized as Nero was, when there is a group of fervent admirers for ever hedging him around with their hosannas, there must always be those who are exasperated by this form of bigotry, and who begin to sneer at its object. And in the case of Nero, there must have been many a singer, many a poet, many an athlete, who was jealous of him and who disliked to be compared unfavourably to him; and there must have been also many a man who felt that the Emperor had overlooked his merits or had blocked his progress.

For some months past conspirators, actuated either by this kind of chagrin and jealousy, or by more reputable motives, had been discussing a plot to assassinate him. Nero had heard vague rumours of this plot at the time of the fire, but, with great bravery, he had ignored them. He was accustomed to plots against his life. His mother, Agrippina, his wife, Octavia, his close relations, Rubellius Plautus, Sulla, Torquatus Silanus, and several others, had wanted to kill him; but he had struck first and thus had saved himself, and he was prepared to strike again.

He knew that trouble was afoot, but he was wholly unprepared for the terrible discovery which he made in the middle of April, A.D. 65, just when this new and lovely Rome was rising out of the ruins of the old, and when his popularity seemed to have been restored. Full of vital energy, bursting with wonderful plans for the future, intoxicated by the joy of creation, thrilled by his ever increasing ability to express himself in song and poetry, he seemed to be upon the crest of his life; and it was at this moment that the shattering blow fell—the discovery of a plot to murder him in which no less than forty-one of his closest friends or attendants were involved.

The revelation of the existence of the plot was made on the very morning of the day upon which he was to have been murdered. As the first light of dawn spread across the sky, a certain Milichus, freedman of a wealthy senator named Flavius Scævinus, appeared at the gates of the palace in the Servilian Gardens, just outside Rome on the road to Ostia, where the Emperor was staying during the building of the Golden House; and after some difficulty in inducing the guards to take him seriously, he was conducted in to Nero, who, it may be supposed, was aroused from sleep to hear the grave tidings which the man declared to be so urgent.

Milichus stated that his master, who was notorious for his indolence and his depraved life, had lately appeared to be sobered by some serious matter which was upon his mind, and had been in suspiciously close consultation with Caius Calpurnius Piso, a famous and popular senator who was widely believed to be aiming at the imperial throne, and with his friend Antonius Natalis. Yesterday, said Milichus, Scævinus had been shut up with Natalis for many hours, and then had come home and had made his will, after which he had drawn from its scabbard a particular dagger which, as he had often told his friends, was a sacred weapon dedicated to some great deed, and had instructed Milichus to sharpen it. An exceptionally sumptuous dinner was ordered, during which Scævinus, very preoccupied and grave, had given freedom to his favourite slaves and had presented money to the others. Finally, he had ordered bandages and appliances for stanching blood to be prepared.

Milichus said that he could not speak with certainty, but that, putting two and two together, he had formed the opinion that an attempt on the Emperor's life was to be made at the opening of the games in the newly built Circus Maximus which was to take place that day. He had talked the matter over with his wife, he said, and she had advised him to tell his suspicions to Nero for what they were worth.

An order for the arrest of Scævinus was at once issued, and when he was brought to the palace he was confronted with his freedman, but defended himself so well that Nero began to doubt the story, and sent for the wife of Milichus to find out whether her tale corroborated that of her husband. This it proved to do, and the woman urged that Natalis, with whom Scævinus had been closeted so long, should be sent for. Her advice was taken, and when Natalis and Scævinus, examined in separate rooms, were each told to give an account of their interview, their two stories were found to disagree entirely. Thereupon Natalis was shown the instruments of torture, and was told that unless he immediately confessed he would be put to the rack; and at this he seems to have replied that he needed no such inducement to tell the truth, but would gladly reveal the whole plot, in which he had played no guilty part. He then dumbfounded Nero by impeaching not only Piso and Scævinus but also the venerable Seneca who, he declared, was deep in the conspiracy against his friend and former pupil. Nero could hardly believe it. Seneca!—the man whom he had loved and enriched, and who was now supposed to be devoting his time to philosophic meditation and to the quiet writing of ethical and moral essays. For the moment he was too stunned to take any action against the philosopher; and he turned to the re-examination of Scævinus, telling him that the game was up and that Natalis had confessed.

At this Scævinus, vainly hoping to gain a pardon by making a confession, named several of his accomplices; and as, one by one, the Emperor's most intimate and trusted friends were impeached, Nero's heart must have sunk, under this rain of cruel blows, into the very depths of disillusionment and distress. History has recorded the names of forty-one conspirators—eighteen other senators besides Scævinus himself, seven private gentlemen, eleven military officers, and four women; but it seems that the wretched man did not at the moment betray the entire number. The leader of the conspiracy proved to be the above-mentioned Piso, against whom Nero had often been warned but whom he had refused to suspect. Piso owned a charming villa at Baiæ, and the Emperor, when he was at that resort, was in the habit of visiting him there with the greatest informality, for he loved the beauty of the place and enjoyed the company of its owner. Piso, like Nero, was a great lover of the stage, and used to act tragic parts with distinction at the musical and dramatic entertainments which he and the Emperor organized in Rome or Baiæ. He was a man of culture, famous for the magnificence of his parties, and, if somewhat lax in his morals, a brilliant personality nevertheless. For many weeks during the past winter Nero had been staying at Baiæ, and had seen a great deal of this man: in fact, he felt so much at home in Piso's villa that he always dispensed with all his attendants and guards, and used to bathe there, or amuse himself in the gardens or the house, like any private individual. Piso's wife was a charmingly scandalous lady of great beauty and little chastity; and Nero had always much enjoyed her unconventional society.

With dismay the Emperor now heard that the conspirators had originally proposed to murder him at Piso's villa while he was thus unguarded; and he shuddered to think how near to death he had been. Scævinus, however, confessed that Piso had objected to this plan, because he felt that an assassination which was supposed to be an act intended for the good of the State, ought to be openly carried out in Rome, and not in a private house, where the breaking of the sacred laws of hospitality would cause the deed to seem like a dastardly murder. Nearly all those in the plot, however, were members of the fashionable society gathered then around the Emperor at Baiæ; and many of them, Scævinus said, had felt that it was very risky to postpone the assassination until the court's return to the capital.

Their anxiety had been increased, moreover, by the action of a lady named Epicharis, who was in the plot, and who was the mistress of Mela, Seneca's younger brother. One day at Misenum, she happened to be talking to a high naval officer, one Volusius Proculus, and, finding that he was nursing a grievance against the Emperor, she urged him to foment a mutiny in the fleet, telling him that there were those who would make it worth his while, and revealing the existence of the conspiracy, though without naming the conspirators. The officer, in duty bound, reported the conversation to Nero, who caused Epicharis to be arrested and examined; but she declared that Proculus must have been dreaming and that she knew nothing about any such plot. Instructions were therefore given that she should be kept under surveillance, and there the matter dropped; but Scævinus now admitted that the lady was indeed one of the conspirators, and that her arrest had caused them such apprehension that they had determined to act as soon as possible after their return to Rome.

One of their members, a military officer named Subrius Flavius, had proposed to stab Nero while he was singing on the stage, for this singing was in his eyes the Emperor's main offence; but in the end it was decided that he should be murdered, as Milichus had guessed, in the Circus Maximus at the inauguration of the games that day, and Scævinus admitted that he had caused his dagger to be sharpened for that purpose. It had been arranged, he said, that a senator named Plautius Lateranus, an ardent Republican, who was a man of gigantic stature and immense physical strength, should approach Nero with a petition, and, kneeling at his feet, should suddenly seize him by the legs and throw him, whereupon Scævinus was to stab him, while those officers of the Guard who were in the plot, and who would be standing near, would keep off any defenders and would also help to dispatch their imperial victim. Meanwhile, Piso was to wait at the temple of Ceres, on the slope of the Aventine, near the Circus, with Antonia, daughter of the Emperor Claudius and widow of Sulla who had evidently been recalled from banishment; and as soon as the deed was accomplished he was to go with her to the Prætorian barracks in the expectation of being proclaimed Emperor on the understanding that he would divorce his wife, and marry Antonia, so as to provide himself with some sort of legal right to the throne to augment the claims of his popularity and his exceptionally noble lineage.

If Piso were not accepted as Emperor, Scævinus explained, it was expected that Seneca, old as he was, would be acclaimed, although the people might prefer Lucius Silanus, son of Marcus Junius Silanus whom Agrippina had poisoned at Nero's accession because of his descent from Augustus.

Meanwhile, immediately on the arrest of Scævinus and Natalis, some of the other conspirators hastened to Piso to beg him to go at once to the Prætorian barracks, and to employ his oratory, for which he was famous, in persuading the troops to dethrone Nero. That was their only hope of escape from death, they frantically pointed out. An immediate revolution alone could save them; and they declared that there was some chance of success, for neither "that actor," Nero, nor Tigellinus and his following of libertines and harlots, would put up any fight. Piso, however, refused to attempt to avert his doom. He went quietly to his room, and wrote a will "full of odious flattery of Nero," [5] which Tacitus thinks he was inspired to do by the hope that the Emperor would for that reason deal more kindly with his wife. This lady, however, who is described as having no morals and not much else to recommend her except her beauty, was going to be divorced by Piso, as has been said, so that he might marry Antonia; and her husband's tender consideration for her seems, therefore, to be an improbable explanation of his honeyed words. It is more likely that, remembering Baiæ, he was ashamed of the part he had played in the conspiracy.

A few hours later a detachment of soldiers arrived at his house bringing Nero's invitation to him to die like a gentleman by any means he might choose. Thereupon he opened the veins of his wrists and quietly expired. His wife went unharmed: she, the pretty creature, had been a pleasant hostess to Nero on many an occasion, and it was obvious to him that she had had nothing to gain by the assassination.

At the palace the cross-examination of Scævinus was still in progress when news was brought that Piso was dead. Nero then ordered the arrest of the various persons inculpated, and gave instructions that Epicharis, the woman whose indiscretion had nearly led to an earlier exposure of the plot, should be rigorously examined, for, as mistress of Seneca's brother, she would probably know whether Seneca were really guilty or not. That was what he wanted most of all to find out: was his old friend really a traitor? The evidence of Natalis was not altogether convincing, but Epicharis, being a woman, could surely be induced to talk and thereby to settle the question one way or the other. He told Tigellinus to go and see to the matter; but after the lapse of an hour or two, it seems, Tigellinus returned, saying that the woman had utterly refused to speak, although they had racked her and lashed her and burnt her with hot irons.

Meanwhile, however, a closer examination of Natalis had revealed the fact that Seneca had warned Piso that they must not be seen together, and had said that his safety depended on Piso's. On top of this came the news that the philosopher, who had been staying at his country house in Campania, had, during the morning, returned unexpectedly to his suburban villa, four miles from Rome, obviously so as to be on the spot in case he should be hailed as Emperor.

Poppæa had now joined her husband in the room where the examinations were being held, and at this damning piece of evidence against Seneca she and Nero decided to send a messenger to him at once, demanding to know whether he had truly made this remark to Piso, and, if so, why. The messenger selected was an officer of the Guard named Gavius Silvanus, who, himself, was one of the conspirators, as yet undenounced. He took with him a detachment of soldiers, and, arriving at Seneca's villa in the late afternoon, surrounded the house, and then delivered Nero's message. Seneca had already heard that the plot had been discovered, and knew that there was no escape. For years his philosophic spirit had contended with his ambitions. Knowing and enjoying the peace of mind which waits upon the man of small possessions, something within him had yet induced him to accept vast riches; loving the simple life, he had nevertheless availed himself of the luxuries of the palace; and now, while extolling the beauties of quiet rustication, he had been forced by the unrest within him to come to Rome to be ready to accept the lordship of the earth.[6] Well . . . !—this, he said to himself, was the last time that his philosophy should thus be flouted: he would go now to his long rest without complaint; he would die like a second Socrates, and the scene of his death would be for ever remembered.

He told Gavius Silvanus to return to Nero, and to say that he could not deny the words. This the officer did, and when Nero asked him whether, then, Seneca appeared to be making ready to commit suicide, he replied that he did not know, but that the philosopher showed no regret for what he had done, nor revealed any excitement or fear. Nero then told him to go back to Seneca, and to see that he put an honourable end to his life.

Gavius Silvanus, however, did not return directly to Seneca's villa: he stopped on the way at the house of Fenius Rufus, who, it will be recalled, was the colleague of Tigellinus in the dual command of the Prætorian Guard, and who was another of the still undetected conspirators. The purpose of his visit was to ask his superior officer whether he should obey Nero's orders; but Rufus, trembling for his own skin, could do no otherwise than tell him to do so.

Seneca received his death-sentence calmly. He called his secretary to him so that he might make his will, but this was disallowed, and thereupon the philosopher, a little vain-glorious in this supreme hour, turned to his household and said that since he was debarred from rewarding their services, he would bequeath them that which alone was left him—the example of his life. Seeing that they were weeping, he rebuked them, saying: "Where is your philosophy?—where are the rules of conduct in times of distress which I have taught you these many years? Who did not know that Nero had a violent disposition? What else could be expected of the man who killed his mother and his brother[7] than that he should also kill his old tutor?"

He then embraced his wife, Paullina, and, struggling to control his emotion, begged her not to grieve for him but to console herself by the contemplation of his virtuous life. Paullina, however, cried out that she would die with him, but I think it is to be supposed that she regretted her impetuosity when her husband said: "Very well, if you prefer the renown of dying with me . . . ," and told the doctor to open the veins of her wrists. His own wrists were cut at the same time, but as the blood did not flow freely, other veins were also opened, after which he bade Paullina farewell, and caused her to be removed to another room, where, it seems, her servants quickly induced her to bind up her wounds. At the same time a messenger hastened back to the Emperor to tell him that Seneca was dying and that Paullina had proposed to die too; at which Nero, in one of those explosions of generous feeling which usually broke up his most angry impulses, sent the man flying back to tell Paullina's servants to save her life at all costs; and it may be added that she survived her ordeal, although her pallor thereafter indicated that she had never quite recovered from the loss of blood.

Seneca, meanwhile, told his physicans to hasten his death by giving him a dose of hemlock, as had been done in the case of Socrates; but this, too, proved slow in its action, and he was therefore placed in a warm bath, the usual expedient in such cases. Flicking the bloodstained water over the servants who stood around him, he told them that it was a libation to Jupiter the Deliverer; after which he lay still, awaiting death which would not come. Somebody then suggested that they should carry him into the sweating-room of the baths, and suffocate him with steam; and this being done, Seneca at last obtained his release from the world he had despised and at the same time had loved so well.

Far into the night the examination of the prisoners at the palace continued. Rufus, still undenounced, had now taken his place at the Emperor's side, hoping against hope that he would not be betrayed; and presently while his colleague, Tigellinus, was away trying to make the heroic Epicharis speak, he found himself in command of the Guard. Just behind the Emperor stood Subrius Flavius, that senior officer who had wished to stab Nero while he was singing on the stage, and nearby were other officers who were in the plot.

Presently Scævinus, who was again being examined, seems to have fixed his eyes pleadingly upon this Subrius Flavius, who thereupon put his hand upon the hilt of his sword and glanced at his commanding officer, Rufus. Both these men, it will be recalled, as well as others in the room, were in the plot, but Scævinus had very naturally refrained from betraying them, hoping for just that action on their part which now seemed imminent; and he must have held his breath as he saw the officer's hand steal to his sword. A nod from Rufus, and the unsuspecting Nero would have died.

But the signal was not given. Rufus, it seems to me, had another plan by which to save himself. Piso and Seneca who could most fully have betrayed him, were dead; but Scævinus, he believed, did not know so very much about his (Rufus's) guilt, and what he did know he would not be likely to tell, since his one hope was that these officers of the Guard would murder Nero as he sat there. Rufus therefore deemed it best to throw himself vigorously into the cross-examination of Scævinus, at the same time winking at him, no doubt, to let him understand that he was only acting a part and that if Scævinus did not betray him he would do what he could for him. It was a risky proceeding, but the immediate murder of Nero would be still more dangerous, for Tigellinus and the loyal officers and men might exact a speedy vengeance.

Scævinus, however, felt himself already doomed, and, misunderstanding the motives of Rufus, and being pressed by him for more information, sarcastically replied: "My dear Rufus, nobody knows more about the matter than yourself. Prove your gratitude to so good an Emperor by telling him all you know."

At this, Nero leapt round upon the traitor, who showed such extreme alarm that his guilt was obvious, and he was at once pinioned by a faithful soldier named Cassius, a man of immense strength, always in attendance on the Emperor. By this time, of course, several of the other conspirators had been brought to the palace, and one in particular, a man named Cervarius Proculus, silenced Rufus's protestations of innocence by angrily inculpating him beyond denial. Thereupon he was condemned to death, Nero giving him time only to write his will, into which, says Tacitus, the wretched man "crowded his lamentations."[8]

It was not long, however, before Scævinus, seeing that there was no hope now of Nero being murdered, accused Subrius Flavius also, who, as just related, had been so near to killing the Emperor. At first this veteran officer declared his innocence, and, referring to Piso and some of the elegant men of fashion who had been in the plot, said: "Do you think it likely that I, a soldier, if I had planned so daring a deed, would have leagued myself with civilians and effeminate persons like these?" His fellow-conspirators, stung by his words, hastened to tell all they knew against him, and it was revealed that, after Nero had been assassinated, he was going to murder Piso also, and attempt to obtain the nomination of Seneca as Emperor.

"But why?" asked Nero, "did you object to Piso?"

"Because," the officer replied, "he acted tragedies upon the stage. If a singer like you were deposed only to be succeeded by a tragedian, the disgrace would continue as before. I once loved you, Nero, above all men. I loved you, and I hoped you would prove to be a good Emperor. You had not a soldier more true to you while you deserved to be loved. But I hated you from the time when you became a chariot-driver and a singer.[9] You killed your mother and your wife; it was you who set fire to Rome. . . ."

That was enough; for "it was well known," says Tacitus, "that nothing which was said during the trial fell so painfully upon Nero's ears." Subrius Flavius was at once handed over to Veianus Niger, one of his brother officers, who was ordered to see to his immediate execution. Niger therefore marched his men by lantern-light to a neighbouring field and dug a grave, after which he led the condemned man to the spot to be beheaded. Upon seeing the grave, Subrius Flavius sharply reprimanded the soldiers, telling them that it was too small, not deep enough, and did not conform to military regulations. Niger then said to him: "Extend your neck bravely"; to which Subrius Flavius, seeing that Niger was trembling, retorted: "I only hope you will strike as bravely." A moment later his severed head and his body fell into the grave.

Meanwhile, Sulpicius Asper, Maximus Scaurus and Venetus Paulus, all officers of the Guard, were accused and found guilty, much to the horror and amazement of the Emperor, who now realized for the first time how near he had been to death, these men having been in attendance on him until that moment. "But why did you want to kill me?" he said to Sulpicius Asper, and he was cut to the quick when the man replied: "There was no other way of preventing your disgrace," thereafter going to his doom without another word. The death of the gigantic Plautius Lateranus followed. He was the man who was to have thrown Nero to the ground; and the Emperor treated him with particular severity, ordering him to be taken away to the place where slaves and low criminals were executed, and giving him no time even to bid farewell to his family. His executioner, a certain Statius, an officer of the Guard, was also one of the conspirators, but Lateranus did not betray the fact. Statius, however, was so upset that, in the feeble light of the lantern, his first blow only felled his victim and inflicted a gaping wound, apparently across the collarbone; whereupon Lateranus picked himself up calmly bent his head forward once more, and in silence received the second stroke.[10]

During the examination of the accused, the name of Atticus Vestinus, at that time Consul, was mentioned. He is said to have been innocent, but, in the excitement of the time, his guilt appeared to be certain, Nero's dislike of the man, who had openly insulted him, perhaps contributing to the conviction that he was in the plot. The Emperor therefore sent an officer and no less than five hundred men to arrest him, for Vestinus kept a large number of young men in his service as a bodyguard, and it was thought that they might put up a fight. The officer found the Consul giving a dinner-party in his house, probably, as Tacitus suggests, in order to present an appearance of unconcern; and when the soldiers entered, they locked up the guests in the dining room, while Vestinus himself was called out, and a doctor was sent for. Vestinus knew at once that he was being offered the alternative of suicide, and, without expressing a word of regret, seated himself and held out his wrists for the doctor to operate upon; nor was it long before in continued silence he died. The news was then conveyed to Nero, and he was asked what should be done with the imprisoned guests, all of whom had been left in the dining room expecting death at any moment.

The Emperor replied that they were to be kept there for the time being; and therewith the examination of the conspirators continued. Scævinus, having told all that he knew, was at length taken out into the darkness and beheaded, but Natalis was pardoned, as also was Statius. Gavius Silvanus, the officer who had carried the death-sentence to Seneca, was acquitted, but, knowing himself guilty, at once killed himself. Statius, also, although pardoned, could not endure to live in disgrace, and committed suicide.

At last, after midnight, the court adjourned; but just before Nero went to bed he remembered the guests of Vestinus locked up in their late host's dining room. "I think they have paid dearly enough for their consular dinner," he said, smiling grimly, and he gave orders that, guilty or innocent, they should all be released.

The next morning opened with a remarkable incident. Tigellinus, who had recently developed tuberculosis, as a result, it was believed, of his immoralities, could hardly have slept that night; and at daybreak he gave orders that the wretched woman Epicharis should be brought to him to be re-examined under torture. After her agonies of the previous day, however, she could not walk, and was therefore placed in a curtained litter carried by four soldiers. At the end of the journey the curtains were drawn back, and, to the astonishment of the soldiers, she was found hanging by her girdle from the top of the litter, quite dead. She had not been able to endure the thought of being tortured again, and although she could hardly move her dislocated joints, she had managed to tie the girdle to a horizontal pole above her, and, placing her neck in the noose, had throttled herself.

When the court reassembled, evidence was taken in regard to the complicity of the poet Lucan in the affair. Lucan, or, to give him his correct name, Marcus Annæus Lucanus, was born at the end of A.D. 39, and was therefore about two years younger than Nero, who had taken a particular interest in him because he was the son of Seneca's younger brother, Mela (the man of whom the heroic Epicharis had been the mistress). Nero had praised his poetry, had found him a salaried government-post, and had received him into his intimate circle of friends. At the "Neronia" contests in A.D. 60 Lucan had recited a panegyric in praise of his benefactor whom he then adored with all the fervour of his poet's heart. To him Nero was a superman, a very god on earth; and in the first books of his famous *Pharsalia,*[11] he describes the Emperor as a glorious divinity, an Apollo, who has brought peace and prosperity to the world. But presently a coolness had developed between them which gossip unkindly attributed to Nero's jealousy of Lucan's greater poetic gifts, but which was more probably due to the poet's "immense vanity," as Suetonius says; and in the later books of the *Pharsalia* the writer began to abuse the Empire, if not directly the Emperor himself, and poured out his longing for a re-establishment of the Republic.

This, of course, was treason, and, seemingly with the consent of Seneca, his uncle, the young man was forbidden to publish any more of his dangerous works. After that he issued privately a poem in which he attacked Nero in the foulest language; and his participation in the conspiracy followed naturally. He became, in fact, one of its active leaders, and he used to boast that one day he would cast Nero's severed head at the feet of his friends.

He was now arrested and brought before the court, whereupon he showed the utmost cowardice, and, hoping to save himself by inculpating others, accused his own mother, Acilia, of being a party to the conspiracy. Nero treated this accusation with contempt, and took no steps whatsoever against the lady; but Lucan he sent back to his home, giving him permission to put an end to himself in whatever way he chose. Thereupon the young man, recovering his courage, ate a hearty meal, and then opened his veins, quoting with his last breath some of his own lines describing the death of a wounded warrior.

Afranius Quintianus, a senator notorious for his effeminacy, was next tried and condemned to death, after which twelve other senators, including Crispinus, Poppæa's first husband, were mercifully sent into exile. Claudius Senecio, one of Nero's best and oldest friends, was then discovered to have played an active part in the plot, and was allowed to kill himself. Four other gentlemen of the court, and two more officers of the Guard, were next proved guilty and condemned to death; four officers were cashiered; and one gentleman, besides Natalis, was pardoned. The charge against Antonia, daughter of the Emperor Claudius, was suspended for the time being; and one other woman-conspirator, Cædicia, wife of Scævinus, was sent into exile although she had merited the death sentence.

Thus, of the forty-one conspirators, eighteen met their deaths, seventeen escaped with banishment or degradation, five were pardoned or acquitted, and one was not sentenced. When it is remembered that Nero was to have been brutally murdered on the very day on which the plot was discovered, that most of the conspirators were his personal friends whose treachery was due to nothing more than jealousy or annoyance, and that the Emperor's chief offence in the eyes of the remainder, for which he was to be stabbed and hacked to death, was that he was an artist, it will be admitted that the sentences were remarkably lenient for that age. The picture sometimes presented to us of the three judges—Nero, ferocious and fiendish, Poppæa, feline and cruel, and Tigellinus, diseased and sadistic—is one which fades away under the scrutiny of historical criticism; and in its place there rises a vision of an utterly disillusioned and wretched young Emperor and his terrified wife, trying to deal justly with a pack of assassins of whom only two or three were actuated by any idealistic sentiments. Nero had ruled for over ten years, and though the deaths of traitors in the imperial family had made sombre his record, there is not a single instance known to history of his condemnation of any man without justification. His mercy had been altogether exceptional—astonishing, indeed, as compared with that shown by other Emperors; and in dealing with this fearful conspiracy his behaviour, in extreme peril and under the utmost provocation, must commend itself to the unbiassed critic as that of a just and brave man.

CHAPTER XVI

The "Neronia" of A.D. 65—The Hunt for Dido's Treasure—The Death of Poppæa, Autumn A.D. 65—Further Conspiracies—The Death of Petronius, A.D. 66—The Coming of King Tiridates to Rome, early Summer, A.D. 66—Nero's Departure for Greece, Autumn, A.D. 66.

THE punishment of the conspirators caused at first an outburst of popular indignation in Rome, and, to quote Tacitus, "the Emperor was mercilessly abused by the people, who said that he had put innocent men to death for motives of fear or jealousy." Nero therefore issued a long statement, giving the evidence against the accused or their own confessions, and "at that, all who took the trouble to ascertain the truth of the matter, came to realize that a conspiracy had indeed been formed, matured, and suppressed."[1]

The Senate and those in responsible positions, on learning how imminent had been the danger, returned thanks to the gods for the Emperor's escape with such fervour that Nero could but think their loyal sentiments were genuine, and he was much comforted by them. Even the relatives of the conspirators, trembling for their own skins, and indignant at the foolhardiness which had imperilled them, tried with sickly smiles to show their delight at his safety, "falling at his knees, and wearying his hand with kisses." Public thanksgivings, of course, were decreed; and special honours were paid to the god of the Sun for the reason that there was a shrine dedicated to him in the Circus Maximus where the murder was to have been committed, he being therefore thought to have caused the plot to miscarry. The dagger of Scævinus was solemnly dedicated to Jupiter Vindex in the Capitol; the month of April, in which the conspiracy was discovered, was named Neronius in the Emperor's honour; special chariot-races were instituted in commemoration of his escape; and Cerialis Anicius, the Consul elect, moved a vote that Nero should be deified, and that a temple should be at once erected to him, at the charge of the State, "a motion," says Tacitus, "by which he meant to intimate that Nero had grown beyond the pinnacle of mortal greatness, and already deserved that worship given to the gods which is not usually paid to an Emperor before he has ceased to sojourn among men." Nero, however, had no wish to be a god, and he vetoed the proposal.

Milichus, the man who had revealed the plot, was richly rewarded; Tigellinus was thanked and decorated; the soldiers of the Guard who, in spite of the treachery of some of their officers, had remained absolutely loyal, were each given a present of money and a perpetual ration of corn; and various persons received rewards according to their services.

The quinquennial Games, the "Neronia" as they were called, which a year ago had been postponed, it will be remembered, because Nero was not in voice, were now due to take place; but the Senate, knowing that the late conspiracy had been initiated partly by those who considered a minstrel Emperor to be an anomaly disgraceful to Rome, tactfully suggested that he should accept the prize for singing and declamation without bothering to compete for it. The suggestion must have touched Nero on the raw. Did they think he had been so intimidated by the conspiracy that he would in future refrain from singing? Were these Philistines going to be allowed to silence his voice, and cause him to give the impression that he admitted the impropriety of his art? Did they perhaps think that his voice was not worth hearing?

Angrily and defiantly he replied that he would most certainly sing. "I am quite prepared to compete for the prize," he said, "nor do I need the protection of the Senate. Any honours that my vocal talents may receive must come to me not by your favour but by the unbiassed decision of the proper musical judges."

The courage of his convictions which he thus displayed pleased the masses, who fought for seats at the performance with such violence that a number of people were crushed to death, while the clothes of a large part of the audience were disheveled, if not torn to rags and tatters. When Nero appeared upon the stage he received an ovation. "Give us the benefit of all your accomplishments!" the audience shouted to him; and Tacitus, in recording the fact, says with hushed horror: "Those were their very words!"[2] He then sang song after song to them, accompanying himself upon the harp, and strictly conforming to the rules of the contest. When he had finished, he went down on one knee and held out his hand like a suppliant, this being the gesture which etiquette required of a competitor; and instantly there was a very thunder of applause. "You would have supposed," says Tacitus, "that the people were delighted, and perhaps they were, since they seem to have been insensible to the disgrace of it."[3]

On this occasion that rhythmic kind of clapping which has already been described was again employed, and it is said that those members of the audience who had not learnt the art were greatly embarrassed, for if they clapped out of time somebody would be sure to thump them on the back, and if they kept silent their enthusiastic neighbours would abuse them as traitors or dolts. The contests continued almost without interruption from noon to late at night; and so eager were the people to hear the Emperor out, either from enjoyment or loyalty, that nobody dared to draw attention to himself by leaving his seat, the result being that several cases of dangerous illness were afterwards reported. There was one man who fell asleep, and was denounced to Nero therefore as a palpable traitor; but the Emperor, of course, paid no attention to the matter. That man was Vespasian, afterwards Emperor of Rome.

In the end the prize was awarded to Nero; but whether the judges were influenced in their decision by the popular enthusiasm and the desire to please both the Emperor and the people, or whether Nero's voice was really the finest in the world, as the crowds declared, will never be known. At any rate, after being awarded the victor's crown, he hastened onto the stage, bursting with excitement, his face beaming and nearly as red as his hair, and told the audience of his success, thanking them from his heart for their appreciation. It must have been almost incredible to recall the fact that a few days previously he had so narrowly escaped being murdered for his minstrelsy.

If, after this popular triumph, he still felt any depression it must have been dissipated in May or June by the thrilling discovery that Poppæa was again going to have a baby. Another exciting event also took place at about this time. A certain Carthaginian, one Cesellius Bassus, had formed a theory that the treasure of Queen Dido, the founder of Carthage, was buried in some caves which were situated on his property; and this well-known form of delusion so worked upon his mind that at last he came to Rome—just before the Games—to tell the Emperor that he knew positively where untold quantities of gold were stacked in huge bars and ingots. Nero was badly in need of money after the rebuilding of Rome; and he now therefore sent some ships and men across to Carthage to secure the treasure, which soon became the subject of the wildest and most confident talk. Everybody, including the Emperor, believed that very soon this vast wealth would be discovered and brought to Rome; but the enterprise, unfortunately, followed the normal course of such treasure-hunts. First one place and then another was tried in vain, thousands of natives being employed in the excavations; and at last the disillusioned promoter of the scheme, the imaginative Cesellius Bassus, in the anguish of his disappointment, killed himself.

The news of his failure and death reached the Emperor in August or September of this year 65, and threw him into the depths of depression, for he had already run up huge bills in connection with the decoration of the new palace, in anticipation of the coming of Queen Dido's gold, and now he did not know where to turn for money. He was irritable and his nerves were on edge; but his consolation at this time was the pleasant thought that his beloved Poppæa was going to present him with this second child who, he hoped, would prove to be the son and heir he longed for. One day, probably in September, he came back from the races very much later than he had said he would, and Poppæa angrily stormed at him, whereupon either in fun or in annoyance, he made a silly lunge at her with his foot. She was nearer to him than he had realized, and the impact caused a miscarriage. To his horror, complications set in; and after a few days of almost unbearable anguish for him, Poppæa died in his arms.[4]

Nero's grief was frantic. Appalled at the thought of allowing her loveliness to be consigned to the flames, he sent for some Egyptian embalmers who were in Rome and told them to preserve her body by the lengthy process by which the bodies of the ancient kings and queens of Egypt had been preserved; and on the day of the funeral, many weeks later, Egyptian incense was burnt in such clouds that the quantity used was estimated as more than that yielded by the incense-groves of Arabia and Egypt in an entire year.[5] The embalmed body was laid in the tomb of the Julian family; and Nero himself, making no attempt to hide his tears, delivered her panegyric, referring in broken tones to her beauty and gifts, and to her exalted fortune in having been the mother of a child, Claudia Augusta, already enrolled amongst the gods. The people, however, did not share their Emperor's grief; and there was some murmuring when she was now deified, and a temple erected in her honour. Poppæa had been unpopular since the death of Octavia, and her behaviour at the recent trial of the conspirators had been regarded as cruel and relentless by those who did not appreciate the court's general leniency on that occasion. Much was said, then and later, against her for which there seems to have been little justification; and there was even some talk of her having been poisoned by an enemy. Her age at her death was thirty-four years, and thus her prayer that she might die before her beauty began to fade was answered with fatal precision. Nero's twenty-eighth birthday occurred in December, a few weeks after her funeral.

During the winter of this year A.D. 65 and the early spring of 66, he was depressed and overwrought. His bitter sorrow, and the loneliness of his days without Poppæa, drove him almost out of his mind. He had no close friends, except Petronius, nor cared to make any since the revelation of the treachery of those he had loved and trusted. The gaunt and consumptive Tigellinus was not his intellectual equal, and was rather an agent in devising entertainment for him than a friend in whom he could confide. The man's mind seldom ranged in its search for palliatives further than prurience and inebriation. Want of money had brought the work upon the palace, the Golden House, in which Nero was so interested to a standstill, and, as a matter of fact, it was never finished. He felt, moreover, that he had lost the sympathy of the people, and the state of his nerves was such that, through his frequent tears, he saw nothing around him but hostility and pitilessness. It seemed evident to him that nobody loved him except when he sang to them; and just now he was too unhappy to sing. He heard that all sorts of jokes were being made at his expense, and from time to time rude rhymes about him were found written upon walls, or were secretly published and passed from hand to hand.

"Amidst all his misfortunes," writes Suetonius,[6] "it was strange and very remarkable that he bore nothing more patiently than this scurrilous language and the general abuse of him, treating no class of persons with more gentleness than those who assailed him with invective and lampoons." Even when information was laid before the Senate, naming the actual authors of these libels, he would not proceed against them. Once, however, a comedian named Datus, who had to say the lines "Goodbye, Father; goodbye, Mother!" in a play in which he was acting, pretended to be eating something which disagreed with him as he said the first two words, and, with the other two words, made the motions of a swimmer, his reference being, of course, to the poisoned mushrooms given to Claudius and to the shipwreck of Agrippina. Nero banished him from the capital for his audacity.

To add to his and the nation's troubles the plague

broke out in Rome, and something like thirty thousand people died within a few weeks, the streets being filled with funerals and the houses with corpses awaiting burial. From all directions came the sounds of wailing, and in every open space the funeral pyres smoked and crackled. The rumour spread that Nero, having failed to exterminate the citizens by fire, was attempting to poison them off; and when a number of high-born children and their attendants died after eating some sort of poisonous food accidentally served to them at a picnic, the distracted parents saw in the tragedy the hand of Nero bent on destroying the old aristocracy.

Then came a terrific storm which devastated Campania, wrecking the villages, uprooting the trees, and playing havoc with the crops; and in Rome, too, its violence was felt, though not with such severity. Shortly afterwards news arrived that Lugdunum, the modern Lyons, which had been the richest and finest city in Gaul, had been totally destroyed by fire—in which connection Nero's generosity was once more shown, for he insisted on making a donation to the homeless townspeople, and sent back to them the money which they had contributed to the fund for the rebuilding of Rome. The gods, said the people, were evidently angry.

Rumours of rebellion were once more rife in the city; and the foolish talk of certain sections of society which accused Nero of the deaths of various people who had actually died of the plague, caused renewed threats to be made against his life. His unpopularity was never general, but the length to which his vilification in some quarters was carried is revealed in the ridiculous story that it was his intention to deliver his enemies to be devoured alive by an Egyptian freak then being exhibited in Rome, who lived on raw meat and could kill animals with his teeth.

Such gossip disgusted the Emperor with Rome, and he went to stay for the remainder of the winter at Naples, where the Greek population understood and loved him; and he instructed the Senate, while he was away, to take into its own hands any cases of incipient rebellion which might come to its notice. He knew well enough that there were such cases, but he did not wish to give his enemies cause for their attacks upon him by acting, himself, against the traitors: he would leave it, this time, to the Senate.

There was a certain Caius Cassius Longinus, a wealthy lawyer who had been governor of Syria under the Emperor Claudius, but was now old and nearly blind. He had always shown such dislike for Poppæa that Nero had refused to allow him to attend her funeral; and his attitude to Nero himself had never been friendly. Two very damning pieces of evidence against him were now reported. Firstly, he had placed conspicuously amongst his family portraits a bust of the famous Cassius who was one of the murderers of Julius Cæsar; and he had inscribed this figure with the words "The Leader of the Party," and was in the habit of showing such veneration for it that his approval of the assassination of the Dictator, and hence of the attempted assassination of Nero, seemed to be a natural conclusion. And, secondly, he had lately made a great friend of Lucius Silanus, the last of the unfortunate Silani family, the descendants of Augustus, and had drawn his friends' attention to him as a fitting leader of a movement to dethrone Nero. Lepida, the young wife of Cassius Longinus, was the aunt of Lucius Silanus and was said to be also his mistress; and these two were reported to have practised "horrible magic rites" for the purpose of putting a curse upon Nero. A plot to place Silanus on the throne appeared to have so far matured that he had already chosen his "cabinet"; and three other persons, two of them Senators, were implicated.

Nero therefore sent a letter to the Senate pointing out these supposed facts, and asking that the persons involved should be suspended from participation in affairs of State. The Senate investigated the matter, and exiled both Cassius and Silanus, the former being shipped off to Sardina (where he remained unmolested until pardoned by Vespasian a few years later), and the latter being sent to the little town of Barium (Bari) in the south-east of Italy. A few weeks later, however, an officer and a few soldiers were sent by the Senate to Silanus, apparently to remove him elsewhere; and this officer strongly "advised him to commit suicide by opening his veins,"[7] since his continued existence was disturbing the peace of Rome, where there seems to have been an agitation in his favour. "I have made up my mind to die," Silanus replied, "but I am not going to allow a scoundrel like you the glory of compelling me to do so." He then sprang towards the door of the room in which they were standing, and, when intercepted, struck out with his fists in his desperate attempt to escape; but he was killed in the struggle, and the officer, having reported the matter to the Senate, was exonerated. The other persons implicated in this plot appealed from the Senate to Nero himself, who let them off.

Shortly after this an accusation of treason was brought against Pollitta, the widow of the traitor Rubellius Plautus, her father, Antistius Vetus, her grandmother, Sextia, and Publius Gallus, a friend of theirs; and it was privately made known to them that the Senate was going to hasten the trial of Vetus and had already determined to punish him with death. At this Pollitta went to Naples to plead with Nero to ask the Senate to pardon him. "Denied access to the Emperor, she besieged his gates, sometimes imploring him in the piercing tones of female grief, sometimes assailing him in accents of bitter reproach,"[8] but at last when Nero had refused to intervene in the actions of the Senate, she returned to her father, and told him that the only honourable thing for them to do was to kill themselves, rather than to await their trial. Vetus therefore gave away every penny of his fortune and all his furniture to his domestics so that there should be nothing for the State to confiscate; and the three of them then opened the veins of their wrists, and, each getting into a warm bath, and "praying with rival earnestness for a quick and easy exit of the soul," gazed thereafter at one another until their sight grew dim. When their deaths were announced to the Senate, they were posthumously decreed guilty and sentenced to be executed as traitors; but Nero, on hearing of this, very considerately ordered the sentence to be erased from the books, and, for the sake of their fair memories, caused it to be written that they had been "honourably granted uncontrolled option in regard to the manner of their death." Publius Gallus, although found to be a close friend of the late Fenius Rufus, one of Nero's would-be murderers, was punished only with exile.

But still the rumours of plots continued, and presently it was reported to the Senate that a rebellion was being planned by Ostorius Scapula, a high military officer who had distinguished himself in the wars in Britain, but who of late had been under a cloud because he had allowed lampoons against Nero to be read at his dinner-parties. Another man involved in this indictment was Publius Anteius, who had once been a great friend of Agrippina, and, after her death, had with difficulty concealed his enmity towards the Emperor. As soon as these two men learnt that their plans had been discovered Anteius killed himself by taking poison, and Ostorius Scapula waited only for the arrival of the soldiers, and then, ordering a slave to hold a sharp dagger to his throat, flung himself upon it.

Shortly after this it was discovered that Crispinus, the former husband of Poppæa, who had been one of the members of the Piso conspiracy but had been let off with exile by Nero, was again plotting against the Emperor. He killed himself as soon as he was accused, and his guilt was vouched for by Mela—Seneca's brother and father of the poet Lucan—who was indicted at the same time and died thereafter by his own hand. Before committing suicide Mela also revealed the fact that the senator, Cerialis Anicius, who had proposed that Nero should be deified, as recorded at the beginning of this chapter, was himself a conspirator against the Emperor's life; and this man, likewise, committed suicide on hearing that he was discovered.

These widespread plots brought Nero back to Rome; and when the trouble had subsided he set out for Naples again in the company of his old friend Petronius Arbiter. Petronius, it will be recalled, was one of the men whose society Nero had sought when he first came to the throne; and though his appearances in the pages of history are few, it seems that he was the Emperor's frequent companion—a fact which had lately brought him into conflict with Tigellinus, whose less elegant attempts to amuse Nero were considered to be rather vulgar by this acknowledged Arbiter of taste. The concealed struggle, in fact, between Tigellinus and Petronius must have been a matter of common knowledge at the court at this time.

Tigellinus had been a fisherman and a horse-breeder, and Nero's great liking for him had its sources amidst those rougher features of the Emperor's character which the refinements of polite society had never quite eradicated. As in the case of most artistic geniuses, Nero was always a little more vulgar, a little less elegant, than the intellectuals who admired him. There was one side of his nature which was simple, crude, and unpolished; and to this side the Sicilian horse-breeder appealed. Petronius, on the other hand, was so exquisitely trained in all the refinements of the artistic life and of the pursuit of pleasure that Nero is said to have "esteemed nothing elegant or delicately luxurious which had not been commended to him on the judgment of this Arbiter"[9]; and thus there must have been a constant swing to and fro on the part of the Emperor between the influence of these two men. Petronius was always so bored and languid that Tigellinus must have been the favourite when Nero was in one of his enthusiastic moods; and one gathers that even the Emperor's singing, with its evident popular appeal, was more to the taste of the Sicilian than to that of this exquisite Roman.

Parts of the comic romance, the *Satyricon,* written by Petronius have come down to us; but while the work is exceedingly amusing and brilliant it is so thoroughly indecent that, as the French historian, Victor Duruy, remarks, one reads it but one does not talk about it. It tells the adventures of a group of young men of dissolute habits whose only deity appears to be Priapus; but although there have been some attempts to identify the leading characters with Nero and his friends, it is more probable that they are imaginary. At the same time the story reflects the immorality of society, and especially the court, in those days; and if Nero himself is to be regarded as having been always too busy and too hard-working to make more than brief excursions into the pale realms of sexual depravity, the general atmosphere of his circle must, nevertheless, have been one of frank indecency. Nobody at the palace believed in the gods, and although Nero had a strong sense of the occult, and was often uncomfortably aware of the supernatural, Petronius was a complete materialist. "No one believes in heaven or hell nowadays," he makes one of his characters say, "or keeps the fasts, or cares a fig for Jupiter. In the olden times it was different. Our noble ladies, with thoughts pure, would go and pray for rain, for instance, and down it would come in buckets-full, and they would come back like drowned rats. But now there is no help from heaven for us sceptics: the gods are old and gouty, and our fields lie and bake."

During this journey to Naples a night was spent at the town of Cumæ, north of Misenum, where Petronius seems to have had a villa; and in the evening one of the slaves at the house went to Tigellinus and told him that his master had been involved in the Piso conspiracy and had secretly been in consultation here with Scævinus on many occasions. In amazement, but not without a feeling of triumph, Tigellinus reported the matter to Nero, whose disillusionment was thus completed. Petronius!—his own familiar friend, a traitor! The blow must have been almost crushing; but for the moment he took no steps against the accused, except to tell him that he need not come to Naples.

Petronius realized, of course, that he had been betrayed, and after Nero's cavalcade had departed in the morning, he called his friends to a sumptuous midday meal with him, during which he retired for a while, and caused the veins of his wrists to be opened and then bandaged up again. All his life he had been notorious for his cynical disregard of danger and his fashionable air of ennui; and now he determined to play with death and to derive what pleasure he could from the novelty of dying. Returning to the repast he told his guests what he had done; and whenever their melancholy solicitude bored him he removed the bandages and allowed the blood to flow, but applied them again at the introduction of any interesting topic of conversation.

Before he had become too weak to stand he took a short stroll in the afternoon sunshine through the streets of Cumæ; and after he had returned to the house he enjoyed a little nap. Then he sent for some of his slaves, rewarded one or two of them, and told his steward to give others a good beating. Next, he dictated a letter to Nero, telling him many home truths and making sarcastic remarks about the inartistry of some of the Emperor's affairs of the night, about which he had been privately told by a certain lady named Silia, the wife of a senator, she being in the habit of amusing herself with Petronius without the knowledge of Nero.

He then removed the bandages once more, and asked his friends to read some poetry to him. Just as his life was ebbing away he noticed at his side a beautiful vase, a work of art which Nero had always coveted; and, extending his hand, he deliberately knocked it off the table, smashing it to atoms, so that it should not pass into the Emperor's possession.

The news of his death, confirming as it did his guilt, must have been a great shock to Nero; and the abusive letter must have stung him sharply. He guessed that it was Silia who had been telling tales about him, and he angrily sent her about her business, forbidding her to show her face in Italy again; but this outburst cannot greatly have relieved his wounded feelings. What was it about him, he must have asked himself, that had induced his dearest friends to associate themselves with his enemies, the traditionists, in these plots against him?—and we, today, can but ask the same question. Classical historians have declared that his chief faults were his cruelty, his immorality, his vanity, and his disregard for the dignity of his imperial position. But emphatically, he was not cruel, nor was he even severe until these plots against his life began to beset him. He was not more immoral than Petronius, Senecio, and other conspirators, who could not therefore have been actuated by a sentiment of disgust. He was certainly not vain, for his lack of self-confidence, as revealed in his fear of the musical critics, was notorious. All his friends were stage-struck, and Piso, the arch-conspirator, acted as publicly as Nero sang; and therefore it was not his disregard for imperial decorum which led them to want to murder him.

To my mind it is clear that while the old-fashioned aristocracy desired his removal, as has been said, because he was the relentless enemy of the conventions for which they stood, because he was felt to be endangering the morale of Rome and the dignity of his office, and because he had wasted, or was likely to waste, public funds, the treachery of his immediate circle must have been caused by individual enmities and ambitions outside these considerations. Piso may have envied him his throne itself; Petronius may have hated him as a rival art-collector, or may have differed with him to the point of exasperation in matters of taste; another may have been jealous of him in connection with some woman; another may have nursed a grudge against him for some supposed insult. Only the traditionists command the forbearance of history in their murderous plots: there is nothing to be said for the others.

There are still three deaths to record which took place during this dark and unhappy phase of Nero's life. The first was that of Thrasea Pætus, a dour senator whose stern condemnation of the Emperor had been openly displayed in Rome for many years. At the time of Agrippina's death he had walked out of the Senate to mark his disapproval; he had taken exception to the Festivals of Youth and had refused to attend them; he had objected to the deification of Poppæa, and had not even gone to her funeral; he had absented himself from the Senate when the annual vows of allegiance to Nero were made, and when the prayers for his safety and for the preservation of his "divine voice" were offered up; and so forth.

The Senate itself undertook the trial of this disgruntled man, who was described as a menace to peace; and at the same time it brought charges of disaffection against his son-in-law, Helvidius Priscus, and against a group of their friends. A certain Eprius Marcellus was the prosecutor on behalf of the State. "If only, instead of showing his disapproval," he argued, "Thrasea would come here and tell us what reforms he desired, all would be well. But he condemns the whole system by sullen silence. Is it the fact that Nero has given us peace throughout the whole world that excites this man's displeasure? He seems to mourn over the public prosperity of our times; he disregards the laws, and insults the city of Rome itself; and he seems so to loathe the State that surely it would be better for him to sever all connection with it by his death."[10]

The Senate rightly condemned him as a public enemy, however sincere his purpose, but he was permitted to commit suicide in lieu of execution; while Helvidius and the others were banished or pardoned. There followed, almost immediately, the trial of Barea Soranus and his daughter, Servilia, the former being accused of having been concerned in the abortive rebellion of Rubellius Plautus, and the latter of using magic against the Emperor. Both were found guilty by the Senate, and were given permission to end their lives in whatever manner they chose. It is possible that the death of Antonia, daughter of the Emperor Claudius, and widow of the traitor, Sulla, is to be assigned to this period and to be connected with these trials for treason, for Suetonius states that she was found guilty of that charge and executed.[11] But the statement is unconfirmed, and it is quite likely that she died a natural death.

In these trials Nero was not actively concerned, but it is to be presumed that the sentences had his approval, for he was still worried and depressed by these menaces to his life, and he knew not whom to trust. Now, however, the dark clouds suddenly lift, and from the spring of A.D. 66 until the end of his reign the chronicle of his life is practically free from these unpleasant tales of executions and suicides. His grief at the loss of Poppæa was now sufficiently softened by time for him to decide to marry again, for he was eager to have children; and he chose as his new Empress a lady named Statilia Messalina, daughter of Statilius Taurus who had been Consul in A.D. 44, and widow of Atticus Vestinus, the Consul who had been made to commit suicide as one of the supposed members of the Piso conspiracy. Hardly anything is known about her beyond the fact that she failed to bear Nero a child, and that she survived him. She is said to have been his mistress before he married her; and if this be so the union may have been something more happy than a *mariage de convenance,* in spite of the little our authorities have to say about it.

In the speech of Marcellus to the Senate, recorded above, grateful mention was made of the fact that Nero had brought peace to the world; and it is an interesting commentary on the character of the Emperor that, as Suetonius says, "he never entertained the least ambition or hope of augmenting or extending the frontiers of the Empire" by military exploits.[12] He did not ever see himself as a leader of armies, nor did he have any desire to be hailed as a conquering hero—a fact which indicates, by the way, that his love of the stage was not caused by his reaction to the glamour of theatrical display or by a liking for heroics, but by a genuine artistic impulse. He was unquestionably a man of peace, and he seems to have regarded as one of his finest achievements the closing of the temple of Janus, the traditional signal that the entire Empire was at peace, which was able to be done twice in his reign, once in A.D. 64,[13] and once again in this year 66.[14] This tendency towards pacifism, or, rather, this absorption in matters which he considered more important than fighting, appears to have been one of the reasons why he was disliked by the conventional elements in Roman society, who were born and bred in an atmosphere of militarism; and these men of the old school of blood and iron must have looked with contempt at the shut doors of the temple of Janus. A few years before this, Nero had talked of withdrawing the legions from Britain[15]; and for some time past he had been closely engaged in attempting to make a lasting peace with Rome's hereditary enemies at the other end of the Empire—the Parthians.

Success had at last crowned his efforts in the latter direction, and in the early summer of A.D. 66 he had the great satisfaction of receiving in Rome the homage of Tiridates, the brother of the King of Parthia, who had been made King of Armenia by the latter, but had been driven out by the Roman general Corbulo. A promise had been made to him that if he came to Rome his throne would be restored to him, and he had therefore set out in the autumn of A.D. 65, making a leisurely and royal progress which occupied no less than nine months.[16] Three thousand Parthian horsemen and almost as many Romans accompanied him, while his servants and attendants were a legion in themselves; and from the moment when this vast company crossed the Armenian frontier into Roman territory its provisions and other expenses were charged to the public treasury of Rome.

Tiridates was a handsome and intelligent young man, and made a very gallant figure as he rode on horseback along the splendid Roman highways from city to city. His wife rode beside him, but as Parthian women were not allowed to show their faces to the public, the Queen wore a helmet-like headdress of gold under which her features must have been almost completely eclipsed. Having been fêted and lavishly entertained all through Asia Minor and Greece, the royal couple were met, somewhere in the neighbourhood of the later Venice, by one of the gorgeous imperial chariots or carriages, and in this they were conveyed down the east coast of Italy and across to Naples where Nero was waiting for them.

There was a slight contretemps when Tiridates was being ushered into the Emperor's presence, for it was observed that he was carrying his dagger, and he was requested to deliver it up in accordance with court etiquette. This he refused to do, but, after much argument, he consented to allow the scabbard to be nailed up in such a way that the weapon could not be drawn; and with that he was taken into the imperial presence, where, forgetting his dignity, he dropped on his knees, quite overcome by the spectacle of the glittering group around the Emperor and by Nero himself, flaming-haired, muscular, and magnificently robed and bejewelled.

For some days he was entertained in Naples, and Baiæ; and then Nero conducted his guests to Rome, where the crown of Armenia was going to be presented to Tiridates in public. This ceremony was performed early one summer morning in the Forum, which was decorated for the occasion with bunting and laurels, and was crowded with spectators, there being people, too, at every window and on the house-tops. Nero was enthroned upon the rostrum, surrounded by troops and senators; and Tiridates, having been led up to him through rows of soldiers, again did obeisance, whereupon Nero raised him up and kissed him, at which such a shout rent the air that the visitor was almost scared out of his wits. He recovered himself presently, however, and made a polite little speech, saying that Nero was his overlord and, in fact, his god; to which the Emperor replied that he was glad he thought so and had come to Rome to do his homage in person, and thereupon he declared him King of Armenia. Tiridates seated himself at Nero's feet, and the Emperor placed the Armenian crown upon his head.

They then went to the theatre, the whole interior of which, including the seats, had been gilded. A great purple awning was stretched across the arena from one side of the building to the other, to keep the sun off, and on this awning a huge figure of Nero driving a chariot was embroidered, with golden stars gleaming all about him. After the performance there was a great banquet, and later the Emperor sang for his guest, who, however, was somewhat shocked; and, finally, Nero drove a chariot for his edification, wearing his racing-colours, namely, green, and a charioteer's cap.

A round of festivities followed, and when Tiridates

at last set out on his return journey, he took with him not only huge presents from his host in goods and cash, but also a number of Roman artists and craftsmen to beautify his capital, the name of which he changed from Artaxata to Neronia. Just before he left, Nero begged him to initiate him into the mysteries of Mithraism, a religion which was already spreading from Persia into Greece and Italy, and ultimately became the great rival of Christianity[17]; but the venture was not very successful, perhaps because a neophyte was supposed to renounce before the initiation all the sinful lusts of the flesh.

So much money had Nero spent upon his guest that the day of the public ceremony described above came to be known in Roman history as "The Golden Day," and as a result of this expenditure the treasury found itself very nearly bankrupt. Yet the game was well worth the candle, for the impression left on the mind of Tiridates by his visit was so deep, and his respect and affection for Nero so genuine, that both Armenia and Parthia, formerly Rome's most dangerous enemies, kept the peace for the next fifty years. The whole incident, in fact, is regarded by historians as Nero's masterstroke of diplomacy, the greatest triumph of his reign; and although its importance was deliberately underrated by classical writers who could see no good in him whatever he did, the modern critic can hardly fail to recognize in Nero's dealings with Tiridates the touch of a master hand, whereby tens of thousands of lives were saved in the years to come.

The remainder of the summer was spent by the

Emperor in Naples and its vicinity; and now, with the whole Empire at peace and the conspiracies at home crushed out of existence, he gave himself up wholly to his art. Again and again he sang to enthusiastic audiences, hour after hour he spent in practising; and at last, feeling that his voice was now at the height of its beauty and power, he decided to go over to Greece to compete at the famous musical contests and particularly at the Pythian, Isthmian, Nemean, and Olympian "Games." The Greeks had ever been his most fervent admirers: they understood music, and, what was more important, they understood the temperament of an artist. *They* would not, he felt, attempt to assassinate him because he did not conform to the stock idea of what an Emperor should be, nor would they malign him and invent ridiculous stories about him. They would see that it was his object to bind the whole world in loyalty to him, not through military force but by means of the power of song; and their chief men would welcome him with a warmth unknown to the cold heart of patrician Rome.

Excitedly he made his plans. His wife Messalina and Tigellinus were to accompany him; his freedmen, Helios and Polyclitus, would remain at home to act for him, and Nymphidius, the successor of Fenius Rufus as joint-commander of the Prætorians, would keep the city in order. All was in readiness by the autumn, and on September 25th, A.D. 66, three months before his twenty-ninth birthday, he set out from Rome upon what proved to be the most amazing tour ever made by a reigning sovereign.

CHAPTER XVII

The Tour through Greece—The Death of Corbulo—The Liberty of Hellas—The Return to Rome, February, A.D. 68—The Revolt of Vindex—The Revolt of Galba—The Dethroning of Nero, June, A.D. 68.

THE story of the life of Nero now becomes that of a popular and successful singer who happened also to be an Emperor; and a superficial examination of his character might suggest merely that he had not allowed the duties of his position to interfere with the pleasures and the excitements of his musical career. He remained in Greece for nearly a year and a half, and during that period he was so occupied with his singing that he could not possibly have had time to do more in regard to the governing of the Empire than sign a few documents and give a few general orders—a fact which suggests at first a culpable negligence.

Instead of remaining in Rome or near it and devoting himself to affairs of State, he chose to tour Greece, singing at every musical festival in the country and giving so many performances that he won over eighteen hundred prizes in less than eighteen months; and it is not surprising that he paid the penalty. He was dethroned in the end, not because he was cruel or unjust, as was later pretended, but simply because music had taken possession of him to the exclusion of almost everything else; and his critics are unanimous in blaming him for his frivolity in allowing himself to become absorbed in anything so trivial.

But a closer examination of the evidence shows that Nero regarded his singing with the utmost seriousness. Nothing could shake his belief, in these last months of his life, that music was the most important thing on earth, and that it was his sacred duty as an Emperor who happened to be endowed by the gods with the gift of song to use that gift as a means of uniting humanity in loyalty to the imperial throne. He believed implicitly that he was crowning the achievements of the Cæsars by singing to his own people and to the conquered nations of the world; and so wholly had this thought taken possession of his mind that he was genuinely amazed at any suggestion that an Emperor had more important matters to attend to. Like every true artist, he believed that Art was a greater thing than the majesty of government; and his concert-tour in Greece, which he hoped to extend to other parts of the world, was undertaken by him not only in anticipation of the thrill of singing, but in a spirit of exalted emotion which, perhaps, only an artist can understand and distinguish from monomania. Nero is not unique in having believed that the making use of a great gift or talent is its possessor's duty; but he stands alone as a ruler who, having been brought up amidst the splendour and the pageantry of a mighty court, and having experienced the fullness of the power thereof, yet deemed the appeal to the world by song a grander endeavour.

He was attended on his tour by a host of officials and helpers, including a body of those Augustani whose business it was to lead the applause and to make themselves useful about the theatre; and there were also numerous musicians and actors in his train. He landed first on the island of Corcyra, and there sang before the altar of Jupiter Cassius. Thence he made his way to Olympia where he caused a special theatre to be built. Each city of any size, of course, announced a musical festival, and Nero accepted all their invitations to compete thereat, as well as at the four great contests already mentioned, the dates of which were shifted so as to meet the requirements of his itinerary. Only Athens and Sparta he refused to visit. It was said, but with small probability, that he dreaded going to Athens, because the Furies were supposed to dwell there who, in the old legend, dogged the footsteps of Orestes, the son of Agamemnon, after he, like Nero, had put his mother to death; but the reason given for his avoidance of Sparta is a more likely one, namely that he did not approve of, nor feel inclined to submit to, the discipline of the Spartan laws.

At every city at which he sang he won the prize—here a chaplet of laurel or parsley, there a garland of olive or fir; and although it is to be supposed that these prizes were given as a matter of courtesy, the enthusiasm of the audiences suggests that generally, if not invariably, his voice was actually better than those of the other competitors. His victories were always announced by a herald, that strong-voiced friend of his, Cluvius Rufus, who used to cry: "Nero Cæsar wins this contest to the glory of the Roman people and of the world that is his."

At first his nervousness was again noticeable, and his eager desire to obey all the rules of the contests and not to be shown favour was widely commented upon. Sometimes, according to the custom of that age, he wore a mask when acting a part, and when he was impersonating a female rôle he sometimes used a mask in the likeness of Poppæa. . . . "But how can one endure," writes Dion Cassius, [1] "to hear about an Emperor listed on the programme amongst the competitors, practising and singing songs, wearing his hair long like a musician, walking about with only one or two attendants, and eyeing his rivals anxiously? What victory less deserves the name than that by which Nero received a garland and lost the crown of statecraft? In this way he lowered himself from his eminence of power, and lost the dignity of his sovereignty to beg in the rôle of a slave, to be led like a blind man, to conceive, to bear children, to go mad, all of which he enacted time after time in the stories of Œdipus, of Thyestes, of Hercules, and of Orestes. All the situations that common actors simulate in their acting, he would undertake to present. Yet these proceedings the soldiers and all the rest saw, tolerated, and approved, calling him Pythian Victor, Olympian Victor, National Victor, Supreme Victor!"

Not all the Greeks were good listeners. There was one man, for instance, who frowned so heavily and applauded so little, that Nero, taking offence, would not receive him afterwards. "But where shall I go, then?" asked this personage in dismay, when he was turned away from the Emperor's door by a freedman. "Go to hell!" the freedman replied. On the whole, however, the tour was an immense success, and after a few months Nero must have begun to feel sure that he was in truth the greatest singer the world had ever known. He was not vain, but the ovations he was everywhere receiving could hardly have failed to turn his head; and though he set out for Greece diffident and nervous, long before his return he had become self-confident and aglow with pride. The words "my public" were ever on his lips, and the more his audiences applauded, the more eager he was to satisfy them. He worked like a slave, singing in public nearly every day, and rising early in the morning or sitting up late at night to practise and rehearse.

In his leisure hours he amused himself by driving a racing-chariot, and his skill was such that at Olympia he entered his name as a competitor in the races, and even drove a chariot with a team of ten horses—a feat of skill which won him much admiration. In one of these races his chariot overturned, and he was flung out, narrowly escaping being trampled upon by the oncoming horses. He picked himself up and resumed the race, but he was so dazed that he could not finish the course; and the judges, diplomatically declaring that the accident had not been his fault, and that he was obviously winning when it occurred, awarded him the prize. "In these races," says Dion Cassius,[2] "he would sometimes allow himself to be defeated in order to make it more credible that he really won at other times"—a remark which, when allowance is made for the adverse prejudice of the writer, suggests that Nero not infrequently gained his victories without the tactful aid of the other competitors.

He spent much time, also, in watching the wrestling matches, a sport at which he was himself very proficient; and he would often enter the ring in his excitement and pull a contestant forward when he was backing too far away from his opponent. He wanted very much to enter the wrestling competition himself; but it may be supposed that even *he* realized what a very bad impression would be created were he, the Emperor of the Earth, to be heavily thrown by his opponent.

At this time he must have been in splendid condition, for daily he went through his physical drill—in which regard it may be mentioned that there exists a vivid little description of him, standing in the gymnasium, naked except for a loincloth, singing lustily as he did his exercises.[3] For fear of impairing his voice he was obliged to be abstemious, and to lead a very regular life; and the later stories of his orgies and debauches may be set aside as being in complete disagreement with the accounts of the care he had to bestow upon himself, of his perfect health, and of the amount of hard work he was obliged to put in. Yet there is one fact to be recorded which reveals him at this time in a curious light.

As has already been pointed out, it was the custom in those days, and particularly in Greece, for a man of fashion to declare himself in love with some beautiful youth, and to take him about with him wherever he went. As a young man Nero had played with this irregularity, because he wished to be *à la mode*, but his love for Acte and afterwards for Poppæa had checked any possible tendencies he may have had in that direction. Now, however, his normal masculine instincts were again deflected by some oddity in his nature sanctioned by Greek custom, and he began to lavish his affections upon a youth named Sporos, who, in appearance, reminded him so much of Poppæa that he used to call him Sabina, Poppæa's second name. The oddity, however, may have been not altogether in Nero's nature but rather in the physical character of Sporos, for there is some evidence to lead us to suppose that he was hermaphroditic, [4] and certainly he lacked the physical organs of a male. One of the new Empress Messalina's ladies-in-waiting, Calvia Crispinilla by name, looked after the boy, and attended to his extensive wardrobe; and this fact may be interpreted either as an indication that he was at first merely a sort of ornamental adjunct, or as evidence of an inurement to sexual peculiarities hardly intelligible to the minds of today. Gossip said that Nero went through a mock marriage with Sporos, and gave a feast in honour of the ceremony at which his friends congratulated the boy-bride, and offered the customary wishes that the union might be blessed with offspring. In this connection it may be mentioned that a certain man having been asked what he thought of such a marriage, replied that it was a pity Nero's father had not also been satisfied with a wife of that kind.

While the Emperor was thus touring through Greece the inevitable plot was being hatched against him by the supporters of tradition, and the imperial agents reported that the leaders of the conspiracy were the two brothers, Sulpicius Scribonius Rufus and Scribonius Proculus, both Governors of western provinces, and Corbulo, the famous general in the East. Nero therefore sent orders to them to come to him in Greece; and the two brothers, not waiting for the Emperor to receive them, killed themselves as soon as they knew that they had been betrayed. Corbulo had been under suspicion for some time, and the evidence against him was so strong that on his arrival at the port of Corinth Nero sent a message to him at once, offering him the privilege of choosing his own mode of death. Thereupon he instantly stabbed himself, uttering one word in Greek, which is to be translated "It serves me right," and which has left posterity wondering ever since whether it were a confession of guilt, an admission of the foolishness of having put himself in Nero's hands, or an expression of regret for not having killed him long ago. Personally, I think he meant to say that he was rightly served for having mixed himself up in some immature plot or other, and for having come to Greece at Nero's command instead of attempting to save himself by heading an immediate revolution.

The autumn of A.D. 67 found the Emperor at Corinth, and here he began the cutting of a canal through the Isthmus, so as to spare the ships the long voyage around the coast of Sparta in their journeys between the east and the west of Greece. The work, however, was left unfinished by Nero's successors, and the canal was not cut until the year 1893.

On November 28th, after winning the prize at the

Isthmian Games held at Corinth, Nero, hot, excited, and beaming with pleasure, went onto the stage and announced that he had bestowed "freedom" upon the whole of southern Greece, that is to say the Peloponnesus or Achaia. This "freedom," which corresponded to what we should now call Dominion Status, meant the country's right to control its own affairs within the Empire, and no such gift had ever before been made to a large area of this kind, only certain cities having been thus honoured. Nero, however, loved the Greeks, and wanted to show his appreciation of the manner in which they had received him and had applauded his singing; and he therefore took this unprecedented step, much to the dismay of the conservative Romans. The charming little speech he made on this occasion has been preserved, and was as follows[5]:—

"Hellenes!—it is an unexpected gift that I am going to make to you—except that there is nothing which you might not expect from my good will towards you. Yes, it is a gift such as you yourselves might never have dared to ask for. Hellenes!—you who inhabit Achaia and the Peloponnesus!—receive your liberty and your exemption from all imperial taxes! It is a liberty which never, not even in your most prosperous days, did you all enjoy; for you were slaves either to foreigners or else to one another. Ah me!—I wish that I were making this gift while Hellas was still prosperous: that would have given me even more happiness, and, indeed, I owe a grudge on this account to time because it has forestalled me and has squandered away the fullness of the boon. Yet it is not now because of pity, but because of my affection for you, that I bestow this gift upon you; and I thank your gods, whose care for me both on land and sea I have never found to fail, for having enabled me to do you this great favour. For other men before now have given freedom to cities; but Nero alone has liberated a Province!"

The enthusiasm of the assembly, of course, was overwhelming, and soon Nero was actually deified by the Greeks as "Zeus, Our Liberator." On the altar of Zeus in the chief temple of the city they inscribed the words "To Zeus, Our Liberator, namely Nero, for ever and ever"; in the temple of Apollo they set up his statue; and they called him "The new Sun, illuminating the Hellenes," and "the one and only lover of the Greeks of all time." All this, of course, was very gratifying; but Nero preferred to be adored as an artist rather than as a Philhellene.

His attitude in regard to his singing is very strikingly revealed in a letter he sent to Helios, his "viceroy" in Rome, who had warned him that he ought to come back. "Though now," he wrote, "all your hopes and wishes are for my speedy return, surely you ought rather to say and hope that I may come back with a reputation worthy of Nero"—a musical reputation, that is to say. He could not understand how Helios, or anybody else, could think affairs of state more important than his engagements to sing to his people, nor the imperial crown more splendid than the singer's chaplet of victory. He did not realize how serious was the discontent in Rome, particularly owing to the mismanagement and injustice of Helios; and when at last, early in A.D.

68, a few weeks after he had celebrated his thirtieth birthday, he found this man on his doorstep, having raced over from Italy to implore his master to come home, he was startled and much put out. He had planned to visit his friend Tiridates, in Armenia, and even to go on to the frontiers of the Parthians. He had hoped, also, to sail over to Egypt, the traditional home of music. He consented, however, to abandon these plans and return, because he felt that, if the fears of Helios were well-founded, the cause of the unrest in Rome could only be the inability of the populace to realize his vocal triumphs in Greece. They did not understand, evidently, that the artistic world was at his feet, and that Art was all that mattered: he must certainly go home and explain his point of view to the sadly uncultured men of Rome, making them understand that an Emperor's victories in the glorious realm of music were more to be reverenced than those on the field of battle.

After a stormy voyage he landed once more in Italy, probably in February, A.D. 68, and went straight to Naples, entering the city in a chariot drawn by milk-white horses, through a gap specially made for the purpose in the wall of the city, it being a traditional and symbolical custom of the Greeks thus to pull down the ramparts of war to let Art's victors in. From Naples he proceeded to Antium, his birthplace, and to Alba, making a similar entry into these towns; and at last he arrived in Rome, where his entrance was effected once more through a breach in the wall, much to the astonishment of the citizens who had never heard of the custom.

A grand procession had been organized, and, notice of his coming having been given betimes, a great welcome was accorded him. At the head of the procession walked the men who were carrying the eighteen hundred and eight chaplets and garlands which the Emperor had won in the Greek contests, and behind them a second army bore aloft the placards upon which were written the names and nature of the contests, each followed by the words: "Nero Cæsar won the victory in this competition, being the first Roman to do so since the world began." Next came Nero himself, flushed and smiling, and waving his hand to his dear public. He was clad in purple sprinkled with gold stars, and carried the Pythian laurel, while upon his red head was a wreath of wild olive. He was riding in the golden chariot which had been used by the Emperor Augustus in his military triumphs, and beside him sat Diodorus, the world's most famous harpist, who, it seems, had often acted as his accompanist. Behind him marched his Augustani, and the Prætorian Guard.

The entire Senate received him in the Forum, and thence went with him to the Capitol. The streets were decked with garlands and bunting, and strewn with saffron, and the smoke of sweet-smelling incense went up in clouds from thousands of censers. "Hail, Olympian Victor!" cried the multitudes. "Hail, Pythian Victor! Augustus! Augustus! Hail to Nero who is the god Hercules! Hail to Nero who is the god Apollo! Our one national Victor, the only one from the beginning of time! Augustus! Augustus! O divine Voice! Blessed are they that hear it!"

"Those were their very words," says Dion Cassius,[6] not knowing, any more than we do now, what to make of it all, and being quite unable to say whether this were a spontaneous ovation or a rehearsed piece of flattery. For my own part, I should imagine that the lower classes were delighted to have their Emperor back, both because it was good for trade, and also because the government of Helios and the Senate had been harsh and unpopular; and that many of the upper classes were really impressed by Nero's triumphal tour of Greece, and were more or less sincere in their welcome and their plaudits. But there must have been a great many people who were bitterly hostile, partly because of the iniquities of his agents—of which Nero, however, was quite unaware—and partly because of their contempt for music and musicians, and their despair at the Emperor's absorption in these things; while many more there must have been who were utterly perplexed, and could only shake their heads and say that it was all very un-Roman.

At the end of the ceremonies Nero was conducted to his new palace, the Golden House, which was not yet finished, but was habitable; and when he had inspected it he made the jovial remark that he now had a house fit for a gentleman. He was tremendously elated by his reception, and he must have laughed at Helios for his fears. Even here in Rome, he felt, the people acknowledged that he was the great *maestro;* and before he retired to rest that night he caused his eighteen hundred prizes to be hung all round his bedroom, so that he could see them when he woke up in the morning. Later he had them hung around the Egyptian obelisk which stood in the Hippodrome; and during the following days he drove his chariot in various races around that course, perhaps being anxious to prove to the Romans that he was a man as well as a musician. If this be so, however, he defeated his purpose by taking Sporos about with him openly, and by embracing him in public. There is, as has been said, a doubt whether Sporos were really a boy at all; but the public did not doubt his sex, nor does the suggestion of a physical abnormality of this kind remove from our minds the discomfort which the subject in any case arouses.

At the beginning of March he went back to Naples; but in the third week of that month, on the anniversary of his mother's death, he received news that Caius Julius Vindex, Governor of Gallia Lugdunensis (the province of Gaul of which Lyons was the capital), had raised the standard of revolt. Vindex himself was of Gallic birth, although his father had been a Roman senator, and was descended from the ancient kings of the province; and the despatches stated that he had called the tribesmen to arms and had been joined by such troops as were stationed in the neighbourhood. The speech which he made to his followers can hardly have been reported to Nero, but it was recorded at the time when it was made, and is given by Dion Cassius.[7]

"It is our duty to revolt," said Vindex, "because Nero has ruined the whole Roman world, because he has put to death the best men in the Senate, because he killed his mother, and because he does not preserve even the semblance of sovereignty. Murders, confiscations of property, and other outrages, of course, have often been committed by many other persons; but how can one find words to describe the rest of his conduct as it deserves? My friends, I have seen, believe me, I have seen that man—if he *is* a man, in view of his relations with Sporos and Pythagoras—in the arena of the theatre or in the orchestra, sometimes playing the harp, and wearing the dress of a musician or of an actor. I have often heard him sing, I have heard him declaim, I have heard him speaking lines from the tragedies. I have seen him in chains, I have seen him dragged about, I have seen him pregnant, I have seen him in childbirth, going through all the situations of legend by speaking or being spoken to, by posturing or being postured at. Who, then, can call such a person Cæsar or Emperor or Augustus? Let no one, on any consideration, so abuse those sacred titles! They were held by Augustus and by Claudius, but this fellow might more properly be termed Thyestes, or Œdipus, or Alcmeon, or Orestes, for these are the characters he impersonates on the stage, and it is their titles that he has assumed, rather than the others. Therefore, now at last let us rise against him. Come to the aid of your own country and of Rome, and rid the world of him!"

In this speech it is interesting to observe that Nero's great crime was his singing and "operatic" acting on the stage. The cruelties of which he was later accused are not referred to, for the good reason that, in spite of all that is said against him, he was not cruel. Vindex, obviously, did not think of him as a human monster:

he thought of him as a morally depraved singer and play-actor, devoid of dignity.

Nero received the news of the rising very casually: he was used to conspiracies, and he had unbounded belief in his good luck. And, after all, if he were dethroned, what would it matter? He would then be able to pursue his musical career with so much the less interruption. An astrologer had once warned him that some day he would lose all his money, and he had replied, "An artist can make a living in any country." Another astrologer had told him, however, that though he might lose his Roman throne he would gain the dominion of the East; and all the fortune-tellers had predicted a long life of happiness for him. The news, therefore, did not trouble him unduly. He was watching some gymnastic contests just after luncheon when the despatches arrived, and, having read them, he turned his attention to the athletes again, and presently joined in the sports himself.

At dinner that night more serious news arrived, at which he began to swear at the rebels in a loud voice; but his friends immediately reminded him that he was going to sing to them the next day, and begged him not to strain his vocal cords by thus cursing his enemies. For eight days he took no steps whatsoever to suppress the revolt; but when at length he heard that Vindex had spoken of him as "that wretched musician," he lost patience. "I am not a wretched musician," he declared indignantly; "I am a very great one," and he turned to his friends, asking them if they knew a better. "Nothing so much galled him," says Suetonius,[8] "as to find his music thus disparaged, and he hotly denied his lack of skill in an art in which he had, indeed, arrived at such perfection." He then sent a letter to the Senate, telling them to take all the necessary steps for the crushing of the rebellion; and he apologized for being unable to come at once to Rome himself, explaining that he was not in very good voice at the moment—as though the only reason for his return to the capital was that he might sing there.

Then came the news that the elderly and trusted Lucius Sulpicius Galba, Governor of Hispania Tarraconensis (northern and central Spain), was in communication with Vindex, who had offered to make him Emperor. An astrologer had once warned Nero to beware of "seventy-three years," and he had assumed that that was to be an age in his own life at which some danger was to be feared; but now, on remarking that Galba was surely an old man, he received the reply that his age was seventy-three years, at which he started back in dismay.

At last, early in April he went to Rome, and was much comforted to hear on his arrival that Verginius Rufus, the Governor of Upper Germany, was marching with the troops under his command, including the Fourth, Twenty-first, and Twenty-second Legions, to attack Vindex. The situation seemed hopeful, and Nero soon resumed his care-free attitude, attending to his public duties and giving sumptuous dinner-parties to his friends, at which he sang amusing songs at the expense of the rebels. He went incognito to the theatre, and on one occasion sent word round to a certain actor who had been much applauded, jokingly, or perhaps, spitefully, telling him that he was evidently having it all his own way now that he (Nero) was too busy to appear on the stage. He was also present at the dedication of the temple to the deified Poppæa, who was now identified with Venus, just as Cleopatra had been, in the days when Julius Cæsar had set up her statue in the Venus-shrine which he had built in Rome.

The days passed, and matters seemed to be going well. News arrived that on April 2nd Galba, at a public meeting in Spain, had refused to allow himself to be proclaimed Emperor, but had said that he would abide by the wishes of the Senate; and at the same time came despatches stating that Verginius Rufus was closing in on Vindex. The Prætorian Guard in Rome, under the command of Tigellinus and Nymphidius, had declared their loyalty, and the legions elsewhere had not mutinied. One day Nero sent hastily for some of the leading senators to come to the palace, but after a brief discussion of the situation he dismissed the subject impatiently, and made them all come with him to view a new pipe-organ, worked by water; and for a long time he discoursed to them upon the principles and the difficulties of the contrivance. It was apparently an improvement on the first hydraulic organ invented by Ctesibius in Egypt three centuries earlier; and Nero was very excited about it. "I will give a public demonstration of it in the theatre," he said, adding, with a smile, "that is to say, if Vindex will permit me."

Early in May, however, the appalling news reached the palace that Galba and the Spanish provinces had thrown in their lot with Vindex; that Otho, the former husband of Poppæa, who was still Governor of Portugal, had joined them; and that Rubrius Gallus, who had been sent with reinforcements from Rome, had gone over to the enemy. At this, Nero fainted dead away. When he came to his senses, he tore his clothes and beat his brow, crying out, "It is all over with me!" One of his nurses, who had lived in the palace ever since he was a child, and had never ceased to love him, threw her arms around him, whispering to him that other princes before him had survived such disasters; but he only moaned, "I ought to be dead: I am wretched beyond all measure, because I have lost an empire and am still living!"

A few days later, however, came the tidings that Vindex, who had now begun to call Nero by his family name, Ahenobarbus, as though he were already dethroned, had been shut out of Lugdunum (Lyons) by the loyal inhabitants, and was about to be attacked in the open by the Legions from Upper Germany. Shortly afterwards the news arrived that Vindex had been defeated and killed.

Nero was elated, and the resilience of his nature caused him soon to forget his gloom. He would go himself to Gaul, he declared, and win the hearts of the defeated rebels by singing to them. The troops should move on towards Spain, against Galba and Otho; and he would follow, appealing to the malcontents by means of musical and theatrical entertainments. He said to his friends one day after dinner: "As soon as I arrive in Gaul, I will make my appearance amongst the disaffected troops, unarmed, and with tears in my eyes. I will talk to them and sing to them, and after I have won them to repentance, I will call for public rejoicings next day, and I shall sing them songs of triumph—which, by the way, I must now go and compose."[9]

Eagerly he began to plan a grand tour of the West which should be like the tour he had recently made through Greece. His first care was the provision of carts in which his musical instruments and his stage scenery were to be carried. He then began to drill a great body of chorus-girls, dressing them as Amazons, cropping their hair, and giving them stage-swords and shields. They were to be employed in some spectacular production which he had in mind, and for which, it seems, he was now feverishly composing the words and music. He ordered all the men of means in the country to supply him with slaves to act as stage-hands and "supers"; and, having very little of his private fortune left, he exacted contributions from his tenants in the form of one year's rent in advance.

His plans, of course, were ridiculed in Rome, and his agents' attempts to raise money for the undertaking brought down the people's wrath on his head. A shortage of corn existed at the time, and there was danger of a famine in the city. Just then a large vessel arrived from Egypt, heaped high with what appeared to be corn; but when the cargo began to be unloaded it was found by the hungry people on the quay to consist of yellow Nubian sand, which the Emperor had ordered some time previously as a covering for the floor of his gymnasium, and their rage vented itself in curses and threats. Lampoons were scribbled on the walls. Upon the head of one of his statues a toy chariot was placed, to which was attached the inscription: "Here's a race for him to run: let him race off and never come back." A sack was hung around another statue, with the words: "You deserve the sack!" —to be tied up in a sack and drowned being the punishment of those who killed their parents. When he sent for his friends they begged to be excused for one reason or another, and even Tigellinus was conspicuously absent. His adoring Augustani, and all his admiring circle, melted away.

His bitter enemies, the upholders of the aristocratic idea, saw their great opportunity, and by spreading fearful rumours about him, worked up the hatred of the crowd. They said that he intended to burn Rome for the second time, to massacre the Senate, to let wild animals loose in the city, and so forth. They declared that the gods were against him, and that the omens were bad; and it was now recalled that on his last appearance on the stage he had stumbled just when, in the rôle of Œdipus, he was saying the words, "Wife, mother, father, force me towards my doom." Somebody spread the story that the doors of the mausoleum of Augustus had flown open of their own accord at dead of night, and that a voice had issued from it, crying "Nero! Nero!" In consequence, everybody was nervous and over-wrought, except the Emperor himself, who was busily engaged in preparing his musical tour, and was convinced that the rebellion would soon be over. He made a public vow that if his troubles were successfully overcome he would give a performance in the theatre upon the organ, the flute, the bagpipes and the harp, and would act and sing the rôle of Turnus which he proposed to adapt from Virgil and set to music.

Then, on the evening of June 8th, letters were brought to him announcing that Verginius and his legions had renounced their allegiance, and that the western provinces had proclaimed Galba Emperor. Nero was eating his dinner at the time, but springing to his feet, he kicked over the table before him, dashed two priceless cups to the ground, and tore the letters to pieces. He then hastened to his room, vainly hunted everywhere for the snake-skin charm which he used to wear as a child, and, seizing a little golden box containing poison, rushed out of the palace, and ordered his servants to take him to the Servilian Gardens, his villa on the road to Ostia. He had for long intended, in case of trouble, to take ship for Egypt, where, he once said to a friend, "this little artistic gift of mine will support me"; and his object in going to this villa was to be near the port of Ostia. As soon as he reached the house, in fact, he sent a trusted freedman to the harbour with orders to make ready a vessel; and then, calling to him the officers of the detachment of Prætorian Guards then on duty in the Servilian Gardens, he asked them whether they would come with him on this voyage. To this wild suggestion, one of the officers replied by quoting a line from the *Æneid:* "Is it then so hard a thing to die?"[10]

But Nero had not yet given up hope. He sent

another freedman back to the palace, it seems, to fetch a few necessities, and to bring Sporos to him. He was not in the least interested in his wife, Messalina; but the sexless Sporos was evidently dear to him, and, if anything can serve to make palatable to the mind a subject so liable to cause disgust, it is the fact that this strange little eunuch, or hermaphrodite, or whatever he was, clung to him faithfully to the end, although it would have been so easy for him to slip away.

Presently Nero changed his mind in regard to an immediate voyage: it was no good going as a fugitive, for there would be a price upon his head. Instead, he decided to address the people, or the Prætorian troops, telling them that he was willing to abdicate in favour of Galba, and that if he were given the governorship of Egypt, he would be a loyal servant of the new Emperor. With this idea in his head, he sat for some hours composing the speech he proposed to make, and, after his death, it was found in his writing-case. Later, however, he began to realize that the mob would probably kill him before he could address them; and, abandoning the plan, he went to bed, his mind now turning over the project of escaping to Parthia.

At length he fell asleep, but was awakened about midnight by a crash of thunder; and in the silence which followed there came to his ears the sound of tramping feet. Rushing out of the villa, a flash of lightning revealed to him the soldiers of the Guard marching away, and he realized that they had received orders to come back to barracks. Who had given those orders?—Tigellinus or his colleague Nymphidius? He despatched two or three of his few remaining servants to tell these two and some of his other trusted officials to come to him; but soon the messengers returned saying that they could get no replies. At this he boldly went out into the storm himself, with three or four attendants, and made his way to such houses of his friends as were in the neighbourhood, but the doors were shut and barred, and nobody would admit him. What had happened, though he did not know it, was that Tigellinus and Nymphidius had both told the Prætorian Guard that Nero was about to take ship for the East, and that their loyalty to him was no longer called for; whereupon the troops, feeling themselves as it were deserted by their Emperor, had given their allegiance to the agents of Galba, their decision being quickly made known to the chief men of the city.[11]

Returning, now in despair, to the villa, Nero found that all the servants had fled; and thereupon he made up his mind to kill himself. He hurried into the room where he had been sleeping; but the decamping servants had stolen the gold box containing his poison, and had stripped the place of all its valuables, even the bedclothes having been taken. He then rushed about the house calling for Spicillus, the gladiator, or somebody to come and kill him; but the last-left of his servants refused to help him, at which he cried out, "What!—have I neither friend nor enemy?" He thereupon made his way amidst the thunder and lightning to the bank of the river at the end of the deserted garden, and was about to drown himself when Phaon, a faithful freedman, coming after him, offered to hide him in his house, some four miles north of the city, and it seems that he had some definite plan for his escape.

Nero eagerly accepted the offer, and, taking Sporos with him, set out on horseback with Phaon, another freedman named Epaphroditus, and one attendant, his head muffled up in spite of the closeness of the night, an old cloak concealing his tunic, and a handkerchief held before his face. It was necessary to traverse the city from end to end, but the hour, the storm, and the crisis had combined to empty the streets, and the four galloping horsemen passed like phantoms, peeped at from windows but unmolested. As they went by the Prætorian Barracks on the slope of the Quirinal, to the north of the Palatine, they heard the shouts of the soldiers, and knew that they were drinking the health of Galba and destruction to Nero. Once a pedestrian called out to them: "Is there any news of Nero?"—and they noticed another man who pointed to them, and said to his companion, "They are in pursuit of Nero."

Suddenly the Emperor's horse shied at a carcass which lay in the road, thereby causing the handkerchief to be lowered from his face; and at that moment an old soldier passed by, recognized him by the light of a lantern, and saluted. Somehow or other, however, they managed to reach the Colline Gate at the northern end of the city, without being intercepted, and to pass out into the open country; and when at length they came to the turning which led down to the house of Phaon they dismounted, and with much difficulty made their way amidst bushes and briars and across a reedy marsh to the back of the building. Here Phaon advised Nero to climb down into a cavernous sand-pit at the end of the garden, but he started back, exclaiming, "No!—I'll not go underground while I am still alive"—a remark which indicates that his bizarre sense of humour had not deserted him. He consented, however, to sit down and wait, while Phaon went into the house to make arrangements for his concealment; and being very thirsty he dipped his hand into a tank of dirty water, drank a little from the hollow of his palm, and said with a smile, "So this is Nero's celebrated *decocta!*"—that being the term denoting the boiled, filtered, and ice-cooled drinking water used at the palace.

Dawn was now breaking, and in the dim light Nero began to pull out the brambles and thorns which were sticking in his cloak; but while he was so doing Phaon returned, saying that he had enlarged a ventilation hole in the wall of one of the back rooms of the house and that through this Nero could crawl without any of the household knowing of his presence. Having done as he was bid, the imperial fugitive found himself in a small room, upon the mud floor of which Phaon had placed a mattress and a coverlet. Some coarse bread and tepid water was offered to him; but though both hungry and thirsty, he only drank a little of the water.

Epaphroditus, who for some reason wished him dead, now urged him to release himself from this miserable situation by committing suicide in the customary manner, whereupon he nodded, and asked him and the others to dig a grave here in the mud-floor of the room, and he told them that he had noticed some slabs of marble stacked in the garden which would serve to line it. They dug the grave in silence, Nero's eyes fixed upon them. He asked them, then, to fetch the water and the materials necessary for the washing of his body after death; and at each request the tears welled into his eyes. Many times he sighed: "*Qualis artifex pereo!*"—"What an artist perishes in me!" But still he hesitated to die.

Soon after sunrise, somebody in Phaon's employ at the palace sent a messenger to him with a letter giving him the news. Nero snatched it from Phaon's hand as he brought it to him to see; and there he read that he had been declared a public enemy by the Senate which had met during the night, that a search was being made for him, and that he had been sentenced to die by "the ancient Roman method of execution."

"What sort of method is that?" he asked, in horror.

"The prisoner," said Epaphroditus, "is stripped naked, his neck is fastened in a forked stake, and he is whipped to death."

At this Nero picked up two daggers which he had brought with him, but, having felt their points, put them down again. "The moment is not yet come," he said.

He knew that he ought to kill himself at once, and yet he hesitated: there was still the faint hope that he might escape. He took up a dagger once more, and laid it aside again. He told Sporos to begin to sing the death-chant. He asked if anybody present intended to kill himself too, and, if so, he begged them to do it first, in order that he might see how it was done. But nobody moved: all eyes were fixed upon him in silence.

"This is disgraceful!" he groaned wiping the sweat from his face. "I ought not to be still alive. It is not seemly, Nero!—it is not seemly. One ought to be brave in a situation like this. Come: courage, man!"

As he spoke, the sound of galloping horses fell upon his ears, and when Epaphroditus had told him that it was the soldiers, who, informed of his place of hiding, were coming in search of him, he assumed his last theatrical attitude, and, quoting the words of Homer,[12] whispered dramatically: "The sound of swift-footed steeds strikes upon mine ears!" Then, saying again, "Jupiter!—what an artist is lost to the world! —what an artist!" he snatched up the dagger and, with the aid of his freedman, drove it into his throat.

A few moments later, as he lay bleeding to death, a military officer burst into the room, and pulling off his cloak, applied it to the wound in an attempt to stanch the blood. "Too late!" Nero gasped. "Is this your loyalty?" A moment afterwards he passed into unconsciousness.

By a curious coincidence this day, June 9th, was the anniversary of the enforced suicide of Octavia.

CHAPTER XVIII

The Reign of Galba, June, A.D. 68—The Reign of Otho, January, A.D. 69—The Return of Nero—The Apocalypse—The Sources of Information—Nero as Antichrist.

THE story of Nero's suicide was soon conveyed to Rome, and was received at first with very mixed feelings. Suetonius [1] says that the people danced with delight, but Tacitus, [2] on the contrary, tells us that though the most solid elements of society were pleased, the masses were plunged into grief. The situation, in fact, was difficult to gauge, for the crowds were divided, some pulling down the Emperor's statues and cursing his memory, others bewailing his loss and blaming his ministers for the tragedy. When the Prætorian Guard learnt that Nero had not fled to Egypt as their commanding officers had told them, they were ashamed and angry, and declared that they would never have renounced their allegiance to him if they had not believed that he had already abdicated. [3]

The opinion of the lower classes seems to have been that the Emperor's agents rather than he himself had been to blame for any ills which they had suffered[4]; and the mob made an immediate attack on these men, some of them being beaten or stoned to death in the streets. Aponius, one of Nero's secret police, was knocked down, and a passing cart heavily laden with stones was deliberately driven over him, crushing him to death. Spicillus, the Emperor's favourite gladiator, who had deserted his master on the previous evening, was attacked in the Forum and the crowd pushed over one of Nero's statues so that it fell upon him and killed him. An important senator named Mauriscus, in fact, warned the Senate that the masses were so much in two minds about the crisis that it looked as though they would all soon be wishing Nero alive again.

A widespread feeling of pity for the Emperor developed during the day. When he had left the palace on the previous evening, people now said, he had not fled: he had gone quite openly to the Servilian Gardens. In the night he had boldly ridden right through the city to the house of Phaon, hoping that his well-wishers would come to his aid there in the end; but when the Senate had declared him a public enemy he had honourably killed himself. He had behaved with bravery, as befitted the last of the glorious Julian line. How peaceful and prosperous all these years of his reign had been! It was only during and since his tour in Greece that his agents—Helios and such-like—had pillaged the people; and that was not his fault.[5] How handsome he had been; what a splendid figure of a young man![6] True, he had been obsessed by this mania for music; but his voice had certainly been wonderful. If only he had marched against the aged Galba at once, he would have crushed the rebellion with ease; for who wanted this old man as Emperor?

Icelus, Galba's chief agent in Rome, was so impressed by this attitude of the mob, that although some sections of the people, as has been said, were overturning Nero's statues and abusing his memory, he decided to allow him a proper funeral. He and Nymphidius, the joint-commander of the Prætorians—the sole commander, rather, for he had made the consumptive Tigellinus retire from active service—were in control of affairs in Rome; but Nymphidius is not stated to have visited the scene of the tragedy. Icelus alone, in fact, appears to have gone to Phaon's house; but instructions were given that the body of Nero was to be treated with respect. Icelus had found Sporos sitting there weeping, and Nymphidius had afterwards sent for the strange little creature and had taken him into his own house; but there is no mention of the fate of Phaon. The two old women, Ecloge and Alexandra, who had nursed Nero when he was a child, had been allowed to go and prepare his body for the funeral; and, during the day, the Emperor's former mistress, Acte, who happened to be in Rome at the time, had gone to help them.

There is a tradition, it may be mentioned, that a few years before this the sorrowful Acte had been converted to Christianity by St. Paul; but the only evidence for the story is a statement made by St. Chrysostom [8] that a lady thus converted, who is not named, had been Nero's mistress. Her identification with Acte is not unlikely; and, if it be so, there is a curiously dramatic quality in the imagination's picture of the convert recommending to Christ the soul of her imperial lover whom her fellow-Christians, as will presently be recorded, were already beginning to regard as Antichrist.

The funeral probably took place towards the evening of the same day. The body, carried upon a couch, was covered by a rich white material interwoven with gold-thread; and after the cremation—the place of which is not recorded, but was perhaps Phaon's garden—the ashes were taken by Acte and the two nurses to the family tomb of the Ahenobarbi in a garden on the Pincian Hill. A few months later, it may be added, a porphyry casket was placed here for the ashes to rest in, before which a marble altar enclosed by a marble balustrade was erected. During the day Icelus set out for Gaul to carry the news to Galba, to whom he ultimately reported that he did not speak from hearsay of Nero's death, but had visited Phaon's house and had seen the body.[9] As soon as he had gone, however, Nymphidius attempted to have himself proclaimed Emperor, for he had always contended that he was the son of the Emperor Claudius, his mother having been a beautiful woman who had from time to time taken the fancy of that Emperor and, indeed, of most of the officials of his court—but the likeness of Nymphidius to Claudius, though striking, was not more remarkable than his resemblance to a certain gladiator whom his mother had admired.

He was not as popular as he had imagined, however, nor was it thought delicate of him to take Sporos about everywhere with him, dressed as a girl, and now named Poppæa; and when it was suggested that he, Nymphidius, should be raised to the imperial throne, an important military officer, named Antonius Honoratus, made a speech to the Prætorian Guard begging them not to forswear their oath to Galba. "Nero's misdeeds," he said, "gave some justification for your former renunciation of allegiance, but you have no such excuse for betraying Galba. The death of a mother, the blood of a wife, and the degradation of the imperial dignity upon the stage and amongst actors, were then your justifications, and even so we did not desert Nero until Nymphidius had made us believe that Nero had first deserted us and had fled to Egypt. Shall we, therefore, to appease the spirit of Nero kill Galba? Rather let us kill Nymphidius, thereby doing to him only what he deserves, and at the same time both revenging Nero's death and showing ourselves loyal to Galba." [10]

This speech, made by a man evidently troubled at Nero's death, shows, as did the speech of Vindex, that the late Emperor's great crime was his work upon the stage. It is to be noticed, by the way, that he was not at this time thought to have murdered Britannicus: the deaths of his mother and of Octavia were alone brought up against him. The speech shows, too, that Nero was ill-served by Nymphidius, and that if only he had gone personally to the Prætorian Guard for protection he would not have been dethroned. Its effect upon the troops was decisive, and Nymphidius was killed shortly afterwards.

Several legions in Italy and the provinces were slow to acknowledge Galba, many of them "lamenting the loss of Nero." [11] and the widespread love for the memory of Nero caused him the greatest alarm; and when at length he arrived in Rome he was so uncertain of the temper of the troops that he used his own legions to carry out the most terrible massacres amongst the soldiers whose allegiance was in question. He also put to death without mercy a number of Nero's late officials, including Helios. Tigellinus, however, he spared, in spite of the mob's demand for the death of this man who, they said, was responsible for Nero's unpopularity and yet had deserted him in the end.[12] Galba, however, explained that Tigellinus was a dying man, being wasted with consumption; and thus, for the moment, he escaped.

The new Emperor's general severity caused him to become very unpopular, and his grim and wrinkled old age "was a subject of loathing to men who were accustomed to the grace and youth of Nero."[13] He seemed to be niggardly and hardly even decent; for the prodigality and sumptuousness of Nero, so long as it was paid for out of his own money, had always been admired by the people. Presently the reaction set in, and Nero began to be idealized into the most wonderful of men. After a reign of six months, Galba was murdered, in January A.D. 69, and on the returning wave of Nero's popularity, his former friend, Otho, once the husband of Poppæa, was carried to the throne. Otho's brief association with Galba was cleverly obscured by his present adulation of Nero; and he won the mob at once by permitting them to re-erect Nero's statues, and to heap flowers on his tomb. Galba's head was struck from his dead body and was placed, as a token of revenge accomplished, upon the grave of one of Nero's favourite slaves whom Galba had executed, the implication being that the head of an Emperor was not too high payment for the life of even a slave beloved by the celestial Nero.

Otho at once began to restore to office some of Nero's freedmen and officials who had escaped Galba's severity; and in particular he reinstated Flavius Sabinus as Governor of Rome, a post given to him by Nero, and taken from him by Galba. Tigellinus, however, was still bitterly hated, and his fate was terrible. He was now suffering from rapid consumption and other incurable diseases, to which were added the diseases of his mind which drove him, as Plutarch says, to "unhallowed and frightful excesses among impure prostitutes, and to which even at the very close of life his lewd nature clung and in them gasped out, as it were, its last—these being in themselves the extremest punishment and equal to many deaths." [14] The people demanded his death, and at last Otho sent for him, whereupon he cut his throat with a razor.

The new Emperor not only proposed to replace all Nero's statues, "as a public measure," but even set up again some of those of Poppæa, just to show that he bore no ill-will to her imperial husband for having taken her from him. He also took possession of Sporos, whom Nero had loved, and called him his little Queen and Empress, though at the same time, but without success, he tried to induce Nero's widow, Messalina, to marry him. "In flattery and as the highest honour," as Suetonius says, [15] Otho was given officially the name "Nero" by the people, "as a mark of additional splendour," [16] and he is said to have used it at first in signing state documents. "With a view to popularity," says Tacitus, "he proposed to celebrate the memory of Nero with public honours." He readily obtained a grant of money to finish the Golden House as a sort of Neronian memorial; but the work was never completed. It may be mentioned in passing, also, that the Fourteenth Legion gave its allegiance to Otho expressly because he showed a love for Nero which they themselves had never ceased to feel.[17]

The overwhelming evidence of his great popularity now that he was gone has been generally overlooked by historians, whose fixed idea has been that he was a monster; but I feel it to be full justification for the interpretation of his character and his actions given in the foregoing pages. The memory of a cruel tyrant, of a fool whose mere vanity made him think he was a great singer, would never have aroused the enthusiasm of the people in this manner; and the delirious excitement caused by the incident about to be recorded is, in itself, the strongest evidence that Nero, with all his faults and eccentricities, was somehow not hateful.

At the beginning of A.D. 69, just before Galba was murdered, the whole Empire, save for the old school in Rome, was aroused to the highest pitch of excited happiness by the announcement that Nero was not dead, but had appeared in Greece on his way to the East. For some time there had been rumours that he had not died of the wound which, with the aid of Epaphroditus, he had inflicted upon himself, and that he had been spirited away. Icelus had stated that he had seen the body, but it was quite possible that Nero had then been only unconscious. It was recalled that the officer who had entered the room just after the Emperor had stabbed himself had endeavoured to stanch the blood, and perhaps his efforts had been successful. Nero's words to him—"Too late! Is this your loyalty?"—were curiously suggestive that the man—who perhaps was now dead [18]—had, actually, been loyal to him, and had promised to come to help him to escape, but had only arrived after Nero had given up hope. The conduct of Epaphroditus had been very suspicious: he had evidently wanted Nero to die, and perhaps he had falsely told the Emperor that the approaching horsemen were coming to arrest him, not to save him, and had rushed him into attempted suicide, or, maybe, had stabbed him himself, knowing that he was going to be rescued. Epaphroditus, presumably, had since disappeared, and could not be questioned; but I may add that a few years later, in the reign of Domitian, he was hounded down and executed for his part in the affair, and since Domitian was an admirer of Nero it may be that the real charge against him was that of trying to prevent the Emperor's escape.

The body taken out to be cremated was covered by a pall, and might have been that of somebody else, substituted. Nero might have remained concealed in some other part of Phaon's house until his wound was healed, and might then have been taken on board a ship and conveyed to the East. "The accounts of his (supposed) death," says Tacitus, [19] "had been various, which caused the more people to assert that he was alive, and to believe it."

Such were the rumours in Rome, but the truth will now never be known. The story that a man is still alive, who has been much beloved and has met an end open to doubt, is a frequent occurrence in history, and is almost invariably a delusion born of deep affection; but the account of Nero's supposed reappearance is circumstantial and lends some colour to the public belief that he had not died in Phaon's house. Tacitus, who, on the contrary, was of opinion that the supposed Nero was an impostor, gives the story as follows[20]:—

"There was a certain slave from Pontus, or, according to some writers, a freedman from Italy, who played the harp with skill and had a good singing voice. With these talents, and having also a face that resembled Nero, he very nearly succeeded in the imposture that he was the Emperor. By immense promises he gathered to his party a number of deserters, and with these as a crew he took ship, but was driven by adverse winds to the island of Cythnus (in the Ægæan Sea). At that place he fell in with a party of soldiers on their return from the East, and some of these he enlisted, while others, who refused to join him, he ordered to be executed. Having plundered some merchants and armed the stoutest of their slaves, he endeavoured to persuade Sisenna, a military officer from Syria who had happened to land on the island, to join him; but Sisenna, fearing danger from so audacious an adventurer, made his escape. A general state of excitement seized the inhabitants of the island, for numbers who hated the existing rule and wanted a revolution, were elated to find the name of Nero on all tongues again. The fame, indeed, of this pretended Nero gained strength every day, but by a sudden accident the illusion vanished. It happened that Asprenas, whom Galba had appointed Governor of Galatia and Pamphylia, arrived at the island with two galleys from the fleet at Misenum escorting him. Thereupon the impostor, calling himself Nero, summoned the commanders of the ships to attend him, their lawful prince, and, with an air of dejection, implored their assistance, by the duty which they owed him, and prayed for safe conduct either to Syria or to Egypt. These commanders, either wavering in uncertainty or intending to deceive, asked for time to consult their subordinates, and promised to return when they had made up their minds. But Asprenas was duly informed of what had occurred, and, at his suggestion, the pretended Emperor, whoever he was, was seized and put to death. The person of the man, his eyes, his hair, and the wildness of his expression, were remarkable. His body was conveyed to Asia, and afterwards sent to Rome."

Now, it seems very unlikely that an impostor would have sent for these naval commanders, knowing, as surely he would have known, that, coming from the naval base at Misenum so much frequented by the Emperor, they must have been personally acquainted with Nero; on the other hand, the action of Asprenas, who was one of Galba's men and had left Italy before he had been killed, is consistent with one who had recognized Nero and had wanted quickly to be rid of him. It must be remembered that Nero had been dethroned but six months before, and only a year ago had been touring Greece, where he must have been known by sight to hundreds of thousands of his people, so that an imposture would have been particularly hopeless, more especially since Nero's features, physique, mannerisms, hair, voice, and talents were all very individual.

I do not think that any historian has even suggested that the man was anything but an impostor; but it seems to me not at all impossible that he really was Nero, who had recovered from his wound and had escaped only to meet a miserable end on this little Ægæan island. Whether this be so or not, however, the story that Nero was alive has a particular interest for us because it was believed by the author of the Book of Revelation, the Apocalypse, which was written in all probability just before Galba's death.[21] The authorship of the Apocalypse is unknown, its attribution to St. John being a later appendage to the title; but, whoever he may have been, as a Christian he was actuated, of course, by a horror of Nero, the Emperor who had first persecuted the Christians, and he believed that he was not dead but was about to return to Rome.

In Greek the name "Nero" was "Neron," and his Greek subjects generally spoke of him as "Neron Kaisar," that is to say "Nero Cæsar." In Hebrew, wherein certain vowels are not expressed in writing, the name is spelt "Nron Ksr"; and these letters correspond to the numerals 50, 200, 6, 50, 100, 60, 200, which add up to 666, the number assigned to the apocalyptic Beast, who was therefore none other than Nero—an interpretation of the cypher upon which scholarship is pretty well unanimous. This Beast is described as having been "wounded unto death, but his deadly wound was healed, and all the world wondered after the

Beast."[22] He was "the Beast that was, and is not, and yet is";[23] and the author of the book adds: "Let him that hath understanding count the number of the Beast, for it is the number of a man, and his number is Six hundred and sixty and six."[24] Perhaps in reference to Nero's hair, he states that the beast was red, and that it had seven heads which were mountains—the seven famous hills of Rome—and ten horns, probably a round number for the provinces of the Empire.[25]

He then says that "there are seven kings: five are fallen, and one is, and the other is not yet come; and the Beast that was, and is not, even he is the eighth, and is of the seven."[26] The "five who are fallen" are evidently the five first Emperors, Augustus, Tiberius, Caligula, Claudius, and Nero; the "one who is" is Galba; the "one who is not yet come" is Otho, who, at the time when the book was written, was already being talked of as Galba's successor; and "the eighth" is Nero again, who is about to return and is "of the seven."

The author of the Apocalypse also refers, so it seems, to the Parthians, into whose country Nero had thought of escaping, for he speaks of the angel "pouring out his vial upon the great river Euphrates, and the water thereof was dried up that the way of the Kings of the East might be prepared."[27] Now, it will be remembered that Nero had made a friend of Tiridates, the Parthian King of Armenia, and that the Parthian royal house had the greatest respect for Nero; and when the news of his dethronement and supposed death reached them, they sent messengers to Rome, as Suetonius tells us, "earnestly requesting that due honour should be paid to Nero's memory." And later, on hearing the story that he was still alive, they were very nearly induced to take up arms to help him.[28]

Nero's honour, however, was for the moment safe in Rome, and before the news of this second death of his had been received, the people waited longingly for the tidings of his return. "Sometimes," says Suetonius,[29] "they placed his image upon the rostrum in the Forum, dressed in robes of state; at other times they published proclamations in his name as if he were still alive and would shortly come back to Rome and take vengeance on all his enemies." Realizing the adoration which was now felt for Nero, Otho did all he could to be like him; but in April A.D. 69, after a reign of three months, he came to blows with Vitellius, another emulator of Nero, and very nobly killed himself to avoid general bloodshed, whereupon Vitellius became Emperor.

"Vitellius," says Dion Cassius,[30] "delighted in and commended the name and the life and all the practices of Nero." He imitated him closely, and greatly pleased the public by offering sacrifices to Nero's spirit in the Campus Martius, making all the priests and people attend. "And at a certain solemn banquet, he called out to a musician who had much pleased the company, 'Sing us one of the songs of the Master,' and upon his beginning some songs of Nero's he started up in the presence of the whole assembly, and could not refrain from bursting into applause, and clapping his hands." This piece of evidence shows clearly that not only was Nero loved, but he was loved as the master-singer. It is touching to read, too, that at this time and for many years to come the tomb where his ashes were supposed to lie was decked with spring and summer flowers. [31]

Vitellius was dethroned and killed at the end of the year 69, and after him reigned Vespasian, who attempted to check this Nero-cult and to encourage the opposite view held by the traditionists. Titus was the next Emperor, after whom, in A.D. 81, Domitian succeeded, and revived the admiration for Nero. In A.D. 88, a certain Terentius Maximus, a middle aged man who came from Asia Minor, declared himself to be Nero, whom he resembled in features and voice. [32] He gathered a considerable following, and made his way to Parthia, where he was kindly received; and although some twenty years had elapsed since Nero's dethronement, the Parthians still reverenced his memory so greatly that they seriously considered how best to restore this man, whose protestations they believed, to the imperial throne, and were even ready to go to war for him. At length, however, the fraud was discovered and they handed him over to the Romans, who, presumably, put him to death.

There appear to have been other impostors, too, who thus traded upon the popular belief that Nero was still alive, but as time passed he became a kind of supernatural being, eternally young, who would one day return unchanged by the years. Dion Chrysostom, for example, writing in the reign of the Emperor Trajan (A.D. 98 to 117), refers two or three times[33] to Nero, and says: "Still even at this time all men long for Nero to be alive, and most men actually believe to this day that he is living." I commend this seldom remembered passage to those who doubt my lonely contention that he has been so much maligned by history as to make the accepted picture of him nothing but a caricature.

In conclusion it will be as well to discuss briefly the sources of our information in regard to him.

The poet Lucan, nephew of Seneca, wrote his famous *Pharsalia* during the years before the great conspiracy of A.D. 65; but though it contains a great deal of extravagant flattery of the Emperor, critically of no use to us, it passes into vague abuse owing to its author's quarrel with him. Little can be gleaned from it beyond the fact that Lucan was genuinely attracted to him at first, and repelled by him afterwards. The epigrammatical poet Martial, who, as a young man of twenty-three, was in Rome during the last year or so of Nero's life, says nothing for or against the Emperor except to call him "cruel" in his treatment of Lucan.[34]

An important source of information, from which I have quoted extensively, is the tragedy *Octavia,* which, as has already been said, is traditionally attributed to Seneca but was probably composed a few years after Nero's death, perhaps by Curiatius Maternus, from material left by Seneca.[35] Far too little attention has been given to this striking play, nor has its great value as a supplement to the historic material been appreciated; for though it has not much poetic merit, it gives with great sympathy and impartiality the points of view of Nero, Octavia, Poppæa, and Seneca. Although Octavia storms at Nero as a brutal tyrant and as the supposed murderer of Britannicus, his own lines reveal him as an understandable despot fighting to defend the woman he loved against the unbalanced hatred of Octavia.

One of the writers most important to us is the Jew, Flavius Josephus, who was certainly in a position to be well informed in the matter. In A.D. 63, at the age of twenty-six, he went to Rome to plead the cause of some of his countrymen who had been sent there for trial; and he had the good fortune to become acquainted with a Jewish actor named Aliturius, a man much liked and admired by Nero and his wife Poppæa. By him Josephus was introduced to the Empress, and presumably to the Emperor, with the result that Nero very graciously pardoned the imprisoned Jews, and Poppæa gave their young advocate a handsome present as a mark of her regard.[36] Josephus afterwards became a personal friend of the Emperors Vespasian, Titus, and Domitian, and lived a large part of his life in Rome, where he must have had every opportunity of hearing what was being said, especially in court circles, of the late Nero's character.

Unfortunately, his writings contain only brief references to this subject. In his work, *The Wars of the Jews,* published about A.D. 75, some seven years after Nero's death, he speaks rather sympathetically of that tragic event, saying with apparent satisfaction that those who occasioned it were in time brought to punishment; and he attributes the blame for the Emperor's misrule to his "unworthy" agents.[37] He also gives the following exculpatory explanation of Nero's actions.[38]

"In many things," he writes, "Nero behaved like one who had become unbalanced by the excessive extent of the pleasures and the riches which he enjoyed, and, owing to that, used his good fortune to the detriment of others. . . . In the end he was so foolish as to become an actor in the theatre." He assumes that Nero was guilty of the murder of Britannicus; and he speaks of his also having killed Agrippina, Octavia, and others who were closely related to him. It is to be noticed, however, that this was written in the reign of Vespasian, who was hostile to Nero's memory.

In A.D. 93, some five-and-twenty years after Nero's death, Josephus published his *Antiquities of the Jews;* but Domitian, who was friendly to Nero, was now on the throne, and Josephus was therefore able to speak his mind. He tells of Nero's kindly treatment of a deputation of Jews which waited upon him to ask that a wall of the temple at Jerusalem which shut out the view from King Herod Agrippa's dining-room windows might be saved from its threatened destruction.[39] He mentions again the murder of Britannicus, but speaks of the deaths of Agrippina, Octavia, and the "many others" who lost their lives, as though they might be regarded as ordinary executions for treason.[40]

Most important for us, however, is his very significant statement, that certain writers of his time in condemning Nero have "so impudently raved against him with their lies that they themselves, rather, are worthy of condemnation."[41] The only other piece of information in this connection to be derived from his writings comes from the same paragraph, where he states that there were in his day several eulogistic accounts of Nero's life in circulation, as untrustworthy, however, because of their evident flattery, as were the above-mentioned tirades of abuse because of their falsehoods.

Plutarch, who was a young man at the time of Nero's death, makes several references to him in his *Parallel Lives,* but does not represent him as a monster, merely saying that "his obsession and folly came not far from ruining the Roman Empire."[42] He mentions as Nero's chief crimes the death of his mother and his wife, and the degradation of the imperial dignity by his singing,[43] but he makes no reference to the death of Britannicus, and, like Josephus, puts the blame for the misgovernment of the provinces on Nero's "iniquitous agents." He tells us that the rebellion which ended Nero's life did so little to relieve general conditions that it came to be regarded as "nothing better than treason"; and in describing Otho's attempt to emulate Nero he takes it for granted that such a course was pleasing to the people.

But though Josephus, Plutarch, and the author of *Octavia,* all writing pretty soon after Nero's death, give no support to the description of the Emperor as an infamous and fiendish character, he is termed "the enemy of the human race" and "the poison of the earth" by Pliny the Elder in his *Natural History,*[44] published nine years after Nero's death; and this author also accuses him of setting Rome on fire. Pliny, however, is not an unbiassed critic; for Nero favoured him by making him Procurator of Spain, in which province the final rebellion originated, and since Pliny retained his office there for three or four years after Nero's end, it is to be presumed that he was a party to the uprising and had to justify himself afterwards by abusing his benefactor. He wrote a history of Nero's reign, which is now lost, and this was probably one of those books said by Josephus to be full of lies.

The poet Statius wrote his book *Silvæ* in the reign of Domitian, some twenty years or so after Nero's death; but, as in the case of his friend Martial, he says nothing of importance about the Emperor except to call him "ungrateful" in one place.[45] It is to be remembered, however, that Domitian did not favour abuse of Nero, and, in fact, defended him so warmly that Juvenal called him another Nero himself, but a bald-headed one.[46]

Tacitus, the historian whose *Annals* give us the fullest account of the reign, was about six years old at Nero's death, and wrote this work about A.D. 115, nearly fifty years later. He was a great friend of the younger Pliny, and belonged to that circle of Roman society which was most hostile to Nero's memory. His account of the reign breaks off at A.D. 66, but the story of the Emperor's life up to that date provides us with a very dark and dreadful picture, Nero's character being only less terrible than that ascribed by this historian to the Empress-Mother, Agrippina. Nevertheless, many of his statements are favourable to Nero, as the references in the foregoing pages will have shown. It is generally supposed that Tacitus derived much of his information from the history written by Cluvius Rufus, which is now lost; but as this writer also held high office in Spain immediately after Nero's death, it is probable that he was of the same opinion as Pliny the Elder. Tacitus seems to have used, too, the history of Fabius Rusticus; but this is likewise lost, and one can only conjecture that it took an unfavourable view of Nero.

Suetonius, who published his *Twelve Cæsars* about A.D. 120, over fifty years after Nero's death, was another friend of Pliny, and, like Tacitus, belonged to that group which Nero had most offended. He accuses him of various crimes, including the burning of Rome, and draws a bizarre picture of him which leaves the impression that, towards the end of his life, he was a thoroughly detestable character; and this writer's enjoyment of prurient gossip has led him to tell some very disgusting details of Nero's supposed immoralities, which, however, pale before those he tells of other Emperors. Nevertheless, he gives us much reason to suppose that, even amongst old-fashioned people, there was a good deal said in favour of Nero; and he explains that these favourable facts have to be considered "separately from the scandalous and criminal part of his conduct."[47]

The work of Dion Chrysostom has already been mentioned; and, after him, we have Pausanias, who, writing a century after Nero's death, describes him as a man of noble character ruined by his upbringing.[48]

The Roman History written by Dion Cassius was published over a century and a half after the death of Nero, and therefore must be based on the works already mentioned. Where it differs from, or is obviously independent of, Tacitus and Suetonius, one may suppose that it repeats the statements of Pliny, Cluvius Rufus, Fabius Rusticus, and others whose histories are now lost. In general he gives an ugly picture of Nero, and it is evident that in his day the views of the Emperor's detractors had gained ground, and that the description of him as a celestial figure was confined to the lower classes.

In the *Life of Apollonius of Tyana,* written by Philostratus during the first half of the third century, some references are made to Nero, with whom Apollonius was contemporary, mostly of a jocularly disparaging kind. He says, however, that Apollonius would never have anything to do with the Emperor Vespasian, for whereas Nero had given liberty to Greece, Vespasian had enslaved it, "thereby proving that Nero was of greater soul than he." Asked by Tigellinus what he thought of Nero, Apollonius replied, "I think him far more worthy than you do"; and he added the witty remark: "*You* consider him worthy to sing; but *I* consider him worthy to be silent."[49]

In the second half of the Fourth Century an outline of Roman history was written by Eutropius; and by this time the idea that Nero was a villain was so fully accepted that this historian dismisses him with the brief statement that he killed many people, set Rome on fire, used perfumes in his bath, disgraced himself by singing on the stage, and, in a word, was an enemy of all good men.[50]

Meanwhile, the early Christian tradition was popularized as Christianity spread far and wide, and Nero became in every way a fiendish monster, in accordance with the apocalyptic representation of him as the Beast. The people's belief that he would one day return caused him to be regarded as the arch-enemy of Jesus Christ whose expected Second Coming clashed with it, and thus the Beast became the false Christ, the Antichrist; and there is no more extraordinary fact to be recorded in connection with Nero than that he thus developed into the rival hope of the world—Jesus Christ being for Christians the divine ideal of the beauties and blessings of the life of self-abnegation and the mortification of the flesh, at that time the key-note of the faith, and Nero being for the pagan masses the ideal of the joys of self-expression and earthly happiness.

Lactantius in the Third Century, St. Chrysostom, St. Jerome and St. Augustine in the Fourth, and others as well, speak of Nero as Antichrist, the Rival of God. "Some suppose," says St. Augustine, "that Nero will rise again as Antichrist; others think that he is not dead, but was concealed so that he might be supposed to have been killed, and that he still lives as a legendary figure, of the same age as that at which he passed away, and will be restored to his Kingdom."[51]

At the end of the Eleventh Century Pope Pascal the Second used sometimes to listen to the crows cawing in a walnut tree which grew on the Pincian Hill near the tomb of the Ahenobarbi, where Nero's ashes were supposed to rest, and where now stands the church of Santa Maria del Popolo. One night he dreamed that these birds were demons in the service of Nero, and that they attended his spirit which for ever wandered over the hill. He therefore tore down the remains of the tomb, scattered the ashes, and built this church; but the crows transferred themselves to other trees, and throughout the Middle Ages they were thought to be the dark servants of the Emperor's ghost which still wandered, and would wander there, until that day when both he and Jesus Christ should return, and Nero Antichrist should be defeated and hurled into the bottomless pit.

The revenge of the traditionists whom the Emperor had flouted was terrible, for they created the picture of him as the enemy of decent humanity; but the revenge of that little band of Christians with whom he had so severely dealt was overwhelming, for they made him the superhuman enemy of God, and, even today, nineteen hundred years later, that dark vengeance still envelops him in a haze of adverse prejudice.

NOTES

CHAPTER I

[1] *Rev.* xiii, 3 and 12.

[2] *Rev.* xvii, 8.

[3] *Rev.* xiii, 18. See the last chapter of the present volume.

[4] Marcus Aurelius, iii, 16.

[5] Sir Charles Oman.

[6] See my *Life and Times of Cleopatra.*

[7] As I have pointed out in the *Life and Times of Cleopatra.*

[8] Suetonius: *Tiberius,* 57.

[9] Suetonius: *Tiberius,* 43.

[10] Tacitus: *Annals,* xiv, 2. He says the fault was hers; but Suetonius, *Caligula,* 24, suggests that her brother encouraged the affair.

[11] Suetonius: *Nero,* 1.

[12] Velleius, ii, 10.

[13] Suetonius: *Tiberius,* 53, says that one of his officers struck the blow.

[14] Suetonius: *Tiberius,* 73.

[15] Tacitus: *Annals,* vi, 50; Dion Cassius: lviii, 28.

[16] Suetonius: *Caligula,* 3.

CHAPTER II

[1] Pliny: *Natural History,* vii, 45.

[2] Suetonius: *Caius,* 24. Caligula's relationship with Drusilla is unquestionable, and therefore that with Agrippina is probably more than mere gossip.

[3] Freedmen, that is to say manumitted slaves, played an important part in Roman history. As the confidants and personal agents of the Emperors they often attained great wealth and power. They owed their freedom to their masters, and hence were likely to be exceptionally faithful.

[4] The worship of Isis was first introduced into Rome about 80 B.C. From the time of Vespasian, who reigned shortly after Nero, her worship spread all over western Europe.

[5] Josephus: *Antiquities,* xviii, 4; Suetonius: Tiberius, 36.

[6] Suetonius: *Caligula,* 22.

[7] He was rescued a month or two later, and in view of the fact that he was even then only 3¼ years of age, it is improbable that the dancer and the barber had "sown the seeds of his later follies" as stated by his German biographer, Hermann Schiller: *Geschichte des römischen Kaiserreichs,* p. 63.

[8] His full name was Tiberius Claudius Drusus Nero Germanicus. He was born on August 1st, B.C. 10.

[9] Suetonius: *Claudius,* 8.

[10] Suetonius: *Julius Cæsar,* 51.

[11] Suetonius: *Claudius,* 27, says he was born on the 20th day of the reign, January 24th having been the first day.

CHAPTER III

[1] Niece, because Messalina's husband, Claudius, was Agrippina's uncle; and aunt, because Messalina was the daughter of Agrippina's husband's sister, Domitia Lepida.

[2] Tacitus: *Annals,* xii, 7.

[3] In later accounts this snake-skin becomes a living serpent.

[4] Suetonius: *Caligula,* 24.

[5] Tacitus: *Annals,* xii, 6, 7.

[6] Claudius and Pallas.

[7] Suetonius: *Augustus,* 43.

[8] Suetonius: *Claudius,* 30.

[9] So Suetonius, *Claudius,* 29; but Seneca, ***De Morte Claudii,*** says 30 Senators and 315 gentlemen.

[10] Suetonius: *Claudius,* 32.

CHAPTER IV

[1] In the Uffizi Palace, Florence.

[2] Juvenal: *Satires,* vi, 120.

[3] Agrippina's complicity in the subsequent plot against Messalina is not actually stated, but seems to me to be apparent.

[4] Suetonius: *Claudius,* 29.

[5] Weigall: *Life of Cleopatra.*

[6] Tacitus: *Annals,* xi, 27.

[7] Tacitus: *Annals,* xi, 30.

[8] Tacitus: *Annals,* xi, 31.

[9] Lucullus, famous for his wealth and his luxurious mode of life, had laid out these gardens about a hundred years previously.

[10] Tacitus: *Annals,* xi, 1.

[11] Tacitus: *Annals,* xi, 35.

[12] Suetonius: *Claudius,* 36.

[13] Suetonius: *Claudius,* 34.

[14] Suetonius: *Caligula,* 36.

[15] Tacitus: *Annals,* xi, 28.

[16] Tacitus: *Annals,* xi, 36.

[17] Tacitus: *Annals,* xii, 3.

CHAPTER V

[1] *Acts of the Apostles,* xxiii, xxiv.

[2] Suetonius: *Claudius,* 28.

[3] Suetonius: *Claudius,* 26.

[4] Tacitus: *Annals,* xii, 3.

[5] Tacitus: *Annals,* xi, 12.

[6] Suetonius: *Claudius,* 39 compared with 26.
[7] Tacitus: *Annals,* xi, 25, last line.
[8] Tacitus: *Annals,* xii, 5.
[9] Father of the Emperor of that name.
[10] Tacitus: *Annals,* xii, 4.
[11] Seneca: *Ludus,* viii.
[12] Ultimately they both met their deaths, as will be recorded in due course.
[13] Tacitus: *Annals,* xii, 22.
[14] Dion Cassius, lx, 32.

CHAPTER VI

[1] The date of his birth is unknown, but in his book *De Tranquillitate animi* (15, 13) he says he can remember hearing a speech of Asinus Pollio, who died in A.D. 5; so Seneca was probably born a year or two B.C.
[2] *Acts of the Apostles,* xviii, 12–17.
[3] Dion Cassius considers him to be an out and out fraud.
[4] His having lent money to the King of the Iceni, in Britain, led to the insurrection of Boadicea, Queen of that country, in A.D. 61.
[5] Seneca: *De Consolatione ad Polybium.*
[6] Tacitus: *Annals,* xii, 7.
[7] Tacitus: *Annals,* xii, 7.
[8] Tacitus: *Annals,* xii, 64.
[9] Tacitus: *Annals,* xii, 65.
[10] Pliny: *Natural History,* xxxi, 2.
[11] The text of Tacitus, *Annals,* xii, 65, is corrupt. It was Claudius, not Narcissus, who said this (Suetonius: *Claudius,* 43).
[12] The reference in Tacitus, *Annals,* xii, 66, to a visit of Claudius to Sinuessa is a copyist's error. The text is evidently corrupt: it was Narcissus who went there (Dion Cassius: lx, 34).

CHAPTER VII

[1] Tacitus: *Annals,* xiii, 3.
[2] Tacitus: *Annals,* xiii, 2.
[3] Tacitus: *Annals,* xii, 65.
[4] Suetonius: *Nero,* 10, 12.
[5] Tacitus: *Annals,* xiii, 3.
[6] Tacitus: *Annals,* xiii, 5.
[7] Dion Cassius, lxi.
[8] Tacitus: *Annals,* xiii, 5.
[9] Tacitus: *Annals,* xiii, 1.
[10] In Seneca's farce on the death of Claudius, described at the end of this chapter, Narcissus reaches Hell at about the same time as Claudius.
[11] *Romans* xvi, 11.
[12] Tacitus: *Annals,* xiii, 1.
[13] Suetonius: *Nero,* 10 to 19.
[14] Tacitus: *Annals,* xiii, 2.
[15] Afterwards Emperor for a few months.

[16] Plutarch: *Galba,* 19.

[17] Suetonius: *Vespasian,* 9. The temple was never finished, and was later almost entirely demolished by Nero, the remains at last being incorporated into a Christian church now known as *San Stefano in Rotondo.*

[18] *Ludus de Morte Claudii Cæsaris.* See the edition by A. P. Ball (Columbia University Press). Adolph Stahr in his *Agrippina die Mutter Neros* (p. 330) argues that the play was not written by Seneca, but he is alone in this contention; and there seems no reasonable doubt of its authorship, although Seneca is never funny in his other writings.

[19] Seneca, of course, would not dare to suggest that poison and not fever had carried him off.

[20] Dion Cassius, lx, 35.

CHAPTER VIII

[1] Tacitus: *Annals,* xiii, 2.

[2] The former is suggested by Suetonius, *Nero,* 28, first sentence, and the latter by the same book, 29, in the reference to Doryphorus.

[3] Tacitus: *Annals,* xiii, 12.

[4] He was Præfectus Vigilum, and to him Seneca dedicates his two books, *De Constantia Sapientis* and *De Tranquillitate Animi.* See also Seneca: *Epist.* 63.

[5] See the play *Octavia.*

[6] Tacitus: *Annals,* xiii, 13.

[7] Tacitus: *Annals,* xiii, 13; xiv. Tacitus says that the historian Fabius Rusticus, whose work is lost, supposed Nero to be the guilty party; and Suetonius (*Nero,* 28) thinks so, too. But Tacitus, on the other hand, quotes the historian Claudius Rufus, whose work is also lost, as saying that Agrippina was alone to blame, and he says that this was the general opinion.

[8] This was a sham pedigree like that invented for Acte.

[9] Tacitus: *Annals,* xii, 53.

[10] Suetonius: *Claudius,* 28.

[11] Tacitus: *Annals,* xiii, 14.

[12] Tacitus: *Annals,* xiii, 14.

[13] Lipsius, Duruy, Henderson and others suggest that the song was the one from the now lost works of Ennius which is quoted by Cicero in his *Tusculanarum Disputationum,* iii, 19, 44.

[14] Tacitus: *Annals,* xiii, 14.

[15] Lucius Silanus, whom she had driven to suicide, and his brother, Marcus, whom she had poisoned.

[16] Suetonius: *Titus,* 2.

[17] Tacitus: *Annals,* xiii, 17.

[18] Tacitus: *Annals,* xiii, 17, says during the same night, and Suetonius: *Nero,* 33, says the following day; so it was probably just before dawn.

[19] Reinhold: *Die römische Kaisergeschichte;* Stahr: *Agrippina die Mutter Neros;* G. H. L.: *Was Nero a Monster?* (Cornhill Magazine, 1863); Fountain: *A Defence of Nero;* Baring Gould: *The Tragedy of the Cæsars.*

[20] Suetonius: *Nero,* 33.

[21] Seneca: *De Clementia.* As Henderson: *Life and Principate of the Emperor Nero,* p. 459, points out, this work was written shortly after December 15th, A.D. 55, for Nero is described therein (ix, 2) as just past eighteen.

[22] See the play *Octavia.*

CHAPTER IX

[1] Dion Cassius, lxi, 8.

[2] Tacitus: *Annals,* xiii, 24.

[3] Tacitus: *Annals,* xiii, 19.

[4] Paraphrased from Tacitus: *Annals,* xiii, 21.

[5] Tacitus: *History,* i, 72.

[6] Dion Cassius, lix, 23.

[7] Aurelius Victor: *De Cæsaribus, epitome* 5.

[8] Suetonius: *Nero,* 23.

[9] Suetonius: *Nero,* 51.

[10] *Corpus Inscriptionum Latinum,* xi, 1414.

[11] Tacitus: *Annals,* xiii, 45, gives her a bad moral character, but this is not confirmed by other writers; and Josephus, who knew her personally (*Antiquities,* xx, 8, 2), calls her a "religious" woman.

[12] Suetonius: *Nero,* 35, says that the boy was afterwards drowned while out fishing, and that Nero was to blame; but the incident itself is not confirmed, nor is Nero's connection with it. He probably died before Nero fell in love with Poppæa.

[13] Suetonius: *Otho,* 3, Dion Cassius: lxi, 11, Plutarch: *Galba,* 19, and Tacitus: *History,* i, 13, all say that Nero arranged Poppæa's marriage to Otho, so as to be able by this arrangement to carry on a secret affair with her himself; but Tacitus afterwards (*Annals,* xiii, 46) corrected this statement, and gave the version I have here followed.

[14] Suetonius: *Otho,* 3.

[15] Paraphrased from Tacitus: *Annals,* xiii, 47.

[16] Tacitus: *Annals,* xiv, 3.

[17] Paraphrased from Tacitus: *Annals,* xiv, 1.

[18] Tacitus: *Annals,* xiv, 4.

CHAPTER X

[1] Horace: *Carmen,* ii, 18, 20–23.

[2] Seneca: *Epistolæ,* li, 1, 4, 12.

[3] Martial, xi, 80, 1–4.

[4] Propertius, i, 11.

[5] Judging by their subsequent actions, but Tacitus: *Annals,* xiv, 7, says it is not quite certain that they were in the plot.

[6] Ovid: *Fasti,* iii, 713, 810.

[7] Suetonius: *Nero,* 34.

[8] Tacitus: *Annals,* xiv, 4.

[9] Dion Cassius, li, 13.

[10] Dion Cassius says that she had been entertained by Nero for some days; but Tacitus, the better authority, says that it happened on this first night.

[11] Tacitus: *Annals,* xiv, 7.

[12] Tacitus thinks that Anicetus threw his own dagger on the ground, pretending that it belonged to the man; Suetonius says that it was Nero who did this; but my version seems more probable.

[13] Suetonius and Dion Cassius, following the tradition that Nero was a human monster, make him callously critical of his mother's body.

[14] For this sentence, Quintilian: *Institutiones Oratoriæ,* viii, 5, 18; for the rest, Tacitus.

[15] Tacitus: *Annals,* xiv, 13.

CHAPTER XI

[1] Suetonius: *Nero,* 35, says that Nero had ceased to have anything to do with her, but the later charge that she was barren seems to contradict this.

[2] Tacitus: *Annals,* xv, 33.

[3] Tacitus: *Annals,* xiv, 5.

[4] Suetonius: *Nero,* 52.

[5] Suetonius: *Nero,* 10.

[6] Of the other nine lines, three are given in the scholiast's note to Lucan, iii, 261; five are, according to the scholiast, quoted by Persius: *Satire* i, 93, 94, 99, 100, 101; and one appears in Seneca: *Quæstionum Naturalium,* i, 5, 6.

[7] Tacitus: *Annals,* xiv, 16.

[8] Dion Cassius (lxii, 19) says that his first shave was the event in honour of which the above-mentioned Festivals of Youth were celebrated; Suetonius, however (*Nero,* 12), says that he was first shaved at the opening of some new baths; but Tacitus makes no mention of the occasion of the shaving. Most probably it took place on his birthday.

[9] Tacitus: *Annals,* xiv, 21.

[10] Suetonius: *Vitellius,* 4.

[11] Tacitus: *Annals,* xiv, 14.

[12] Dion Cassius, lxi, 20.

[13] Dion Cassius, lxi, 16.

[14] Tacitus: *Annals,* xiv, 22.

[15] Aurelius Victor: *De Cæsaribus, epitome* 5.

[16] Weigall: *Wanderings in Roman Britain,* p. 53; Tacitus: *Annals,* xiv, 31.

[17] Dion Cassius, lxii, 2.

[18] Julius Asbach: *Analecta historica Latina,* ii, 8, followed by B. Henderson: *Life and Principate of Nero,* p. 477, suggests A.D. 60 for the revolt; but Tacitus: *Annals,* xiv, 29, indicates A.D. 61.

CHAPTER XII

[1] Dion Cassius, lxii, 13.

[2] It has been pointed out in Chapter I that Cleopatra was a pure Greek, descended from the long line of Greek Kings or Pharaohs of Egypt whose capital, Alexandria, was the great centre of Greek culture.

[3] *Juvenis infandi ingeni.*

[4] Dion Cassius, lxii, 13.

[5] Suetonius: *Nero,* 35.

[6] Tacitus: *Annals,* xiv, 51.

[7] Dion Cassius, lxi, 16.

[8] Tacitus: *Annals,* xiv, 52.

[9] The interview is recorded by Tacitus and I follow Raabe (*Geschichte und Bild von Nero,* p. 277) and Diepenbrock (*Annæi Senecæ Vita,* p. 170) in thinking it genuine history and not historic fiction.

[10] Tacitus: *Annals,* xiv, 53–56.

[11] Suetonius: *Nero,* 35.

[12] Dion Cassius, lxii, 14. He makes this remark apply to Plautus who was executed shortly afterwards, but Tacitus records the remark about the grey hair in reference to Sulla, and I fancy Dion's story must also have referred to him.

[13] Tacitus: *Annals,* xiv, 58.

[14] Juvenal, viii, 39.

[15] Tacitus: *Annals,* xiv, 22.

[16] Tacitus: *Annals,* xvi, 10.

[17] Tacitus: *Annals,* xiv, 63.

[18] Dion Cassius, lxii, 13.

[19] One cannot avoid the passing thought that Poppæa, failing to have a child by Nero, and knowing the importance of having one, had perhaps been driven to an act of unfaithfulness to her imperial lover. Her pregnancy was curiously opportune.

CHAPTER XIII

[1] These words are from the tragedy *Octavia,* and we may assume that something of the sort was said.

[2] Tacitus: *Annals,* xiv, 61.

[3] We return here to the play *Octavia.*

[4] Nero having been adopted as a son by Octavia's father, Claudius.

[5] Suetonius: *Nero,* 29.

[6] Tacitus, however, who records the death of Doryphorus in *Annals,* xiv, 65, names another man, Pythagoras, as the Emperor's companion in vice, *Annals,* xv, 37; and this fact that the story has two versions indicates that it was based on prurient gossip.

[7] Tacitus: *Annals,* xv, 23.

[8] Seneca: *Quæstionum Naturalium,* vi, 1. Tacitus mistakenly dates the catastrophe a year earlier.

[9] Tacitus: *Annals,* xv, 25.

[10] Tacitus: *Annals,* xv, 33.

[11] Tacitus: *Annals,* xvi, 4.

[12] Suetonius: *Nero,* 20, 22.

[13] Dion Cassius, lxi, 20.

[14] Philostratus: *Life of Apollonius,* v, 10.

[15] Tacitus: *Annals,* xv, 33.

[16] Tacitus: *Annals,* xv, 35.

[17] Suetonius: *Nero,* 31.

[18] Suetonius: *Nero,* 24.

[19] Suetonius: *Nero,* 23.

CHAPTER XIV

[1] It is mentioned by Servius in his commentary on Virgil: *Georgica,* iii, 36, and *Æneid,* v, 370.

[2] Suetonius: *Nero,* 30.

[3] Which disposes of the later calumny that he hated all rival musicians.

[4] Tacitus, our best authority, gives a version of the affair (*Annals,* xv, 37), which permits of the above interpretation, but 150 years later the whole thing had become exaggerated into a story of a mixed orgy in which the ladies took the place of the professionals (Dion Cassius, lxii, 15).

[5] Tacitus: *Annals,* xv, 36; Suetonius: *Nero,* xix.

[6] The accounts of the fire are by Tacitus: *Annals,* xv, 38–41; Suetonius: *Nero,* 38; and Dion Cassius, lxii, 16–18.

[7] The Palatine Hill was then called the *Palatium,* and the word at length came to designate the imperial residence itself. Our word *Palace* is derived from this *Palatium.*

[8] Tacitus (*Annals,* xv, 39) says "on the stage of his private theatre"; Dion Cassius (lxii, 18) says "the roof of the palace"; Suetonius (*Nero,* 38) says "a tower in the house of Mæcenas" on the Esquiline. Both the latter, however, must have been obscured in smoke; and Tacitus therefore seems our best guide.

[9] Henderson: *Life and Principate of Nero;* Gibbon: *Decline and Fall;* Merivale: *History of the Romans;* Hertzberg: *Geschichte des römischen Kaiserreichs;* Sievers: *Studien zur Geschichte;* Aubé: *Histoire des Persécutions de l'Eglise;* Schiller: *Geschichte des römischen Kaiserreichs;* Bury: *History of the Roman Empire;* etc.—Renan: *L'Antichrist,* and Ranke: *Weltgeschichte,* however, hesitate to exonerate him entirely.

[10] "Everywhere the sect is spoken against," *Acts of the Apostles,* xxviii, 22. "An odious superstition," Suetonius: *Nero,* 16. "A pernicious superstition," Tacitus: *Annals,* xv, 44.

[11] Tacitus: *Annals,* xv, 44; Suetonius: *Claudius,* 25. The Gospels were not yet written. See Weigall: *The Paganism in our Christianity,* p. 28.

[12] *Acts of the Apostles,* xxviii, 30; *Philippians,* i, 13; iv, 22.

[13] Suetonius: *Claudius,* 25.

[14] Tacitus: *Annals,* xv, 44. The authenticity of the passage, though questioned by Hochart, can hardly be in doubt.

[15] St. Clement of Rome indicates this, although another tradition suggests a later date.

[16] Clement of Rome: *Epistle I to the Corinthians,* vi, 1, 2.

[17] *Revelations,* xx, 4.

[18] The First Epistle General of St. Peter is thought by Lightfoot, Hort, Renan, Henderson, and the majority of scholars, to date from this time. The Second Epistle is now fully recognized to be by another hand, and to date from nearly a century later.

[19] *I Peter,* i, 6, 7; ii, 13, 17, 18; iii, 14, 15, 16; iv, 7, 12, 14, 16; v, 4, 6–10.

[20] An early tradition that he and Paul suffered on the same day seems to be out of the question.

[21] St. Ambrose: *Epistle* 21.

[22] Weigall: *The Paganism in Our Christianity,* p. 81.

CHAPTER XV

[1] The exact height is not known; but Augustus, in his day, limited it to seventy, and Trajan to sixty feet.

[2] Suetonius: *Nero,* 31; Pliny: *Natural History,* xxxiv, 45-47; Spartianus: *Vita Hadriani,* xix, 12, 13.

[3] Dion Cassius, lxv, 4.

[4] Tacitus: *History,* i, 30; *Annals,* xii, 53. Two and a quarter billion sesterces would be about seventeen million pounds sterling, or eighty-five million dollars, but the value of this sum was far greater then than now.

[5] Tacitus: *Annals,* xv, 59.

[6] Seneca's guilt is indirectly affirmed by Tacitus: *Annals,* xv, 60, 65, and directly by Dion Cassius (lxii, 24). Merivale, Schiller, and other modern historians have no doubt of his guilt, and Henderson thinks it probable.

[7] This is probably an addition of Tacitus. Seneca believed Nero innocent of the death of Britannicus.

[8] Tacitus: *Annals,* xv, 68.

[9] Thus, Dion Cassius, lxii, 24. Tacitus: *Annals,* xv, 67, doubtfully adds the rest.

[10] Epictetus: i, 1, 19.

[11] A good translation of the *Pharsalia* is that by E. Ridley. Suetonius has left us a short life of Lucan.

CHAPTER XVI

[1] Tacitus: *Annals,* xv, 73.

[2] Tacitus: *Annals,* xvi, 4.

[3] Dion Cassius (lxiii, 1) also speaks of the "deep disgrace" of it.

[4] Dion Cassius (lxii, 27) thinks the kick may have been accidental; and Tacitus (*Annals,* xvi, 6) says that he was too devoted to her to do her any harm, and he indicates a doubt about the whole story.

[5] Pliny: *Natural History,* xii, 18.

[6] Suetonius: *Nero,* 39.

[7] Tacitus: *Annals,* xvi, 9.

[8] Tacitus: *Annals,* xvi, 10.

[9] Tacitus: *Annals,* xvi, 18.

[10] Tacitus: *Annals,* xvi, 28.

[11] Suetonius: *Nero,* 35.

[12] Suetonius: *Nero,* 18.

[13] *Rivista Italiana di Numismatica,* x, iii, 327. The event is celebrated on coins of this year.

[14] Suetonius: *Nero,* 13.

[15] Suetonius: *Nero,* 18.

[16] For a full account of the visit of Tiridates, see Dion Cassius, lxiii, 1-17; also Suetonius: *Nero,* 13; Pliny: *Natural History,* xxx, 14-17.

[17] Weigall: *The Paganism in Our Christianity,* p. 135.

CHAPTER XVII

[1] Dion Cassius, lxiii, 9.

[2] Dion Cassius, lxiii, 21.

[3] Philostratus: *Apollonius of Tyana,* iv, 42.
[4] Suetonius: *Nero,* 28.
[5] It is inscribed upon a memorial stone which was found at Karditza in 1888, and is published in the *Bulletin de Corr. Hellén,* xii (1888), 510.
[6] Dion Cassius, lxiii, 20.
[7] Dion Cassius, lxiii, 22.
[8] Suetonius: *Nero,* 41.
[9] Suetonius: *Nero,* 43.
[10] Virgil: *Æneid,* xii, 646.
[11] Josephus: *Wars of the Jews,* iv, 9, 2; Tacitus: *History,* i, 5.
[12] Homer: *Iliad,* x, 535.

CHAPTER XVIII

[1] Suetonius: *Nero,* 57.
[2] Tacitus: *History,* i, 4.
[3] Tacitus: *History,* i, 5.
[4] Plutarch: *Galba,* 6. For what happened after Nero's death, see in general Plutarch's *Galba* and *Otho;* Tacitus: *History,* i and ii; Suetonius: *Galba* and *Otho;* and Dion Cassius, lxiv, lxv.
[5] Josephus: *Wars of the Jews,* iv, 9, 2.
[6] Tacitus: *History,* i, 7.
[7] Tacitus: *History,* i, 5.
[8] Chrysostom: *Homilies,* xlvi, 13.
[9] Plutarch: *Galba,* 10.
[10] Plutarch: *Galba,* 17.
[11] Tacitus: *History,* i, 25.
[12] Plutarch: *Galba,* 20.
[13] Tacitus: *History,* i, 7.
[14] Plutarch: *Otho,* 3.
[15] Suetonius: *Otho,* 7.
[16] Tacitus: *History,* i, 78.
[17] Tacitus: *History,* ii, 11.
[18] Galba had put to death many of the Prætorians.
[19] Tacitus: *History,* ii, 8.
[20] Tacitus: *History,* ii, 8.
[21] See the detailed discussion of the subject in Henderson's *Life and Principate of Nero,* appendix B, p. 439.
[22] *Rev.:* xiii, 3.
[23] *Rev.:* xvii, 8.
[24] *Rev.:* xiii, 18.
[25] *Rev.:* xvii, 3–13.
[26] *Rev.:* xvii, 10, 11.
[27] *Rev.:* xvi, 12.
[28] Tacitus: *History,* i, 2.
[29] Suetonius: *Nero,* 57.
[30] Dion Cassius, lxv, 4.
[31] Suetonius: *Nero,* 57.
[32] Dion Cassius, lxvi, 19; *John of Antioch,* fragment 104 (Mueller); Suetonius: *Nero,* 57.

[33] Dion Chrysostom: *Orations,* 21, 31, 32.

[34] Martial: vii, 21.

[35] The Latin text of *Octavia* with English translation will be found in the *Loeb Classical Library* edition of Seneca's *Tragedies,* vol. ii.

[36] Josephus: *Life,* 3.

[37] Josephus: *Wars,* iv, 9, 2.

[38] Josephus: *Wars,* ii, 13, 1.

[39] Josephus: *Antiquities,* xx, 9, 11.

[40] Josephus: *Antiquities,* xx, 8, 2.

[41] Josephus: *Antiquities,* xx, 8, 3.

[42] Plutarch: *Antony,* last par.

[43] Plutarch: *Galba,* 17.

[44] Pliny: *Natural History,* vii, 45–46; xxii, 92; xvii, 5.

[45] Statius: *Silvæ,* ii, 7.

[46] Juvenal, iv, 38.

[47] Suetonius: *Nero,* 19.

[48] Pausanias, vii, 17, 2.

[49] Philostratus: *Life of Apollonius,* iv, 42; v, 41.

[50] Eutropius, vii, 18.

[51] Augustine: *City of God,* xx, 19.

INDEX

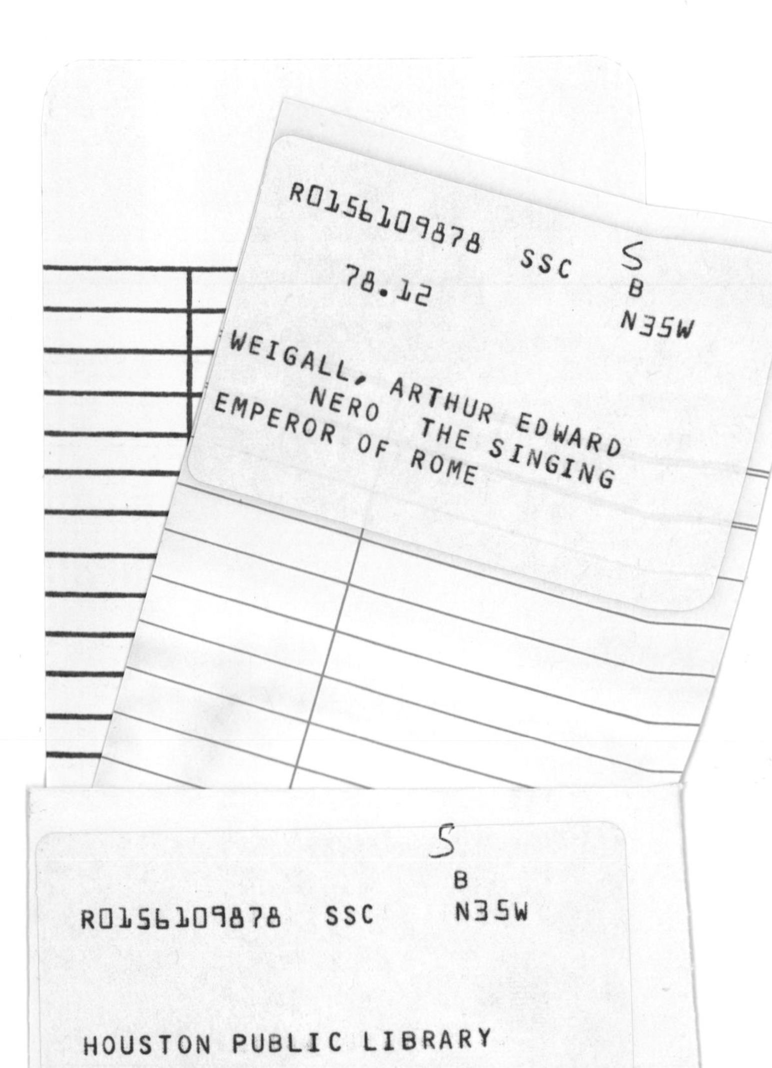
R0156109878 SSC
78.12
S
B
N35W
WEIGALL, ARTHUR EDWARD
NERO THE SINGING
EMPEROR OF ROME